IN THEIR OWN BEHALF

ACC SOCIOLOGY SERIES

John F. Cuber, *Editor*

Alfred C. Clarke, *Associate Editor*

IN THEIR OWN BEHALF

Voices
from
the
Margin

Edited by
Charles H. McCaghy
James K. Skipper, Jr.
Mark Lefton
All of Case Western Reserve University

New York / APPLETON-CENTURY-CROFTS
Division of Meredith Corporation

PRINTED IN THE UNITED STATES OF AMERICA

E 61090

Preface

Social and behavioral scientists have always been intrigued by that behavior which, despite being generally disapproved by society, occurs with inevitable regularity. Regardless of threats of punishment and ostracism, some individuals will inevitably circumvent or violate certain of society's rules. Although they ostensibly remain within the boundaries of society, their behavior very often effectively isolates them from the normative mainstream. Insofar as society is concerned they become, in a word, "deviant."*

Through the years numerous theories have been formulated which attempt to explain what circumstances lead certain individuals to develop behavior patterns often negatively evaluated by society. As social scientists have become more systematic in their investigations, many of the older theories have been discarded, modified, and replaced by ones backed by sound empirical data. Today there exists a vast number of "tools" to probe, index, classify, and scale individuals whose behavior transgresses the "rules" of society. But as sociologists and social psychologists turn more to the "efficiency" of the structured interview and questionnaire as techniques of collecting data, the actual responses of such persons themselves are not taken at face value. The tendency is to either immediately translate them into *a priori* conceptual schema or to declare them largely irrelevant for more general social scientific objectives.

---

* In our use of this term for the purpose of sociological investigation, we emphasize that we do not attach any value judgment, explicitly or implicitly, either to the word "deviance" or to those describing their behavior or beliefs in this book.

Notwithstanding the great heuristic advantages which derive from a de-emphasis of the unique and subjective appraisals by persons regarding their own behavior, the fact is that students of the field endeavor to understand the motivations and drives which prompt individuals to behave as they do. To ignore what individuals say or think about their behavior is to invite facile imputations which often border on reductionism. It is our contention that there is a need to listen more carefully to those who speak from the margin, and try to understand their own perspectives and explanations of their behavior, unhindered (as much as possible) by preconceived albeit sophisticated social scientific models or frames of reference.

It is the purpose of this volume to provide the opportunity to "listen" to, or more exactly, to examine a wide sampling of writing by individuals whose behavior has been variously defined or labelled as "deviant." The selections included were chosen with a view toward providing the reader with enough insight to understand personal justifications of behavior. We do not propose that the selections serve as a substitute for the painstaking efforts of social scientists to understand and explain deviance in contemporary society. On the contrary, they are offered as adjunct critical ingredients which simply cannot be ignored nor abstracted out of existence.

The reader should bear in mind three considerations. First, we have included articles by several groups of people whose behavior is more or less tolerated in the United States. It was decided to include these groups because they represent a minority opinion and because they frequently experience societal reaction as a result of their beliefs.

Second, although the selections are first-hand accounts, they may reflect the intellectual bias of the editors. Were we psychoanalysts, for example, one would probably find more childhood reminiscences. As sociologists, we concentrate on the more immediate rationales and experiences of the writers, emphasizing the learning of deviance and the factors which perpetuate it. An effort was made to select passages in which the authors made direct reference to the experience of becoming and being a deviant. Exceptions to this are those selections which present the more or less formal "platforms" of social and political groups.

Third, the selections should not be interpreted as necessarily representing the rationales or experiences of most of those
whose behavior society regards as deviant. It is quite possible that
those who choose to write about and publish their experiences
may be the product of quite different social and psychological
characteristics and environments than those who do not. Behavioral science has not developed to the point where we can isolate
and control such variables.

When scanning the table of contents, the reader will quickly
note a lack of traditional classification. The selections are listed
only alphabetically by author or editor. To use the usual type
of classification would have violated the orientation of the volume because it would have imposed a bias on the interpretation
of the readings. The reader himself may wish to experiment with
various classifications: type of behavior, type of "behaver," type
of societal reaction, type of rationale, and any others which
might seem appropriate for his purpose.

We wish to express our appreciation to the authors and
publishers who gave us permission to reprint their works. We
wish also to thank William Doll for his long fruitful hours in the
library, Saul Feldman and Arthur Neal for leading us to several
key selections, and to Mrs. Gloria Sterin for her able editorial
assistance. Finally, we want to thank our wives, Dawn, Joan, and
Eva, for their patience and understanding in allowing us to complete this project during the last days of a summer's vacation.

Cleveland Heights, Ohio   C. H. M.
                                                           J. K. S., Jr.
                                                           M. L.

Contents

Contents

IN THEIR OWN BEHALF

1   *Perhaps the United States' most renowned madam*
comments on her "place in the social structure."

Providing a quality service

polly adler

If I was to make my living as a madam, I could not be concerned either with the rightness or wrongness of prostitution,
considered either from a moral or criminological standpoint. I
had to look at it simply as a part of life which exists today as it
existed yesterday, and which, unless there occur changes more
profound than can at present be visualized, will exist tomorrow.
The operation of any business is contingent on the law of supply
and demand, and if there were no customers, there certainly
would be no whorehouses. Prostitution exists because men will
pay for sexual gratification, and whatever men are willing to pay
for, someone will provide.

I had found that being cynical and half-hearted about my
profession had worked out to the disadvantage both of my customers and myself. But if I could think of myself as fulfilling a
need, as one in a long line which stretched back to the beginning
of civilization, then, no matter what stigma attached to my calling, at least I was not "antisocial." I had a very definite place in
the social structure. I belonged, I had a job to do, and I could
find satisfaction in doing it the very best way I knew how.

To the uninitiated it might seem that there can hardly be
much difference in houses, and of course in the bedroom the
procedure is fairly well standarized, varying only with the customer's whim. (This last item would make a book—or, rather, a
whole library—all by itself, and is a subject I will leave to Kinsey
and to Freud.) Actually, however, the atmosphere, surroundings

and quality of entertainment depend on such factors as geography, economics and contemporary tastes. In America today you would find no counterpart of an Algerian peg-house or the Yoshiwara in Japan or the Fish Market in Cairo. In fact, for the most part, the red-light district is a thing of the past. And, in fact, the old-time sporting house has vanished like the old-time saloon. There are no more establishments like the Everleigh Club or like the famous house in St. Louis run by Babe Connors (she of the diamond-inlaid teeth), where Paderewski once accompanied bawdy songs on the piano and in which, so it is said, a Republican platform once was written.

Yet all whorehouses, past and present and wherever located, exist to cater to an instinctive appetite, just as all eating places exist primarily to supply food. But aside from their common reason for being, you will find little resemblance between a "greasy spoon," an automat, and the Colony or Chambord. Similarly there is a world of difference between a two-dollar house and a ten-dollar house, between a twenty-dollar house and what a punning friend of mine once called a *maison carte blanche*. Moreover, just as in top restaurants it is the personality of the maître d' which gives a place its particular cachet, so does the personality of the madam count for a great deal, and in the long run the difference between my place and other houses in the same price bracket was me.

Leaving modesty aside, I still cannot say what, in particular, it was about me which put Polly Adler's house in a class by itself. (I guess maybe I'm too close to the subject to write of it objectively.) But I can say that I did have a somewhat different attitude toward my customers than did the other madams. To me (once I'd dislodged those chips on my shoulders) my patrons were not just ambulatory bankrolls, but individual human beings—social acquaintances and often friends—entitled to the cordiality and consideration one extends to an honored guest. There is a Polish saying: "When a guest enters the house, God enters the house," and this was the golden rule of my hospitality.

The way I looked at it was this: When a woman marries a man she knocks herself out (or should) to gratify his every wish. She will cook to please his stomach, dress to please his eye, behave to suit his mood. After all, why not? Isn't he supporting her? Isn't he giving her his love and respect? Well, I didn't get the love, and I didn't always get the respect, but there were certainly a lot of husbands supporting me, and I figured it was my duty to find out what they wanted and give it to them.

I recall meeting an old-time madam in, of all places, a Turkish bath, and while we were sitting there in the steam room, as was to be expected we got to talking business. "Tell me, Polly," said Evelyn, "what is the secret of your success? I'm a much older hand in the make-believe love game than you, but I've never seen anything like the way you've come to the top. What's the angle?"

"If I have an angle," I said, "it's quality and consideration —the quality of my establishment and consideration for my customers. Bergdorf's and Bonwit's dress their windows attractively to pull in trade. I give my customers an attractive house. People in stores prefer to patronize good-looking, capable sales girls. I give my customers good-looking, capable hostesses. In the finest and most exclusive shops, the customers are treated as privileged friends of the management, their special likes and dislikes are tabulated, and they are given personalized service. Well, that's the way I try to run my business."

Though I didn't go on to say so to Evelyn, there were two other precepts which I applied to running my house: *Cleanliness is next to godliness,* and *Honesty is the best policy.* I was a fanatic on the subject of cleanliness. It was a must that both the house and the girls be immaculate. As for honesty, I considered it a keystone in my relationship with the customers. The men knew they would never be rolled at my house, nor be given a padded check. As my reputation for square-shooting became established, I had a number of customers who would simply hand me a signed blank check when they arrived, and tell me to fill it out in the morning—and they were men whose bank accounts did not contain peanuts. Also, often when a patron had an out-of-town guest whom he wished to be entertained, he would telephone me and name the amount which he was prepared to spend on the evening, and he could be sure his guest would not be short-changed. Sometimes, my patrons made me handsome presents when they were particularly pleased with my brand of hospitality. And if I liked the man I would accept his gift. After all, if

Washington officials can accept deep freezes, why shouldn't I grab off a little ice?

A man's visit to Polly's meant more than just sleeping with a woman. He expected to be amused and even informed. He knew he could count on conversation about the latest plays and the newest books; he would hear fresh and funny stories and anecdotes about the town characters. Good talk and good liquor, good-looking girls in good-looking surroundings, these were the ingredients which went into the making of a good night, and when my men said, "Good night" (though usually it was five or six in the morning), they really meant it had been.

Sunbathers, ahoy!

american sunbathing association

PRINCIPLES AND STANDARDS

Our goal is the healthy mind in the healthy body. This is not only a creed but a way of life. Sun, light and air are vital conditions of human well-being. We believe these elements are insufficiently used in present-day life, to the detriment of physical and moral health. For the purpose of health and recreation and for the conditioning of man to his world we offer a *new social practice,* based on the known wholesome value of exposure to these elements and in the spirit of naturalness, cheerfulness, and cleanness of body and mind that they symbolize. We aim to make the fullest possible use of sun, light and air by a program of exercise and life in the open in such a way as will result in the maximum physical and mental benefit.

We believe in the essential wholesomeness of the human body, and all its functions. We therefore regard the body neither as an object of shame nor as a subject for levity or erotic exploitation. Any attitude or behavior inconsistent with this view is contrary to the whole spirit of the society and has no place among us.

The practice of our physical culture tends toward simplicity and integrity in all ways. We counsel for our members the sane and hygienic life. We reserve the right to impose abstinence from stimulants and intoxicants at our meetings and on our grounds.

We invite to our membership persons of character of all ages and both sexes. Our purposes are not exclusively physical or

Reprinted by permission of The American Sunbathing Association, Inc.

cultural or esthetic but rather a normal union of all these. We make no tests of politics, religion or opinion provided that these are so held as not to obscure the purposes of the Movement. It is intended that the Movement shall be representative of the whole social order.

WHAT WE BELIEVE

We believe in the essential wholesomeness of the human body and all its functions.

We believe in inculcating in all persons a desire to improve and perfect the body by natural living in the out-of-doors.

We believe that sunshine and fresh air in immediate contact with the entire body are basic factors in maintaining radiant health and happiness.

We believe in creating beauty in all things and therefore encourage men and women by daily care and culture to create for themselves the body beautiful.

We believe that the health of the nation will be immeasurably advanced through the wide acceptance of the principles and standards advocated by the American Sunbathing Association.

We believe that presentation of the male and female figures in their entirety and completeness needs no apology or defense and that only in such an attitude of mind can we find true modesty.

THE MAGNA CARTA OF NUDISM

Under proper safeguards and for the public weal we desire:

1. The elimination from our statute books of all legislation that makes social nudism *per se* an illegal thing.
2. The setting aside of at least some part of our public beaches, parks, picnic grounds and recreation centers where nudists may freely live the natural life in the open.
3. The constitutional right of a free press to print text and unaltered pictures which decently and naturally represent nudism as it actually is being lived and practiced.

Today these demands represent the rightful desire of a minority; tomorrow they may represent the priceless heritage of the majority.

THE SCOPE AND AIMS OF MODERN NUDE CULTURE

Modern Civilization with all its artificiality, repressive and inhibitive tendencies, prevents man from using the vital elements under natural conditions as a nude animal. A better adjustment between the artificial and natural elements in life can be attained by the elimination of society's taboo on nudity, replaced by a sincere belief in the essential wholesomeness of the human body in all its functions.

If the individual, in a state of complete nudity, leads a natural hygienic life in the open, has immediate contact with sun, air, light, water, warmth and cold, and takes well-balanced exercises, he will derive great satisfaction, regain hardihood, develop physical fitness, a feeling of freedom, a distinct sense of the enlargement of his personality, and the maximum mental benefit.

The practice of nude culture in a group will satisfy man's gregarious tendency and will—by bringing the whole naked body within the scope of personality—give a more accurate impression and increase the significance of our fellow human beings. It will develop fully the urge for improvement in physical beauty, and enrich the mind by frank discussion, deeper argumentation, closer contact and understanding co-operation.

Complete nudity in association with the opposite sex will furnish adequate knowledge of the physical make-up of the other, will obviate the abnormally erotic effect of the concealment caused by clothing, and will permit the full development of a sex life unhampered by false modesty and unassuaged curiosity. It will bring a mutual selection for mating and procreation based on an appreciative understanding of the complete personality of the mate.

The union of physical, mental, social, and aesthetic purposes in the nude culture movement will have far-reaching results, will develop physically healthier and more mentally capable individ-

uals, and—practiced through generations—will be an important
factor in the evolution of a higher type of mankind.

A PLATFORM OF NUDISM

We maintain that nudism
Looks on life as being essentially pure,
Assists moral and physical cleanliness,
Never degrades—ever exalts,
Keeps our thoughts and actions clean,
Says that the body is more than raiment;

Offers physical, moral and spiritual comfort to all,
Foregoes conventional modesty and induces true propriety, chastity
and morality,
Negatives the contention that the wearing of clothes is a moral or
spiritual necessity.

Locates in one brotherhood all sects and denominations,
Demands pure motives of its adherents,
Inspires pride of body, and is a reminder that a healthy body
should be a universal heritage,
Shows sex to be normally undisturbing and reduces it to its proper
proportion in the scheme of life,
Makes the instruction of the young in the great facts of life a
matter of simplicity, beauty and truth.

DEFINITION OF A NUDIST

A nudist is a person who believes that clothes are neither
normal nor natural to the human being, but may be worn when
special circumstances of environment or physical comfort would
indicate the propriety of so doing. He does not conceive of the
human body as being in anywise shameful in itself but *carefully*
distinguishes between decent and indecent exposure. He accords
to every part of the body an equally normal naturalness wholly
devoid of any vulgarity or obscenity. In this view an elbow, a
pubic arch, or a nose are equally respectable; a thyroid, a testicle,
a mammary are just so many glands each with its particular but
equally splendid function to perform.

The nudist holds that sun and air bathing are essential to

the maintenance of health at its best; that there is no essential reason why the sexes should be segregated since modern psychology furnishes many reasons why they should not be. He therefore believes and practices a nonsegregated or social nudism in games, swimming, sun and air bathing and in outdoor sports generally; while in the home, within the family circle, he cultivates the clothesless life as being the normal life. The nudist believes, and hopes, that the limits within which nudism may be practiced with propriety will gradually broaden until the practice of social nudism becomes an accepted procedure.

3   *A young woman recounts her experiences in obtaining an illegal abortion.*

"I didn't have the baby, I had the abortion"

anonymous

A long-short year ago, the taste of the experience still full upon me, I decided to write an article about abortion. About having an abortion. About my having my abortion: the loneliness of it, the pregnancy books with their terse two-paragraph discussions (dismissals) of abortion, the streets full of baby carriages, the people who helped, the people who didn't. I wanted to say it all, tear it out of myself if I had to.

What with one thing and another, the article spent a year ripening in a desk drawer. Rereading it now, I find much in the article I'd forgotten I felt, and much that I might not feel *now* (Aren't we all older and cooler?)—and also a kind of raw-edged immediacy that makes me think that this piece by my younger self (I feel as though I'm talking about something written by a sister, or a friend) stands up as an emotional document, a reaching out, a way of saying to the many others who need to know it (and will continue to need to know until the setup changes) that someone else was there, and understands.

I think of the experience as beginning with a moment of awful premonition. The gynecologist's office. I don't remember why I was there—just checking on things, maybe. Liking to know that all goes well inside. Yes. And all was well. Then afterward, just talking, the doctor tried to persuade me to take birth control pills. But I (big nature girl) said No, not wanting to tamper with

From *Cosmopolitan*, **163** (July, 1967). Reprinted by permission of *Cosmopolitan*.

something that works so well by itself (I mean, why fool around?) though of course I hated, and hate, using a diaphragm, as who does not. And the doctor, resigned, said, "OK, but please be careful; not a week goes by without one of my girls getting pregnant—last week a graduate nurse, in fact, so please be very careful"—and I said, "Of course," but there was a chilling moment, a flashing premonition that the longing to conceive was strong enough in me to outsmart all thinking and mechanical things.

(This, I think, is the deepest pain of most abortions; girls who "accidentally" get pregnant are so often girls who subconsciously *want* to get pregnant. Do they also want to have babies? But it is not a thought-out thing, it is grounded in the flesh; the whole body moves to receive and to hold. It is the way we are made, the instinct of the structure.)

Yes. And three weeks later I was saying over the phone: "Doctor, I think I'm this week's pregnancy"—and she said, "What?"—and I said, "Don't you remember? You told me not a week went by without one of your patients getting pregnant" —and she said, "Oh no, not you, Anne. How late are you?"—and I said, "A week, and I'm never late"—and she said (in a tired, automatic, chiding sort of way), "Usually never late, you mean." And then she told me that she wanted me to take a pill called Provera, one a day for five days, which would bring on my period if it were delayed for any other reason than It, but that the pill wasn't absolutely certain, and if nothing happened within a week I should have a rabbit test.

So I went to the drugstore, to my nice young-father druggist, wondering how he would feel about it, and gave him a small slip of paper with "Provera" and my doctor's name and number on it; and he called her and had the prescription filled just as if it were for cough medicine or something, while I sat waiting in a chair behind a rack of hair curlers, feeling suddenly very heavy, with hurting feet and infinite stomach.

Meanwhile, Harry. Poor Harry. How terrible for him, and I didn't help. Such bad timing. All this unlovely discovery happening after the finally not-good weekend when it had more or less ended. And I'm afraid I made it worse by shutting him out. Not deliberately; it was just that my universe was suddenly so nar-

row, so secretly magic, sad and blue, that nothing existed outside
my own body. And—I don't know—I suppose maybe I was hating him a little for not being the man I would marry. (There
were so many things not right between us, however much love
there had been.) And he must have been hating me a little, not
so much for my mechanical carelessness and that frightening will
to conceive, as for being younger, so much younger, with so many
more chances to have my six children while he might not so
easily go that way again.

That week, that terrible time of taking pills and having
nothing happen, was maybe the roughest I've ever had. Getting
through work each day required absurd amounts of determination—I was so tired, so utterly weighted down with a kind of
oppressive fatigue like nothing else in this world. I was a gray
thing (The whole world was gray) dragging itself from moment
to moment. That week every woman I saw on the street was
pregnant or wheeling a laughing baby. I kept running into
statistics about how many women had died from abortions the
previous year. I could not stop buying and ingesting books for
pregnant women, obsessed as I was with the world within me.

I suppose it was terrible most of all because it was a time of
such uncertainty, of waiting. Though what uncertainty? I knew I
was pregnant, just as I never thought I was when I wasn't. My
body told me. My breasts. Everywhere. My skin. The heaviness
throughout. Running to the john. The feeling of containing the
whole world in my belly.

Nor was I ever really uncertain about what course to take.
(I thought of a conversation Harry and I had had long before
this happened. "I don't believe in abortion, you know," he said
to me one diaphragmless night when we were wondering whether
or not to. "Neither do I," I said. "Nobody believes in abortion.
People just have them.") What made the abortion the unques-
tioned outcome of this pregnancy—and maybe this sounds hate-
ful, horrible, cold—was a balance of absolute against absolute,
life against life, in which the confrontation of the life not yet
fully realized had to give way to those lives already there. Mine,
Harry's, the woman Harry really belonged with, my parents, my
brother, and then, too, the actual day-to-day life which would be
the destiny of this child. I was too old to do more than play with

the ultraromantic dream of just going out and bearing the baby somewhere, somehow. Even then I loved all my children-to-be too much to think that merely loving them would ever be enough.

But I don't know—how can I make it sound like it was? It was not some mathematical equation, this balancing of absolutes, it was nothing like that at all. I can only say that if you have ever been there, in that no-man's-land, that nightmarish land of absolute confronting absolute, you will understand.

No, the uncertainty was not whether I was pregnant, or what I should do; it was the crueler (because smaller) uncertainty of not knowing who would do the abortion, and where, and when, and how to set it up, and just what it would be like. I wanted to go to the legendary Dr. S.—because I didn't want to die. And because the one other price I didn't want to pay, even though I'm not wealthy, was damage to my ability to carry another child. Blood, pain, sordidness—anything else could be endured. But not that.

All through this waiting week I called Dr. S. First thing when I woke up. Ten times during the day as I ducked out of the office on every possible excuse to head for a pay phone. At night when I came home. But his phone would just ring and ring. Twice I called Information to check on the number—it was extraordinary; both times the operator gave me the number off the top of her head as if I had asked for the listing of the Fire Department or the most popular girl in town. But Dr. S. didn't answer and didn't and didn't until the sound of that ringing began echoing in my head.

Throughout this time there was the deepest loneliness. I would walk along the streets entirely unto myself, everywhere seeing swollen-bellied women, so-much-to-be-envied women, and shop-windows filled with tiny dresses. I thought of a little lace dress I had bought one summer in France for the daughter I would one day have; where was it now?

I suppose I could have cut into the loneliness by talking to other women about the whole thing. Almost everyone I knew (at twenty-three) had had an abortion or knew someone who had. But I just couldn't go to a friend and ask: "What was it like? Did you feel what I'm feeling?"—partly out of shyness and fear of intruding, and more maybe because I couldn't bear to think of it

as just another experience—like going to Europe or smoking pot.
I mean, it wasn't just an abortion. I had conceived. That was the
whole other magic part of it. I had conceived! Somehow it was
much easier to talk to a couple of men I was very close to. And I
came to a whole new appreciation of the sweetness of moving in a
world of sentient men.

Then the week of Provera was more than up, and I knew on
top of knowing (though I didn't yet have the results of the
rabbit test which I had arranged for). I began throwing up in the
morning. I also began to panic. Dr. S. seemed to be out of the
question.

Finally I called my dear friend K. at his office. Saint Abortion. He would help me. He had to help me. His secretary said he
was on vacation (awful moment) but (beautiful moment) she
would have him call me collect in a day or two if I gave her my
name and number. He called me that night, having guessed what
I wanted, and gave me the name and phone number that he had
brought with him across the country in case of calls like mine. A
man who cares that much—this is a great man.

He told me that Dr. M. was very good, that Dr. S.—who had
retired—used to send his overflow to him, that he had helped lots
of girls that K. knew, and everything would be all right, everything would be fine. I dialed the number K. had given me, an
answering service, and left my name and number with a calm-
voiced operator (Did she know?), asking her to have the doctor
call me as soon as she heard from him, it didn't matter how
late.

The call came that 2 A.M. Low voice, Spanish accent, careful.
"Is this Anne?"

"Yes. Is this Dr. M.?"

"Yes. How did you get my number?" I told him. And asked
if he would help me.

"How far along are you?"

"Five weeks, six."

"Can you come tomorrow?"

"Tomorrow I—well, I work. Could you take me Saturday?"
That was two days off. Suddenly I wanted time.

"Saturday—OK. But you'll have to come early. At eight."

"Yes. Fine. All right."

He told me where I was to go—a certain city square in a town just outside New York. I was to be there in time to call him at 7:45 at another number which he gave me. I mustn't be late. I should come with a friend. My stomach should be empty. It would be two hundred fifty dollars (as K. had told me). That was all.

I hung up the phone. The panic was gone. His voice had been kind. I looked at the phone number and directions I'd written down and put the piece of paper in my passport case, home of crucial documents. It would be all right. I felt very lucky. I slept.

The next day I called Harry to tell him what was going to happen. He said he would bring the money over. . . . I felt horrible about the money part. We were so—tentative with each other now. Strangers. We had come so close to something we both had wanted, and now there was this. All I wanted was for it all to be over.

I also called my gynecologist—to ask, crazily, the results of the rabbit test. She said there had been a mix-up in the lab and the report wasn't ready yet. I told her to forget it. "Oh, did your period come?" she asked brightly. "No," I said, with a half-hysterical laugh. "Oh, *that*," she said in a terrible voice which I will never, ever forgive. "OK, dear." And she hung up. Not even asking how I was. And this was a doctor. A woman. A person.

Those last two days before the abortion were strangely easy. The terrible heaviness had left me. Not that I was exactly ebullient, but the panicky uncertainty was gone. And I think I was buoyed up by the idea that if I had to be going through all this, I was getting off relatively easy. Very easy. I wasn't some poor abandoned kid wandering around with no one to turn to; I didn't have to go to my parents (who would have backed me up whatever I decided to do about it and, for that reason and all the others, deserved to be spared this); there wasn't really a money problem; and if I wasn't going off to some nice hospital to have it done under ideal conditions, I still didn't have to go to some horrible butcher who would cut me up into little pieces for the consumption of the headline vultures (the same people who help keep abortion illegal and so much more hazardous and headline-prone than it has to be).

Friday night Harry came over with an envelope full of cash. He didn't stay very long. It was a terrible, hurting moment. I don't think we once really looked at each other.

I had already told Harry that I didn't want him to come with me Saturday; I thought it would be too traumatic if he did. I had begun to be afraid less of what was going to be wrought on my body than of what might be unleashed inside my head. He seemed relieved about this decision. (Though I wonder now if I wasn't cruel in shutting him out so much, and if he didn't feel this.) He was going to the country for the weekend—his casualness reassured me. I mean, he wouldn't plan to be out of town if I were going to die, would he?

After Harry left I wandered around for the rest of the evening. I'd decided to spend it mostly by myself—thinking I would not be exactly great company. I became strangely calm. I read for a little while. Maugham. I always read Maugham in moments of crisis. I thought about straightening up my apartment, sweetly chaotic place, but since women traditionally clean their drawers when they sense they are going to die, I demurred.

I sat down then with a full-enough sense of the daytime television-drama of what I was doing to write my parents and brother a letter—in case. Halfway through I realized for certain that I wasn't afraid because I would be paying much more attention to style if this were to be my last document on earth; that if anything went wrong the blame belonged not to Harry, or the abortionist, or the people who'd helped me, but to the self-righteous and therefore inhumane people who keep the abortion setup the way it is.

I slept, carried through this last night of waiting by the knowledge that it was just that. I woke to the alarm at six, took a long shower, did my hair for a while, brushed some color onto my face, got dressed. I picked out a dress I knew I wouldn't terribly mind never wearing again. I figured (rightly) that I somehow just might not want to put it on after that morning.

Peter, another friend, came for me at seven in a car he had borrowed. I thought it would be best to go with him. There was a loving easiness between us that would not give way before this. And he knew about abortions.

It was raining and cold, but traffic was easy. I wasn't too

tense. I didn't want Peter to worry about me so I concentrated on being relaxed. We made each other laugh. Was I numb? I don't know. I could only think that it would soon be over.

We were early and went into a coffee shop to wait. I sipped weak tea (I hadn't eaten since the noon before) and wondered if everyone knew why I was there. I kept looking at the clock, like a nervous lover. Finally it was time to call. I went outside to a phone booth.

Dr. M. answered. He said I was to wait in front of a certain florist's. I looked through the phone booth window and there it was. He said his assistant would come for me—what was I wearing? I described my raincoat. He said that I must come alone, that I was to give his phone number to whomever I was with and he should call me an hour after I left. I agreed. It didn't matter. I convinced myself that I preferred going alone. (Why subject Peter to more than was necessary?) But the doctor could have said anything and it wouldn't have mattered.

Peter and I waited outside the florist's. It began to feel like a bad movie, almost too ludicrous to be real. I just didn't belong to this. It was too unreal to frighten me.

Ten minutes passed. It was getting to be too long. Then a man came. I think I'd expected a woman. It didn't matter.

"Anne?" Low voice, kind.

"Yes." He took my arm. I just had time to look at Peter over my shoulder. Did I smile? He nodded calmly and said he would call me in an hour.

The man—I never learned his name—led me across the street, holding my arm to protect me from the traffic, and so I could share his umbrella, and perhaps because he was afraid I might faint or run away. It didn't matter. The touch was lovely. Warm. We took a strange gangster-movie route through back alleys and up side streets. Did we talk? I don't remember. Except that he asked me if I was afraid and I said I wasn't. It was all so beyond fear.

We went into an apartment-hotel, through the back door, up the back stairs. He knocked on a door. Dr. M. pulled it open an inch, then all the way, then locked it behind us. I think I shook hands with him. Yes. To confirm—something. He asked if I was afraid. I said I wasn't. He said this was good because it was

so much harder when a girl was hysterical. This made me want
to show all the fiber I'd ever imagined was in me. I made myself
think of all the women in the world who had ever gone through
really grueling things. I wanted to carry it off like a lady.

We went from the little foyer through a curtained doorway
into the main room. For a moment I almost balked. It was a little
room that made me understand what "seedy" meant, an ugly
hotel bedroom distinguished from a thousand others only by the
portable operating table set up in one corner. The table looked
ready for flight. I could see the hinged seam in the middle and
the leather carrying handle. There was something at the foot of
it that looked like an inner tube. And beneath it two plastic
buckets. There was a metal container on a side table with instruments boiling in it. I recognized a hypodermic. I felt an acute
lack of intellectual interest. I looked away.

Dr. M. asked me to take off my panties and stockings and to
lie down on the bed on the other side of the room. He put on a
plastic glove and gave me a brief internal examination. I must
have been a thousand miles away from my body at that moment.
It felt like any other gynecological examination. We weren't
people. Nothing really mattered.

He said that I was only five or six weeks pregnant, as I'd
known, and that it would be easy. I told him I'd rather not have
an anesthetic if I didn't have to, that this was the only part I was
afraid of. I knew as long as I was conscious nothing too terrible
could happen. He said this was fine, better in fact. It would be
over that much more quickly for me.

I got up on the table then, still clothed, but with my dress
pulled up. All of this—my seminakedness, everything—was impersonal beyond description. These weren't—men. Dr. M. tied
my legs, bent at the knees, to posts on either side of the table,
gently, in a way that wouldn't interfere with my circulation. He
said the operation would feel no worse than bad menstrual
cramps and that I should tell him if I wanted him to stop from
time to time. He smiled and said I could use the worst language
I knew—but please not to scream.

Then came the sensation of being pumped up, the dilation
part, and the terrible cramps; and then the scraping, which I
remember not as a feeling but as a wet, wet sound and a metal-

lic smell, metal on metal; then the pumping up, then the scraping. . . .

I didn't scream, I didn't even swear . . . the pain was there, but it was not unbearable; nothing was, because I was alive and it would soon be over and I would yet have all my babies. The assistant was holding my hands. He kept mopping my face. His eyes were worried and kind. When it got too bad I would plead for the doctor to stop, and he would, then it would start again. It was not as horrible as I'd thought it would be, but I wanted it to end. I kept asking how much more. Not much the doctor kept saying; everything was fine. His voice was far away. He was saying that it was important that everything came out. Very kind. "Are you all right?"

Somehow I didn't exist at that moment. Thinking only: It's being done, it's being done, it will be over. Then I could hear myself asking him to stop—was that my voice?—trying not to moan, and he would stop, his face so gentle, and I was alive, and the metal on metal, a hand on my forehead, "not much more now," softest eyes, and then it was over.

I lay on the bed for a while, cotton-stuffed, waiting for the cramps to subside, coming back from that world to this, waiting for Peter to call—the hour hadn't yet passed—making silly conversation, giddy. . . .

Peter called. I told him I was fine, could leave anytime. I still had cramps. What were cramps? I combed my hair, astonished that the face in the mirror was the same, like a sixteen-year-old girl regarding herself after parting with her virginity. The doctor told me to take it easy for a day or two and to abstain from sexual relations for at least ten days. He said that my normal menstrual cycle would resume in about six weeks (It did, to the day), and that I should be careful, because it would be easier for me to get pregnant now. I should go back to him, and not call my doctor if anything went wrong—but nothing would, he assured me.

Then I gave him the money, which he counted with an apologetic money-counting look, put on my coat, shook his hand again, went down the back stairs, out the back door, through the back streets to the car, where Peter was waiting.

right. Nothing else mattered. Peter had coffee waiting. It was great. Everything was great.

There were still some twinges of cramps when I got home, so Peter went to the drugstore and got me a pain-killer. Then I went to sleep, so happy to be in my home, my bed. All was silent, and safe.

I woke up mid-afternoon when Harry called from the country. The cramps were all gone. I think I practically sang over the phone. I wanted to kiss trees, buildings, everything—I was alive! I went out and walked and walked, full of some fantastic energy. Everything delighted me. I felt so lucky to be alive. And intact. I knew I was all right. You are good to me God, I thought. Is it wrong to think of You now?

There was only one bad moment after that. A week or so later I was wandering around by myself—I think I'd just had a fight with someone—and I went into a movie. On the way out I saw K., who'd just gotten my letter thanking him for giving me the abortionist's name and number. We looked at each other and grinned and then started to laugh. We laughed and laughed. Then he went off with his friends and I went home by myself and cried and cried. That night I was the loneliest girl in the world. I wanted the baby so much then. More than I had ever wanted anything, I just wanted that baby.

4   *Jay, a London prostitute, provides information on those who make her profession possible: her customers.*

Streetwalker

One in the morning, and in spite of the lamps Piccadilly is very grey. Most of the sightseers and partygoers have gone home, and the long street is once again in the possession of the night people—the outcasts and the eccentrics, the profit seekers and the escapers, the buyers and the bought.

Across the road I can see the looming darkness of trees, overhung by a heavy autumn sky billowed with rain. The grass is another darkness, subtly different in texture, distinguishable only to eyes used to the night and with time to spare. Few people look into the shadows or step onto the darkness, though. They keep determinedly to the paths civilized by electricity, walking a little faster through unlit alleys and the black, open spaces of the park, as if they would prefer to run.

In my profession, however, there is time to learn the warp and weft of leaf and grass blade, if one cares so to spend it. And nightfall itself holds few terrors, because the dangers of the job are much more immediate and tangible, and the lesser fear gives way to the greater caution.

I always stand here, where Half Moon Street and Piccadilly meet, and every brick of this shop front, every fault in its paintwork, every crack in the pavement is familiar to me. There is a certain safety and advantage in this familarity, too: I know the quickest route to take if I spot the police, the best angle of light from the street-lamp for my face and figure, the most comfortable

From *Streetwalker* (Anonymous). Copyright © 1959 by The Bodley Head. Reprinted by permission of The Viking Press, Inc. and The Bodley Head, Ltd.

section of wall to lean on when the minutes drag. Besides, they expect to find me somewhere near this corner if they come back for more, and a good many of them do.

This is a slack night and spare time must be carefully used. Introspection is obviously to be avoided, but the streets themselves have many things to teach. Learning how to survive in London's grey wilderness and among its people is no easy course, though getting to know the heart of the city and its physical geography, the patterns of its squares and byways, is absorbing.

And so one whiles away the hours until habit and the clock on the car showroom say that it is time to go, time to abandon the street, to plunge into the pulsing jungle of basement club, spieler,* or backroom café, or simply into a warm cab, and then home. Preferably, of course, the time is too busy with money-making to need any other filling.

Twenty yards away, down to my right, Big Barbara is chatting a geezer, though the stream of polished professional patter she is directing at him warrants a less terse description. Barbara is an old hand, with the articulation and the grand manner of a duchess. She swoops on her prey, hand outstretched, smiling with autocratic charm. Taking an arm, she walks him swiftly up and down, outlining her plans and capabilities, hinting at bizarre possibilities and never mentioning money; she might be describing a charity bazaar, and, as it would take a strong man to avoid subscribing in that case, so it takes iron nerve to refuse her actual suggestion. Even more will power is needed to leave her flat with any cash. I wish I knew how she did it—there she goes now, fifty if she's a day, hobbling the only visible sheep to shear him in the befrilled luxury of her pink and mauve bedroom.

To be a successful prostitute, you've got to have at least one of three things: either outstandingly good looks and figure—and many of us are really beautiful; or the personality and individuality to make a man look at you twice, and then come back again and again; or the ability to talk or scare your clients, once you've got them back in your flat, into paying more than the original sum stipulated for extra attentions, or less ordinary functions—you must persuade them into something new, or roll them, steal from them.

* Gambling den.

If you possess all these assets, you have no business being connected with commercial sex at all. Your place in the world is assured, if it is money and power that you want. If you have two of these qualifications, your best bet is to be a telephone number on an agency list, a hostess in a top-rank club, or the mistress of wealthy men. Most of us, however, are endowed with only one of these qualities, and quite a large number have none at all.

A girl in this most unfortunate position should really consider going home to her parents, or marrying the first reasonable man who comes her way, to whom she will probably make a passable wife. She certainly shouldn't waste her time on the streets, because, unless you can earn ten pounds a night without much difficulty, it isn't worth it. The toll is much too heavy.

If I fit into any category I suppose it is the second. I'm certainly not beautiful to look at and I'm twenty-two, which, while being by no means old, is still four or five important years more than some. My figure isn't bad, and I've got the smallest waist in Piccadilly after midnight, but that isn't enough to qualify in the first section.

As far as the financial wizardry is concerned, I'm useless. I've never learned to haggle, and I don't think I shall ever be able to do so now. I prefer to put a price-tag on myself, so to speak, before leaving the street, and then take that amount without asking for more. I'm no good at rolling, either, not because I believe it to be morally wrong, for it seems no crime to take from a man who is buying this particular commodity, but because I'm too clumsy. I simply haven't got the courage to be caught tripping over the doormat on my way out with someone's wallet.

Willy, the contraceptive man, is coming in the distance. He must be at least sixty-five, and nobody can remember how long he has been plying this particular trade. He used to be an undertaker, selling this commodity as an extremely profitable sideline, but his firm retired him because his health wasn't good enough for coffin-bearing. However, he makes enough money out of us to keep himself in Wills Whiffs, and to support his wife, an old car, and two Pekinese dogs. I think he'd miss us if he gave it up, anyway. He likes to have a chat in passing, whether his wares are needed or not, and it breaks the monotony to see his sprightly, birdlike figure approaching.

"All right, Jay?" he calls as he passes.

"Yes, thanks. None tonight."

He smiles brightly and passes on up the street, an integral part of the night, the cuckoo who calls the hours for us.

It is remarkable how much of a routine this business of being on the streets can develop into. I go to the same club every night, leave it at a quarter to twelve, wander down Shaftesbury Avenue, across Piccadilly Circus, up Regent Street as far as Air Street, which cuts through to Picadilly itself, and then dawdle along to Half Moon Street, which I reach at about five to midnight.

I stand just inside Half Moon Street until one o'clock, when the crowd has thinned to the buyers and us, the sellers, and when Willy puts in his first appearance, and then move round to Piccadilly to really get to work. At four, as a rule, I make my way back to Soho for a meal before going home.

There is a routine of approach, performance, and farewell, too. Even the smallest action—the call to a cab, the switching on of a light, the pocketing of money, is duplicated time and time again. The same small-talk, the same phrases are repeated, with only slight variations for the differing types of client, who behave with equally monotonous uniformity, within their type.

I've always thought the "Hello, darling! How about a nice time?" sort of approach rather crude. "How about a nice short time?" strikes me as downright bad taste, and as inviting as a slap round the face. What one might call the "filthy picture" one is a little more acceptable: "Why don't you come home with me and look at my photos, books, sketches?" does at least suggest an interesting meal, or one with a piquant sauce to it.

Naturally, it is sensible to promise rather more than one intends to give, especially since one gives the minimum. It is not a good idea to state any definite length of time, because although most men like to leave as soon as they've had what they came for, quite a few are determined to get every penny of what they consider to be their money's worth, or even more, which can be most unpleasant.

If the giving of some sort of time limit seems unavoidable, I find it best to say, "Oh, about half an hour!" with the sort of smile which suggests I might stretch a point, just for them. Actually, it is quite possible to leave Piccadilly, take a cab for the five minutes' drive back to your gaff, or flat—for no flat should be out of five minutes' travelling reach to be practical—get the performance over, and be back on your corner, all within twenty minutes. I know, because I've done it often.

When I first went on the game, it seemed to me that I was meeting a gallery of widely various and interesting people. Turning from bank manager to sailor, from poet to business magnate, playboy to thief held a definite excitement because of the outward trappings of their trades and ways of life. But as the weeks went by, army uniform and Savile Row suit became united as one anonymous garment, hanging over the back of my chair; complexions, features, hair lost their individuality and one face became all faces, one body all bodies, so that even crippled and distorted limbs were not much more distasteful than the flabby, sagging flesh of the old, and the muscular straightness of the young men not much better. Occupation and class lost significance, becoming no more than a rough guide to financial status and a useful subject for small-talk during the moments when conversation was called for.

Not, of course, that I stopped showing interest in clients as individuals—merely, I feign this interest now, and the imitation passes as genuine, so there is no loss on either side. But much more important than what a man does, I have learned, is what he wants from me, how he is going to try to get it, and how little he will be satisfied with.

Since clothes and speech are no certain guide to character or inclination, when a total stranger comes up to me in the street, assessment of his true self and his potentiality has to be largely instinctive. A man who is rude may be naturally aggressive, or he may be disguising shyness in this way. Timidity may be simply what it seems, or it may be a nervous approach to some perverted act long craved for, the outward sign of some inner, contorted desire whose very existence and strength is frightening enough, but whose execution and fulfilment is even more terrifying, though at the same time intensely exciting.

A man who behaves normally and naturally is unlikely to

provide any unpleasantness. A man who haggles about price and conditions, who wants fine details as to exactly what he is going to get, is best left alone, unless it is a very slack night, as is the one with salaciousness over-brightening his eyes, or with hands quick to fumble at you in the open street. And the drunkard, too, is to be avoided, as is the tough, the obviously insane, and the frequently met practical joker.

Once at the gaff, the hurried, the efficient, and the business-like are obviously favourites. Those who refuse to part with their money in advance must be got rid of, as must be those whose peculiarities did not reveal themselves at first meeting. The timid must be reassured of their safety or flattered into feeling that they are the men they want to be. The Don Juans, with prowess to display and achievements to be retailed, must be suffered with patience; the Galahads who, with immense condescension, allow you contact with their persons, counting you lucky to have been favoured and expecting due appreciation for the honour, must also be supported.

Personally, I find what one might term the "post-act" reformers the hardest to bear as, sated, they condemn the means by which they achieved satiation—prostitution and its instrument, yourself, abjuring you to give it up before it's too late, a nice girl like you.

In many if not most cases an encounter such as this slips quickly from a man's mind, and out of consideration or sheer hurry he leaves without delay. Then there are those—and not as many of them as might be expected—who, when they have made use of your physical and agreed-upon services in their various ways, are driven away quickly by disgust at what they have done: for paying for that which should always be a gift or taken by force, for running the risk of passing disease on to wives and sweethearts, for using what another man had probably only half an hour before and what hundreds have used in a twelvemonth.

A fairly large proportion come to us not only for physical relief, but for mental as well, and for sympathy, because of marital or economic troubles, and these are apt to linger. At such times, all one's humanitarian instincts must be fought back if one is not to waste valuable time to give them the comfort they seek. Some, of course, are so nauseating in their self-pity that it is easy to steel oneself against them. Others, though, are genuinely at their wits' end and desperate for help and solace, and few of us are cruel enough to refuse it in these cases.

I think that the release of talking about an unhappy home situation may well have saved many a marriage, and possibly even lives, when nerves have been strained to breaking point. It is well known that it is easier to unburden serious trouble onto a total stranger whose face you need never recall. Easier still to tell a girl whose time you have bought, whom nothing will surprise, and who is in no position to despise you, whatever you've done or want to do.

Others among the malingerers who incite pity are the vast army of lonely, unloved, and unwanted men who come to us seeking an oasis in their loneliness, fooling themselves out of desperation that the friendliness they have bought is genuine, feeling at home in the warm pink glow of a shaded lamp and fire and feminine company, relaxing, replenishing themselves, treating one for as long as they are allowed to as their own, shyly or urgently clinging, and loth to break the spell, to leave their short moment of content, so that in the end one has to be brutal, to remind them of what they are and where they are, and that their time is up.

Really infuriating are those who demand your attention and time until the last pennyworth of their due has been extracted, either because they are mean by nature, or because they are at once intelligent and sadistic enough to know that you long to be rid of their company and of your intense irritation at their continuing presence. These latter derive immense satisfaction from the sight of your annoyance, while the former derive equal pleasure from each moment they get "free." Both need firm handling.

5   *The author, a product of a middle-class family, became involved with a professional criminal. When she
wrote this selection, she was an alcoholic and serving
time for counterfeiting and forgery.*

Why crime . . . snowball!

anonymous

Much has been written on the subject of why people commit
crimes. I am not a psychologist, criminologist or sociologist. I am
a four-time loser. Here is one woman's opinion as to why women
go to jails and prisons.

There are many pat reasons for committing crimes,—environment, association, money, alcohol, drugs, boredom, and love.
Let's take the last one first. With women love seems to be at the
top of the list. You will very rarely find a woman in jail who
doesn't have a man somewhere in the picture. The women who
go to jail for love, or infatuation, or fear, start out looking for
love and understanding, and end up with the wrong kind of
man. There seems to be something fascinating about the man
who isn't a "square." These women are bored and looking for
excitement. This point is brought to light in "Little Things," on
page 15 of this issue.

Crime to a woman is like a snowball; she gets involved with
a man or a wrong crowd and someone gets an idea and away she
goes, not stopping to think of the future—only of the minute.
When she finds herself in prison, she wonders how she got there.
There may be nothing in her background to indicate that she
would end up in jail sometime in her life. This is the average
woman behind bars today.

Emotionally she is and always has been immature, looking

From *The Eagle*, 29 (Summer, 1962). Reprinted by permission of the
Warden, Federal Reformatory for Women, Alderson, West Virginia.

for the pot of gold at the end of the rainbow. This is no reason for her family or friends to think she will end up in jail. There are plenty of women in the U.S. of the same make-up who miss out on being arrested for a crime.

The percentage of women in prisons is on the increase—an alarming fact in itself. I feel there are several reasons. With older women of average intelligence, it is the failure they have made as wives and mothers, in trying to live up to the housewife-mother image set up for them since childhood by books, magazines, TV, and radio—which produces the "I just don't care any more" attitude, bringing them to the courts and jails of this country.

The woman who is not able to compete in this highly competitive business world also adds to the crime figures. Not being equipped to earn a decent wage, she goes out to make some Easy Money, just piling trouble on trouble. I have known many talented, intelligent women in jails saying so many times, "I just can't take the competition out there. I want someone to take care of me for a change."

Many of the women who commit crimes are not prepared to hold a decent job. They have either quit school to get married, or married soon after high school. They have never worked at a job outside the home. When their world of husband and children falls apart, they go hunting for a man who will appreciate them, and the snowball starts rolling.

Another aspect of crime increase among women is the increasing number of juvenile offenders—aged 16 to 21. These girls are different in that they have started the snowball early in life. "A Real Home," on page 18 of this issue, is one illustration of how the snowball starts with a broken home. Then there is the pattern of truancy and petty crimes and running away from home, soon leading to reform school. The girls I have met seem to fall into two groups—a too-strict, small town home, or an overindulgent family. The overly-strict, small town type are looking for freedom and a chance to see the world they have only known from books and magazines. The over-indulged type are spoiled materially, but insecure in parental love, the parents being just too busy to give of themselves to the girl, so she goes looking for attention and love and ends up with the wrong crowd. The story on page 17 of this issue, "The Mother Chain," brings this to mind. The delinquent girl who gets into trouble from her early teens on into adulthood is the one I feel needs guidance and understanding most.

You hear the remark "I did it just for kicks." This is a form of rebellion that teenagers often use to justify their actions. So often what starts out as a joke or a lark ends up in the court room. There goes that snowball again.

The addict or alcoholic woman is another story. She uses drugs or liquor to no end,—except to forget. The snowball gets bigger and bigger until crimes are committed just to get the drugs or drinks she can now not do without. I'm not familiar with narcotics but can speak from experience on alcohol. There is nothing worse than a drunk, and a drunken woman is the worst of all. She may start drinking as an escape from a bad marriage, a rejected love, the guilt from an affair, or the loss of a job—there are all kinds of excuses to start the ball rolling. From the respectable cocktail lounge to the hang-out bar is the usual pattern. Here she does not have to compete, and sooner or later will meet a man who will tell her how wonderful she is and how they can do real well together and make some real money. The same old snowball. She is very lucky if there are only minor scrimmages with the law—too often it means felonies and prison.

This brings us back to the beginning. Most women in prison were looking for something—in most cases love and attention, security, recognition. All the articles mentioned—"Little Things," "Mother Chain," and "A Real Home"—illustrate this. What went wrong, why couldn't they pull themselves out before the snowball got too big? I think it is not so much weakness of character as the loss of a desire to do any better. They went down for the count and couldn't get back up. How many times have I heard women in jail say "I just don't care any more. There isn't anything better for me out there." The husband or boy friend who is waiting (if he waits) is either the one she committed the crime with, or a real square who cannot give her the understanding and moral support she will need.

I am all for getting at this problem at the early stages. But who is to do it? The community, the schools, the social agencies? They can't do it alone. Until the women themselves try to help themselves, there is little that can be done.

6 *The late author and comedian was a deviant, if one were to judge by his arrest record for "obscene" nightclub performances. His comments provide, in the form of social criticism, an incisive look at "deviant" behavior.*

So who's deviant?

lenny bruce

When I talk on the stage, people often have the impression that I make up things as I go along. This isn't true. I know a lot of things I want to say; I'm just not sure exactly when I will say them. This process of allowing one subject spontaneously to associate itself with another is equivalent to James Joyce's stream of consciousness.

I think one develops a style like that from talking to oneself. I don't actually talk to myself out loud—"Hello, Lenny, how are you today?"—rather it's a form of *thinking*. And out at sea you have a lot of time to think. All day and all night I would think about all kinds of things.

Sometimes I would talk out loud up on the bow, where tons of water actually bend the shield plate. You would never figure water to be so hard that it could bend steel, but I've seen it happen.

In the spring, however, the Atlantic Ocean is very pleasant, and the trip isn't so bad. The first land you sight is a thrilling experience. I must have played Columbus hundreds of times. It was really fun, standing those bow watches all alone.

I always felt that the Azores were going to sink, because on the map they're just a bunch of little dots. And everything that's *on* the Azores is shipped in. There was even a Turkish seaman who had gotten an attack of appendicitis on board his ship, and they had let *him* off at the Azores, where we picked him up.

From *How to Talk Dirty and Influence People* by Lenny Bruce, published by Playboy Press. Copyright © 1963, 1965 by HMH Publishing Co., Inc.

He bunked with Caleb and me. He had a little leather bag in which he kept all his wordly possessions. He didn't speak any English, but when he sat down on the bunk, I tried to communicate with him anyway, asking what had happened to him, although we already knew.

People are the same the world over. Just like an old lady from the Bronx, he proudly showed us his appendix scar.

I gave him two candy bars which he devoured immediately, and Caleb gave him soap and a towel. He scowled at us, and I guessed that probably in his country a towel and soap meant only one thing—that you were in *need* of same. I tried to explain in sign language. I sniffed him and smiled, in order to show that we *all* have towels and soap to keep in our lockers *if* and *when* we need them.

He wrote his name in Turkish for us, and we wrote our names in English for him. It seemed to be turning out like a Richard Halliburton story.

But then he opened his little bag and offered us something. I didn't know what the hell it was. It looked like bunches of strips of leather. I asked Caleb if he knew what it was, and he said maybe it was some sort of "good-luck leather." He took a piece and pushed it toward my face, and I pantomimed to the Turk: "Should we eat it?"—and then it dawned upon him that we didn't know what it was.

He gestured for a knife and a cigarette. He took the cigarette and opened it up, dumping the tobacco out on the bench; then he started chopping up the leather and the cigarette tobacco, until he had it evenly mixed. He took a pipe from his bag, filled it, and lit it. Oh that was it—some sort of religious ritual like the Indians have on first meeting—a peace pipe.

The tobacco was rather strong, and we passed it around several times, but when the pipe came to me the fifth time, for no apparent reason Caleb looked hysterically funny to me, and I started to laugh, and Caleb started to laugh, until we were carrying on like a couple of damned idiots.

"Oh, my God, this son of a bitch has us smoking hashish!"

As soon as I got the word out, he nodded and laughed, too. We smoked some more, and when it came time to go on watch, the relief man came and said, "Time to go topside," and I thought that was the funniest goddamned thing I'd ever heard in my whole life.

We laughed so hard that it scared the relief man, and he went away and didn't bother us anymore.

Within a week I could communicate perfectly with Sabu (the name I'd christened him). I made Harpo Marx look slow. I'm sure Vincent Price would have been honored to have me on his team on the TV version of charades.

No matter how hard I tried, though, I couldn't make Sabu believe that it was against the law on American ships to smoke dope. He wanted to know why, and I honestly couldn't tell him. He asked me what *I* used to get high, I told him whiskey, and he was horrified.

Since then, I've learned that Moslems do not drink. But they sure smoke a lot of that lovelorn. It's based on their religious health laws. Imagine that: religious laws to smoke dope. But here's the capper: They're right. Alcohol is a caustic that destroys tissues which cannot be rebuilt. It is toxic, and damages one of the most important organs in the body—one that cannot repair itself or be repaired—the liver. Whereas, for example, no form of *cannabis sativa* (the hemp plant from which marijuana is made) destroys any body tissue or harms the organs in any manner.

This is a fact that can be verified by any chemistry professor of any university in the United States. Nevertheless, the possession of marijuana is a crime:

PUBLIC DEFENDER: Your honor, I make a motion that the prosecution's statement, "Was involved and did encourage others to partake in this immoral degenerate practice" be stricken from the record. The word "immoral" is entirely subjective and not specific.

JUDGE: Objection overruled. Existing statutes give this word, in the context used, legal credence. Can counselor refer to an existing statute that labels marijuna users as moralists?

PUBLIC DEFENDER: Which moralists are we using as criteria? Sherman Adams? Earl Long? Jimmy Walker? Or does the court refer to the moralists who violated Federal law—segregationists, traitorous anarchists that have given ambiguity to the aphorism, "Of the people, by the people, for the people . . ." Or the moralist who flouted Federal law—the bootleg coffers flowing with billions, illegal whiskey drunk by millions. A moral standard that gives mass criminal rebellion absolution? In the realm of this subject, the Defense requests that the six men on this jury be disqualified on the grounds of unfitness.

JUDGE: Can the Public Defender qualify this charge?

PUBLIC DEFENDER: The Defense submits these qualitative and quantitative documents in answer to the Court's query.

JUDGE: (*Reading the documents aloud*) ". . . And these six jurors have sworn in the presence of a notary that their daily alcoholic consumption, martinis for lunch and manhattans before dinner, totals an average of a half-pint per day. Jurist also stated motivations for drinking: 'Gives me a lift.' 'Need a boost once in a while.' 'After a frustrating day at the office a couple of belts lift me out of the dumps.' " I fail to see the merit in your plea to disqualify. What is your point, succinctly?

PUBLIC DEFENDER: One cannot cast the first stone—if already stoned.

(*Dissolve to interior of jury room and new set of jurors.*)

FIRST WOMAN: You know, I was thinking, that Public Defender was right. A crutch is a crutch no matter if it is made of wood or aluminum.

SECOND WOMAN: A couple of those jurors gave me the creeps anyway. That one with the thick fingers looked like a real moron.

THIRD WOMAN: And the other one with those sneaky eyes. I can always tell a person's character by his eyes.

FIRST WOMAN: To serve on a jury in a civil case is easy, but when you're dealing with drug addicts it's rough. This damned jury duty has me a nervous wreck. I had to take five sleeping pills to get some rest last night. You build up a tolerance to the damned things so quickly. I feel miserable today. I'm really dragging.

SECOND WOMAN: Here, take one of these Dexies.

FIRST WOMAN: What are they for?

SECOND WOMAN: They're amphetamine, Dexedrine Spansules. My doctor gave them to me for depression and fatigue. They really give you a lift. I take them all the time except when it's "that time of the month"—then I take Demerol.

THIRD WOMAN: (*Rummaging through her purse and pro-*

ducing a handful of pills.) Do you know what these red-and-white ones are? My neighbor's doctor gave them to her to try out. They're supposed to be for nerves. Better than Miltowns.

SECOND WOMAN: Oh, these are Deprols. Umm, no, wait a minute, I think they're phenobarbs.

(*An elderly woman juror, silent until now, turns and speaks.*)

ELDERLY WOMAN: Come on, ladies. We need a verdict. What are we going to do with this man?

FIRST WOMAN: Oh, yes—the dope addict. How does a person sink that low?

So I do not understand the moral condemnation of marijuana, not only because of its nontoxic, nonaddicting effects as contrasted with those of alcohol, but also because, in my opinion, caffeine in coffee, amphetamine, as well as all tranquilizers—from Miltown to aspirin to nicotine in cigarettes—are crutches for people who can face life better with drugs than without.

Part of the responsibility for our indiscriminate use of drugs is the doctors'. How often does a patient say to his doctor, "Doc, I have this cold coming on—can't you give me a shot?" And the doctor does, although the patient might just as easily get over the cold without it. One of the reasons for this is that the doctor realizes that most people do not feel that they've gotten their money's worth if they haven't gotten "a shot."

But the doctor also knows that constant inappropriate usage of penicillin and aureomycin and other antibiotics is breeding strains of bacteria that are resistant to these drugs, so that not only will their protective qualities be lost in the future if ever they are desperately needed, but more and more people are suffering from dreadful drug "reactions"—swelling, itching, and sometimes even death. And every day the ads and the TV commercials bombard us with new things to swallow so we can take the modern way to normal regularity—things to drink, chew, gargle, stick into ourselves. It's Nature's way . . . .

Surprisingly enough, there are actually psychotics in high public places that have been reported to have *sympathetic* feelings concerning the stiff penalties received by the marijuana users and narcotics offenders. Judging from the newspapers and movies, one would believe that drug users are sick, emotionally

immature, degenerates, psychos, unstable. They are not right in
the head. They are *weirdos*. So, I would assume, they belong in
jail with all the other crazy people.

Or do you believe all that crap about mental-health programs? I mean, you don't actually believe there *are* crazy people,
do you? You don't actually believe people are emotionally unstable, do you? A person is only bad because he wants to be. You
can do anything you want. Anything. You can memorize
12,000,000 different telephone books—all the names inside them.

Or *can* you do anything you want? Do you perhaps believe in
the *existence* of mental illness, but still feel that treatment for
the mentally ill should be duplexed? Good nuts, the ones who
blow up trains with 300 people or repeatedly try to kill themselves, should be sent to Bellevue or other instutitions equipped
with mental-health programs; but bad nuts, who try to kill themselves with heroin or other narcotics, should be sent to jail.

After all, what's the sense of sending a heroin addict to a
hospital for intensified therapy and perhaps curing him in three
years, when you can have him in and out of jail three times over
a period of *ten* years? Then, the last time, you've got him for
good!

I don't know about you, but I rather enjoy the way tax
money is spent to arrest, indict, convict, imprison, parole, and
then re-imprison these people. I'd just piss it away on beer, anyway.

I must admit that, since a certain incident, I've never given
a penny to mental health. I shan't mention the city in which this
occurred because I have no desire to cause any trouble for the
individual involved (although, what with his being a genuine
masochist, he might *love* the trouble). And certainly I have no
moral judgment to bestow on him—which others certainly
would, if they recognized him from my description.

I discovered the truth about this guy through a friend of
mine, this chick who was a hooker; the guy was one of her tricks.
Anyway, this *noffka* told me about a trick who didn't want anything but a good beating. He was willing to pay from $100 to
$500, depending upon how ingenious and sadistic the amuse-
ment she devised for him was each evening.

She described the guy in detail to me: his home, his personal appearance, right down—or up—to his toupee.

Then, another hooker, who, I'm positive, didn't know the first chick, told me about this same trick one night and said that he had asked her to bring her boyfriend along to help work him over. She was a little wary about asking her boyfriend to do this because he was a rather surly type and inclined, perhaps, to get a little carried away with his work, which was important to avoid, because this trick insisted that he was never to be hit above the shoulders. He was an important man and had to travel in respectable business circles, and couldn't afford to have his scars seen in public.

She asked me if I would accommodate her that evening and punch him around a bit. Somehow, I didn't feel quite up to it—I don't know, maybe I'm just a sissy—and I graciously declined her offer. I was sorry about it afterward, because the next day she saw me and complained that they hadn't been paid because, sure enough, her boyfriend had gotten a little overexuberant and given the trick a black eye and a swollen jaw.

Now here's the capper, and I swear it is true. That afternoon there was a meeting of the heads of the mental-health campaign, and I had been asked to contribute my services as a performer to a fund-raising show they were organizing. I attended the meeting with the other acts, planning the billing and staging, and so forth, and we had to wait for about ten minutes for the president of the committee to arrive. I had met the gentleman before, a very imposing, robust businessman with a brusque good nature and a toupee that nearly matched the graying hair at his temples.

Till the moment he walked in, I had never connected him with that trick, nor would I have in a million years. But there he was, black eye, swollen jaw and all. It was like a cheap old Charlie Chan movie; the chief of police turns out to have committed the series of brutal murders.

Immediately everyone displayed great concern over him. "What happened?" "You poor thing!" "Oh, my God, George, look at your eye!"

He sat down wearily and told his tale:

"I was coming out of the Plymouth House last night, about two in the morning, meeting with the board from the United

Fund, you know, and in the parking lot there were these two chaps attacking a young girl. Well, I grabbed one of them and knocked him out and clipped the other one, when six more jumped out from behind a car. You see, it was a setup: the girl was in on it—part of the gang, I guess. The next thing I knew, I was flat on my back. I mean I couldn't handle them *all*."

"Were there any witnesses?" I asked.

"No. At two o'clock in the morning, I might just as well have been alone in the jungle."

"Weren't there any cops around?"

"No. Isn't that the damnedest thing, Len? It's always that way—when you want a cop, you can't find one. They're too busy giving out tickets."

"Well," piped up the inevitable cliché expert, "it's a lucky thing you didn't get killed."

"Yes," he agreed philosophically, "I guess I am lucky, after all."

I thought to myself: He probably would *love* to get killed, if only somehow he would be able to live through it to enjoy it.

I am not trying to project an image of myself as pure, wholesome and All-American. Again, I certainly am not making any value judgment of others and attempting to put myself on a high moral level above anyone else. As I have said, I have indulged myself in houses of prostitution.

I try to keep in mind that the only difference between a Charles Van Doren, a Bernard Goldfine, a Mayor Curley or a Dave Beck, and me, is that they got caught. I am always offended by a judge or district attorney with an Academy Award sense of moral indignation. I have great respect for the offices of law enforcement and preservation, but I'll never forget that William O'Dwyer was the D.A.

I love my country, I would give allegiance to no other nation, nor would I choose any other for my home, and yet if I followed a U.S. serviceman and saw the enemy bind him, nude, face down, and then pour white-hot lead into a funnel that was inserted in his keister, they wouldn't even have to heat another pot for me. I would give them every top secret, I would make shoeshine rags out of the American flag, I would denounce the

Constitution, I would give them the right to kill every person that was kind and dear to me.

Just don't give me that hot-lead enema.

So that's how low I am. That's what I would resort to, to keep that lead out of my ass. I spent four battle years in the Mediterranean and saw starving priests, doctors and judges. I saw ethics erode, again, according to the law of supply and demand.

So I am not offended by war in the same way that I am not offended by rain. Both are "motivated" by need.

I was at Anzio. I lived in a continual state of ambivalence; guilty but glad. Glad I wasn't the GI enjoying that final "no-wake-up-call" sleep on his blood-padded mud mattress. It would be interesting to hear his comment if we could grab a handful of his hair, drag his head out of the dirt and ask his opinion on the questions that are posed every decade, the contemporary shouts of: "How long are we going to put up with Cuba's nonsense?" "Just how many insults can we take from Russia?"

I was at Salerno. I can take a lot of insults.

War spells out my philosophy of "No right or wrong"—just "Your right, my wrong,"—everything is subjective.

After we resolved our conflict with the villainous English, the Indians were next. They had some absurd notion that since they were here before us, they had some claim upon the land.

Setting a precedent for Nazi purging, we proved to those dunderhead Indians the correctness of the aphorism "Possession is nine tenths of the law." If you have any doubts about that, if you're ever in Miami, drive to the one tenth: the Seminole Indian reservation, in the mosquito-ridden, agriculture-resistant Everglades swamps.

The next suffering people we had to liberate were the Mexicans. We took Texas and California. But we always maintained a concept of justice. We left them a land where holy men could walk: the desert.

Later, continuing with our hollow, rodomontade behavior, we involved ourselves in the war to end all wars.

After going out on a limb like that, there were wars that followed nonetheless, especially the one that took courageous

Americans, heroic Russians, invincible Englishmen, and the indefatigable French, who shared moral unity, having God and Irving Berlin on their side, and censuring those who offended the principles of Christianity—the Italians.

The Pope, possessing the clairvoyance of a representative of the Deity, did not flee to Argentina, thereby escaping the fate of Adolf Eichmann.

7 Burroughs reflects on his experiences in the world of junk.

Deposition: testimony concerning a sickness

william s. burroughs

I awoke from The Sickness at the age of forty-five, calm and sane, and in reasonably good health except for a weakened liver and the look of borrowed flesh common to all who survive The Sickness. . . . Most survivors do not remember the delirium in detail. I apparently took detailed notes on sickness and delirium. I have no precise memory of writing the notes which have now been published under the title *Naked Lunch*. The title was suggested by Jack Kerouac. I did not understand what the title meant until my recent recovery. The title means exactly what the words say: NAKED Lunch—a frozen moment when everyone sees what is on the end of every fork.

The Sickness is drug addiction and I was an addict for fifteen years. When I say addict I mean an addict to junk (generic term for opium and/or derivatives including all synthetics from demerol to palfium). I have used junk in many forms: morphine, heroin, dilaudid, eukodal, pantopon, diocodid, diosane, opium, demerol, dolophine, palfium. I have smoked junk, eaten it, sniffed it, injected it in vein-skin-muscle, inserted it in rectal suppositories. The needle is not important. Whether you sniff it smoke it eat it or shove it up your ass the result is the same: addiction. When I speak of drug addiction I do not refer to keif, marijuana or any preparation of hashish, mescaline, *Bannisteria Caapi*, LSD6, Sacred Mushrooms or any other drug of the hallucinogen group. . . . There is no evidence that the use of any hallucinogen results in physical dependence. The action of these drugs is physiologically opposite to the action of junk. A lamentable confusion between the two classes of drugs has arisen owing to the zeal of the U.S. and other narcotic departments.

I have seen the exact manner in which the junk virus operates through fifteen years of addiction. The pyramid of junk, one level eating the level below (it is no accident that junk higher-ups are always fat and the addict in the street is always thin) right up to the top or tops since there are many junk pyramids feeding on peoples of the world and all built on basic principles of monopoly:

1—Never give anything away for nothing.
2—Never give more than you have to give (always catch the buyer hungry and always make him wait).
3—Always take everything back if you possibly can.

The Pusher always gets it all back. The addict needs more and more junk to maintain a human form . . . buy off the Monkey.

Junk is the mold of monopoly and possession. The addict stands by while his junk legs carry him straight in on the junk beam to relapse. Junk is quantitative and accurately measurable. The more junk you use the less you have and the more you have the more you use. All the hallucinogen drugs are considered sacred by those who use them—there are Peyote Cults and Bannisteria Cults, Hashish Cults and Mushroom Cults—"the Sacred Mushrooms of Mexico enable a man to see God"—but no one ever suggested that junk is sacred. There are no opium cults. Opium is profane and quantitative like money. I have heard that there was once a beneficent non-habit-forming junk in India. It was called *soma* and is pictured as a beautiful blue tide. If *soma* ever existed the Pusher was there to bottle it and monopolize it and sell it and it turned into plain old time JUNK.

Junk is the ideal product . . . the ultimate merchandise. No sales talk necessary. The client will crawl through a sewer and beg to buy. . . . The junk merchant does not sell his product to the consumer, he sells the consumer to his product. He does not improve and simplify his merchandise. He degrades and simplifies the client. He pays his staff in junk.

Junk yields a basic formula of "evil" virus: *The Algebra of*

Need. The face of "evil" is always the face of total need. A dope fiend is a man in total need of dope. Beyond a certain frequency need knows absolutely no limit or control. In the words of total need: *"Wouldn't you?"* Yes you would. You would lie, cheat, inform on your friends, steal, do *anything* to satisfy total need. Because you would be in a state of total sickness, total possession, and not in a position to act in any other way. Dope fiends are sick people who cannot act other than they do. A rabid dog cannot choose but bite. Assuming a self-righteous position is nothing to the purpose unless your purpose be to keep the junk virus in operation. And junk is a big industry. I recall talking to an American who worked for the Aftosa Commission in Mexico. Six hundred a month plus expense account:

"How long will the epidemic last?" I enquired.

"As long as we can keep it going. . . . And yes . . . maybe the aftosa will break out in South America," he said dreamily.

If you wish to alter or annihilate a pyramid of numbers in a serial relation, you alter or remove the bottom number. If we wish to annihilate the junk pyramid, we must start with the bottom of the pyramid: *the Addict in the Street,* and stop tilting quixotically for the "higher ups" so called, all of whom are immediately replaceable. *The addict in the street who must have junk to live is the one irreplaceable factor in the junk equation.* When there are no more addicts to buy junk there will be no junk traffic. As long as junk need exists, someone will service it.

Addicts can be cured or quarantined—that is, allowed a morphine ration under minimal supervision like typhoid carriers. When this is done, junk pyramids of the world will collapse. So far as I know, England is the only country to apply this method to the junk problem. They have about five hundred quarantined addicts in the U.K. In another generation when the quarantined addicts die off and pain killers operating on a nonjunk principle are discovered, the junk virus will be like smallpox, a closed chapter—a medical curiosity.

The vaccine that can relegate the junk virus to a land-locked past is in existence. This vaccine is the Apomorphine Treatment discovered by an English doctor whose name I must withhold pending his permission to use it and to quote from his book covering thirty years of apomorphine treatment of addicts and alcoholics. The compound apomorphine is formed by boiling morphine with hydrochloric acid. It was discovered years before it was used to treat addicts. For many years the only use for apomorphine which has no narcotic or pain-killing properties was an emetic to induce vomiting in cases of poisoning. It acts directly on the vomiting center in the back brain.

I found this vaccine at the end of the junk line. I lived in one room in the Native Quarter of Tangier. I had not taken a bath in a year nor changed my clothes or removed them except to stick a needle every hour in the fibrous grey wooden flesh of terminal addiction. I never cleaned or dusted the room. Empty ampule boxes and garbage piled to the ceiling. Light and water long since turned off for non-payment. I did absolutely nothing. I could look at the end of my shoe for eight hours. I was only roused to action when the hourglass of junk ran out. If a friend came to visit—and they rarely did since who or what was left to visit—I sat there not caring that he had entered my field of vision—a grey screen always blanker and fainter—and not caring when he walked out of it. If he had died on the spot I would have sat there looking at my shoe waiting to go through his pockets. Wouldn't you? Because I never had enough junk—no one ever does. Thirty grains of morphine a day and it still was not enough. And long waits in front of the drugstore. Delay is the rule in the junk business. The Man is never on time. This is no accident. There are no accidents in the junk world. The addict is taught again and again exactly what will happen if he does not score for his junk ration. Get up that money or else. And suddenly my habit began to jump and jump. Forty, sixty grains a day. And it still was not enough. And I could not pay.

I stood there with my last check in my hand and realized that it was my last check. I took the next plane for London.

The doctor explained to me that apomorphine acts on the back brain to regulate the metabolism and normalize the blood stream in such a way that the enzyme system of addiction is destroyed over a period of four or five days. Once the back brain is regulated apomorphine can be discontinued and only used in case of relapse. (No one would take apomorphine for kicks. *Not one case of addiction to apomorphine has ever been recorded.*) I agreed to undergo treatment and entered a nursing home. For the first twenty-four hours I was literally insane and paranoid as many addicts are in severe withdrawal. This delirium was dispersed by twenty-four hours of intensive apomorphine treatment. The doctor showed me the chart. I had received minute amounts of morphine that could not possibly account for my lack of the more severe withdrawal symptoms such as leg and stomach cramps, fever and my own special symptom, The Cold Burn, like a vast hive covering the body and rubbed with menthol. Every addict has his own special symptom that cracks all control. There was a missing factor in the withdrawal equation—that factor could only be apomorphine.

I saw the apomorphine treatment really work. Eight days later I left the nursing home eating and sleeping normally. I remained completely off junk for two full years—a twelve year record. I did relapse for some months as a result of pain and illness. Another apomorphine cure has kept me off junk through this writing.

The apomorphine cure is qualitatively different from other methods of cure. I have tried them all. Short reduction, slow reduction, cortisone, antihistamines, tranquilizers, sleeping cures, tolserol, reserpine. None of these cures lasted beyond the first opportunity to relapse. I can say definitely that I was never *metabolically* cured until I took the apomorphine cure. The overwhelming relapse statistics from the Lexington Narcotic Hospital have led many doctors to say that addiction is not curable. They use a dolophine reduction cure at Lexington and have never tried apomorphine so far as I know. In fact, this method of treatment has been largely neglected. No research has been done with variations of the apomorphine formula or with synthetics. No doubt substances fifty times stronger than apomorphine could be developed and the side effect of vomiting eliminated.

Apomorphine is a metabolic and psychic regulator that can be discontinued as soon as it has done its work. The world is deluged with tranquilizers and energizers but this unique regulator has not received attention. No research has been done by any of the large pharmaceutical companies. I suggest that research with variations of apomorphine and synthesis of it will open a new medical frontier extending far beyond the problem of addiction.

The smallpox vaccine was opposed by a vociferous lunatic group of anti-vaccinationists. No doubt a scream of protest will go up from interested or unbalanced individuals as the junk virus is shot out from under them. Junk is big business; there are always cranks and operators. They must not be allowed to interfere with the essential work of inoculation treatment and quarantine. *The junk virus is public health problem number one of the world today.*

Since *Naked Lunch* treats this health problem, it is necessarily brutal, obscene and disgusting. Sickness is often repulsive details not for weak stomachs.

Certain passages in the book that have been called pornographic were written as a tract against Capital Punishment in the manner of Jonathan Swift's *Modest Proposal.* These sections are intended to reveal capital punishment as the obscene, barbaric and disgusting anachronism that it is. As always the lunch is naked. If civilized countries want to return to Druid Hanging Rites in the Sacred Grove or to drink blood with the Aztecs and feed their Gods with blood of human sacrifice, let them see what they actually eat and drink. Let them see what is on the end of that long newspaper spoon.

I have almost completed a sequel to *Naked Lunch.* A mathematical extension of the Algebra of Need beyond the junk virus. Because there are many forms of addiction I think that they all obey basic laws. In the words of Heiderberg: "This may not be the best of all possible universes but it may well prove to be one of the simplest." If man can *see.*

POST SCRIPT. . . . WOULDN'T YOU?

And speaking *Personally* and if a man speaks any other way we might as well start looking for his Protoplasm Daddy or Mother Cell. . . . *I Don't Want To Hear Any More Tired Old Junk Talk And Junk Con.* . . . The same things said a million times and more and there is no point in saying anything because *NOTHING Ever Happens* in the junk world.

Only excuse for this tired death route is THE KICK when the junk circuit is cut off for the non-payment and the junk-skin dies of junk-lack and overdose of time and the Old Skin has forgotten the skin game simplifying a way under the junk cover the way skins will. . . . A condition of total exposure is precipitated when the Kicking Addict cannot choose but see smell and listen. . . . Watch out for the cars. . . .

It is clear that junk is a Round-the-World-Push-an-Opium-Pellet-with-Your-Nose-Route. Strictly for Scarabs—stumble bum junk heap. And as such report to disposal. Tired of seeing it around.

Junkies always beef about *The Cold* as they call it, turning up their black coat collars and clutching their withered necks . . . pure junk con. A junky does not want to be warm, he wants to be Cool-Cooler-COLD. But he wants The Cold like he wants His Junk—NOT OUTSIDE where it does him no good but INSIDE so he can sit around with a spine like a frozen hydraulic jack . . . his metabolism approaching Absolute ZERO. TERMINAL addicts often go two months without a bowel move and the intestines make with sit-down-adhesions—Wouldn't you?—requiring the intervention of an apple corer or its surgical equivalent. . . . Such is life in The Old Ice House. Why move around and waste TIME?

Room for One More Inside, Sir.

Some entities are on thermodynamic kicks. They invented thermodynamics. . . . Wouldn't you?

And some of us are on Different Kicks and that's a thing out in the open the way I like to see what I eat and visa versa mutatis mutandis as the case may be. *Bill's Naked Lunch Room.* . . . Step right up. . . . Good for young and old, man and bestial. Nothing like a little snake oil to grease the wheels and get a show on the track Jack. Which side are you on? Fro-Zen Hydraulic? Or you want to take a look around with Honest Bill?

So that's the World Health Problem I was talking about back in The Article. The Prospect Before Us Friends of MINE. Do I hear muttering about a personal razor and some bush league short con artist who is known to have invented The Bill? Wouldn't You? The razor belonged to a man named Occam and he was not a scar collector. Ludwig Wittgenstein *Tractatus Logico-Philosophicus*; "If a proposition is NOT NECESSARY it is MEANINGLESS and approaching MEANING ZERO."

"And what is More UNNECESSARY than junk if You Don't Need it?"

Answer: "Junkies, if you are not ON JUNK."

I tell you boys, I've heard some tired conversation but no other OCCUPATION GROUP can approximate that old thermodynamic junk Slow-DOWN. Now your heroin addict does not say hardly anything and that I can stand. But your Opium "Smoker" is more active since he still has a tent and a Lamp . . . and maybe 7-9-10 lying up in there like hibernating reptiles keep the temperature up to Talking Level: How low the other junkies are "whereas We—WE have this tent and this lamp and this tent and this lamp and this tent and nice and warm in here nice and warm nice and IN HERE and nice and OUTSIDE ITS COLD. . . . ITS COLD OUTSIDE where the dross eaters and the needle boys won't last two years not six months hardly won't last stumble bum around and there is no class in them. . . . But WE SIT HERE and never increase the DOSE . . . never—never increase the dose never except TONIGHT is a SPECIAL OCCASION with all the dross eaters and needle boys out there in the cold. . . . And we never eat it never never never eat it. . . . Excuse please while I take a trip to The Source Of Living Drops they all have in pocket and opium pellets shoved up the ass in a finger stall with the Family Jewels and the other shit.

Room for one more inside, Sir.

Well when that record starts around for the billionth light year and never the tape shall change us non-junkies take drastic action and the men separate out from the Junk boys.

Only way to protect yourself against this horrid peril is come over HERE and shack up with Charybdis. . . . Treat you right kid. . . . Candy and cigarettes.

I am after fifteen years in that tent. In and out in and out in and OUT. *Over* and *Out.* So listen to Old Uncle Bill Burroughs who invented the Burroughs Adding Machine Regulator Gimmick on the Hydraulic Jack Principle no matter how you jerk the handle result is always the same for given co-ordinates. Got my training early . . . wouldn't you?

Paregoric Babies of the World Unite. We have nothing to lose but Our Pushers. And THEY are NOT NECESSARY.

Look down LOOK DOWN along that junk road before you travel there and get in with the Wrong Mob. . . .

A word to the wise guy.

8 *Chambers, the government's principal witness in the spy trial of Alger Hiss, begins his book with a "Foreword in the Form of a Letter to My Children." Here he describes the visions which led him to become a Communist and the disillusions which followed.*

On entering and leaving communism

whittaker chambers

My children, as long as you live, the shadow of the Hiss Case will brush you. In every pair of eyes that rests on you, you will see pass, like a cloud passing behind a woods in winter, the memory of your father—dissembled in friendly eyes, lurking in unfriendly eyes. Sometimes you will wonder which is harder to bear: friendly forgiveness or forthright hate. In time, therefore, when the sum of your experience of life gives you authority, you will ask yourselves the question: What was my father?

I will give you an answer: I was a witness. I do not mean a witness for the Government or against Alger Hiss and the others. Nor do I mean the short, squat, solitary figure, trudging through the impersonal halls of public buildings to testify before Congressional committees, grand juries, loyalty boards, courts of law. A man is not primarily a witness *against* something. That is only incidental to the fact that he is a witness *for* something. A witness, in the sense that I am using the word, is a man whose life and faith are so completely one that when the challenge comes to step out and testify for his faith, he does so, disregarding all risks, accepting all consequences.

One day in the great jury room of the Grand Jury of the Southern District of New York, a juror leaned forward slightly and asked me: "Mr. Chambers, what does it mean to be a Communist?" I hesitated for a moment, trying to find the simplest, most direct way to convey the heart of this complex experience to men and women to whom the very fact of the experience was all but incomprehensible. Then I said:

"When I was a Communist, I had three heroes. One was a Russian. One was a Pole. One was a German Jew.

"The Pole was Felix Djerjinsky. He was ascetic, highly sensitive, intelligent. He was a Communist. After the Russian Revolution, he became head of the Tcheka and organizer of the Red Terror. As a young man, Djerjinsky had been a political prisoner in the Paviak Prison in Warsaw. There he insisted on being given the task of cleaning the latrines of the other prisoners. For he held that the most developed member of any community must take upon himself the lowliest tasks as an example to those who are less developed. That is one thing that it meant to be a Communist.

"The German Jew was Eugen Leviné. He was a Communist. During the Bavarian Soviet Republic in 1919, Leviné was the organizer of the Workers and Soldiers Soviets. When the Bavarian Soviet Republic was crushed, Leviné was captured and court-martialed. The court martial told him: 'You are under sentence of death.' Leviné answered: 'We Communists are always under sentence of death.' That is another thing that it meant to be a Communist.

"The Russian was not a Communist. He was a pre-Communist revolutionist named Kalyaev. (I should have said Sazonov.) He was arrested for a minor part in the assassination of the Tsarist prime minister, von Plehve. He was sent into Siberian exile to one of the worst prison camps, where the political prisoners were flogged. Kalyaev sought some way to protest this outrage to the world. The means were few, but at last he found a way. In protest against the flogging of other men, Kalyaev drenched himself in kerosene, set himself on fire and burned himself to death. That also is what it meant to be a Communist."

That also is what it means to be a witness.

But a man may also be an involuntary witness. I do not know any way to explain why God's grace touches a man who seems unworthy of it. But neither do I know any other way to explain how a man like myself—tarnished by life, unprepossessing, not brave—could prevail so far against the powers of the world arrayed almost solidly against him, to destroy him and defeat his truth. In this sense, I am an involuntary witness to God's grace and to the fortifying power of faith.

It was my fate to be in turn a witness to each of the two great faiths of our time. And so we come to the terrible word, Communism. My very dear children, nothing in all these pages will be written so much for you, though it is so unlike anything you would want to read. In nothing shall I be so much a witness, in no way am I so much called upon to fulfill my task, as in trying to make clear to you (and to the world) the true nature of Communism and the source of its power, which was the cause of my ordeal as a man, and remains the historic ordeal of the world in the 20th century. For in this century, within the next decades, will be decided for generations whether all mankind is to become Communist, whether the whole world is to become free, or whether, in the struggle, civilization as we know it is to be completely destroyed or completely changed. It is our fate to live upon that turning point in history.

The world has reached that turning point by the steep stages of a crisis mounting for generations. The turning point is the next to the last step. It was reached in blood, sweat, tears, havoc and death in World War II. The chief fruit of the First World War was the Russian Revolution and the rise of Communism as a national power. The chief fruit of the Second World War was our arrival at the next to the last step of the crisis with the rise of Communism as a world power. History is likely to say that these were the only decisive results of the world wars.

The last war simplified the balance of political forces in the world by reducing them to two. For the first time, it made the power of the Communist sector of mankind (embodied in the Soviet Union) roughly equal to the power of the free sector of mankind (embodied in the United States). It made the collision of these powers all but inevitable. For the world wars did not end the crisis. They raised its tensions to a new pitch. They raised the crisis to a new stage. All the politics of our time, including the politics of war, will be the politics of this crisis.

Few men are so dull that they do not know that the crisis exists and that it threatens their lives at every point. It is popular to call it a social crisis. It is in fact a total crisis—religious, moral, intellectual, social, political, economic. It is popular to call it a crisis of the Western world. It is in fact a crisis of the whole world. Communism, which claims to be a solution of the crisis, is itself a symptom and an irritant of the crisis.

In part, the crisis results from the impact of science and technology upon mankind which, neither socially nor morally, has caught up with the problems posed by that impact. In part, it is caused by men's efforts to solve those problems. World wars are the military expression of the crisis. World-wide depressions are its economic expression. Universal desperation is its spiritual climate. This is the climate of Communism. Communism in our time can no more be considered apart from the crisis than a fever can be acted upon apart from an infected body.

I see in Communism the focus of the concentrated evil of our time. You will ask: Why, then, do men become Communists? How did it happen that you, our gentle and loved father, were once a Communist? Were you simply stupid? No, I was not stupid. Were you morally depraved? No, I was not morally depraved. Indeed, educated men become Communists chiefly for moral reasons. Did you not know that the crimes and horrors of Communism are inherent in Communism? Yes, I knew that fact. Then why did you become a Communist? It would help more to ask: How did it happen that this movement, once a mere muttering of political outcasts, became this immense force that now contests the mastery of mankind? Even when all the chances and mistakes of history are allowed for, the answer must be: Communism makes some profound appeal to the human mind. You will not find out what it is by calling Communism names. That will not help much to explain why Communism whose horrors, on a scale unparalleled in history, are now public knowledge, still recruits its thousands and holds its millions—among them some of the best minds alive. Look at Klaus Fuchs, standing in the London dock, quiet, doomed, destroyed, and say whether it is possible to answer in that way the simple question: Why?

First, let me try to say what Communism is not. It is not simply a vicious plot hatched by wicked men in a sub-cellar. It is not just the writings of Marx and Lenin, dialectical materialism. The Politburo, the labor theory of value, the theory of the general strike, the Red Army, secret police, labor camps, underground conspiracy, the dictatorship of the proletariat, the technique of the coup d'état. It is not even those chanting, bannered millions that stream periodically, like disorganized armies, through the heart of the world's capitals: Moscow, New York, Tokyo, Paris, Rome. These are expressions of Communism, but they are not what Communism is about.

In the Hiss trials, where Communism was a haunting specter, but which did little or nothing to explain Communism, Communists were assumed to be criminals, pariahs, clandestine men who lead double lives under false names, travel on false passports, deny traditional religion, morality, the sanctity of oaths, preach violence and practice treason. These things are true about Communists, but they are not what Communism is about.

The revolutionary heart of Communism is not the theatrical appeal: "Workers of the world, unite. You have nothing to lose but your chains. You have a world to gain." It is a simple statement of Karl Marx, further simplified for handy use: "Philosophers have explained the world; it is necessary to change the world." Communists are bound together by no secret oath. The tie that binds them across the frontiers of nations, across barriers of language and differences of class and education, in defiance of religion, morality, truth, law, honor, the weaknesses of the body and the irresolutions of the mind, even unto death, is a simple conviction: It is necessary to change the world. Their power, whose nature baffles the rest of the world, because in a large measure the rest of the world has lost that power, is the power to hold convictions and to act on them. It is the same power that moves mountains; it is also an unfailing power to move men. Communists are that part of mankind which has recovered the power to live or die—to bear witness—for its faith. And it is a simple, rational faith that inspires men to live or die for it.

It is not new. It is, in fact, man's second oldest faith. Its promise was whispered in the first days of the Creation under the Tree of the Knowledge of Good and Evil: "Ye shall be as gods."

It is the great alternative faith of mankind. Like all great faiths, its force derives from a simple vision. Other ages have had great visions. They have always been different versions of the same vision: the vision of God and man's relationship to God. The Communist vision is the vision of Man without God.

It is the vision of man's mind displacing God as the creative intelligence of the world. It is the vision of man's liberated mind, by the sole force of its rational intelligence, redirecting man's destiny and reorganizing man's life and the world. It is the vision of man, once more the central figure of the Creation, not because God made man in His image, but because man's mind makes him the most intelligent of the animals. Copernicus and his successors displaced man as the central fact of the universe by proving that the earth was not the central star of the universe. Communism restores man to his sovereignty by the simple method of denying God.

The vision is a challenge and implies a threat. It challenges man to prove by his acts that he is the masterwork of the Creation—by making thought and act one. It challenges him to prove it by using the force of his rational mind to end the bloody meaninglessness of man's history—by giving it purpose and a plan. It challenges him to prove it by reducing the meaningless chaos of nature, by imposing on it his rational will to order, abundance, security, peace. It is the vision of materialism. But it threatens, if man's mind is unequal to the problems of man's progress, that he will sink back into savagery (the A and the H bombs have raised the issue in explosive forms), until nature replaces him with a more intelligent form of life.

It is an intensely practical vision. The tools to turn it into reality are at hand—science and technology, whose traditional method, the rigorous exclusion of all supernatural factors in solving problems, has contributed to the intellectual climate in which the vision flourishes, just as they have contributed to the crisis in which Communism thrives. For the vision is shared by millions who are not Communists (they are part of Communism's secret strength). Its first commandment is found, not in the *Communist Manifesto* but in the first sentence of the physics primer: "All of the progress of mankind to date results from the making of careful measurements." But Communism, for the first time in history, has made this vision the faith of a great modern political movement.

Hence the Communist Party is quite justified in calling itself the most revolutionary party in history. It has posed in practical form the most revolutionary question in history: God or Man? It has taken the logical next step which three hundred years of rationalism hesitated to take, and said what millions of modern minds think, but do not dare or care to say: If man's mind is the decisive force in the world, what need is there for God? Henceforth man's mind is man's fate.

This vision *is* the Communist revolution, which, like all great revolutions, occurs in man's mind before it takes form in man's acts. Insurrection and conspiracy are merely methods of realizing the vision; they are merely part of the politics of Communism. Without its vision, they, like Communism, would have no meaning and could not rally a parcel of pickpockets. Communism does not summon men to crime or to utopia, as its easy critics like to think. On the plane of faith, it summons mankind to turn its vision into practical reality. On the plane of action, it summons men to struggle against the inertia of the past which, embodied in social, political and economic forms, Communism claims, is blocking the will of mankind to make its next great forward stride. It summons men to overcome the crisis, which, Communism claims, is in effect a crisis of rending frustration, with the world, unable to stand still, but unwilling to go forward along the road that the logic of a technological civilization points out—Communism.

This is Communism's moral sanction, which is twofold. Its vision points the way to the future; its faith labors to turn the future into present reality. It says to every man who joins it: The vision is a practical problem of history; the way to achieve it is a practical problem of politics, which is the present tense of history. Have you the moral strength to take upon yourself the crimes of history so that man at last may close his chronicle of age-old, senseless suffering, and replace it with purpose and a plan? The answer a man makes to this question is the difference between the Communist and those miscellaneous socialists, liberals, fellow travelers, unclassified progressives and men of good will, all of whom share a similar vision, but do not share the faith because they will not take upon themselves the penalties of the faith. The answer is the root of that sense of moral superiority which makes Communists, though caught in crime, berate their opponents with withering self-righteousness.

The Communist vision has a mighty agitator and a mighty propagandist. They are the crisis. The agitator needs no soap box. It speaks insistently to the human mind at the point where desperation lurks. The propagandist writes no Communist gibberish. It speaks insistently to the human mind at the point where man's hope and man's energy fuse to fierceness.

The vision inspires. The crisis impels. The workingman is chiefly moved by the crisis. The educated man is chiefly moved by the vision. The workingman, living upon a mean margin of life, can afford few visions—even practical visions. An educated man, peering from the Harvard Yard, or any college campus, upon a world in chaos, finds in the vision the two certainties for which the mind of man tirelessly seeks: a reason to live and a reason to die. No other faith of our time presents them with the same practical intensity. That is why Communism is the central experience of the first half of the 20th century, and may be its final experience—will be, unless the free world, in the agony of its struggle with Communism, overcomes its crisis by discovering, in suffering and pain, a power of faith which will provide man's mind, at the same intensity, with the same two certainties: a reason to live and a reason to die. If it fails, this will be the century of the great social wars. If it succeeds, this will be the century of the great wars of faith.

You will ask: Why, then, do men cease to be Communists? One answer is: very few do. Thirty years after the Russian Revolution, after the known atrocities, the purges, the revelations, the jolting zigzags of Communist politics, there is only a handful of ex-Communists in the whole world. By ex-Communists I do not mean those who break with Communism over differences of strategy and tactics (like Trotsky) or organization (like Tito). Those are merely quarrels over a road map by people all of whom are in a hurry to get to the same place.

Nor, by ex-Communists, do I mean those thousands who continually drift into the Communist Party and out again. The turnover is vast. These are the spiritual vagrants of our time whose traditional faith has been leached out in the bland climate of rationalism. They are looking for an intellectual night's lodging. They lack the character for Communist faith because they lack the character for any faith. So they drop away, though Communism keeps its hold on them.

By an ex-Communist I mean a man who knew clearly why he became a Communist, who served Communism devotedly and knew why he served it, who broke with Communism unconditionally and knew why he broke with it. Of these there are very few—an index to the power of the vision and the power of the crisis.

History very largely fixes the patterns of force that make men Communists. Hence one Communist conversion sounds much like another—rather impersonal and repetitious, awesome and tiresome, like long lines of similar people all stolidly waiting to get in to see the same movie. A man's break with Communism is intensely personal. Hence the account of no two breaks is likely to be the same. The reasons that made one Communist break may seem without force to another ex-Communist.

It is a fact that a man can join the Communist Party, can be very active in it for years, without completely understanding the nature of Communism or the political methods that follow inevitably from its vision. One day such incomplete Communists discover that the Communist Party is not what they thought it was. They break with it and turn on it with the rage of an honest dupe, a dupe who has given a part of his life to a swindle. Often they forget that it takes two to make a swindle.

Others remain Communists for years, warmed by the light of its vision, firmly closing their eyes to the crimes and horrors inseparable from its practical politics. One day they have to face the facts. They are appalled at what they have abetted. They spend the rest of their days trying to explain, usually without great success, the dark clue to their complicity. As their understanding of Communism was incomplete and led them to a dead end, their understanding of breaking with it is incomplete and leads them to a dead end. It leads to less than Communism, which was a vision and a faith. The world outside Communism, the world in crisis, lacks a vision and a faith. There is before these ex-Communists absolutely nothing. Behind them is a threat. For they have, in fact, broken not with the vision, but with the politics of the vision. In the name of reason and intelligence, the vision keeps them firmly in its grip—self-divided, paralyzed, powerless to act against it.

Hence the most secret fold of their minds is haunted by a terrifying thought: What if we were wrong? What if our inconstancy is our guilt? That is the fate of those who break without knowing clearly that Communism is wrong because something else is right, because to the challenge: *God or Man?* they continue to give the answer: *Man.* Their pathos is that not even the Communist ordeal could teach them that man without God is just what Communism said he was: the most intelligent of the animals, that man without God is a beast, never more beastly than when he is most intelligent about his beastliness. *"Er nennt's Vernunft,"* says the Devil in Goethe's *Faust, "und braucht's allein, nur tierischer als jedes Tier zu sein"*—Man calls it reason and uses it simply to be more beastly than any beast. Not grasping the source of the evil they sincerely hate, such ex-Communists in general make ineffectual witnesses against it. They are witnesses against something; they have ceased to be witnesses for anything.

Yet there is one experience which most sincere ex-Communists share, whether or not they go only part way to the end of the question it poses. The daughter of a former German diplomat in Moscow was trying to explain to me why her father, who, as an enlightened modern man, had been extremely pro-Communist, had become an implacable anti-Communist. It was hard for her because, as an enlightened modern girl, she shared the Communist vision without being a Communist. But she loved her father and the irrationality of his defection embarrassed her. "He was immensely pro-Soviet," she said, "and then—you will laugh at me—but you must not laugh at my father—and then—one night—in Moscow—he heard screams. That's all. Simply one night he heard screams."

A child of Reason and the 20th century, she knew that there is a logic of the mind. She did not know that the soul has a logic that may be more compelling than the mind's. She did not know at all that she had swept away the logic of the mind, the logic of history, the logic of politics, the myth of the 20th century, with five annihilating words: One night he heard screams.

What Communist has not heard those screams? They come from husbands torn forever from their wives in midnight arrests. They come, muffled, from the execution cellars of the secret police, from the torture chambers of the Lubianka, from all the citadels of terror now stretching from Berlin to Canton. They come from those freight cars loaded with men, women, and children, the enemies of the Communist State, locked in, packed in, left on remote sidings to freeze to death at night in the Russian winter. They come from minds driven mad by the horrors of mass starvation ordered and enforced as a policy of the Communist State. They come from the starved skeletons, worked to death, or flogged to death (as an example to others) in the freezing filth of sub-arctic labor camps. They come from children whose parents are suddenly, inexplicably, taken away from them —parents they will never see again.

What Communist has not heard those screams? Execution, says the Communist code, is the highest measure of social protection. What man can call himself a Communist who has not accepted the fact that Terror is an instrument of policy, right if the vision is right, justified by history, enjoined by the balance of forces in the social wars of this century? Those screams have reached every Communist's mind. Usually they stop there. What judge willingly dwells upon the man the laws compel him to condemn to death—the laws of nations or the laws of history?

But one day the Communist really hears those screams. He is going about his routine party tasks. He is lifting a dripping reel of microfilm from a developing tank. He is justifying to a Communist fraction in a trade union an extremely unwelcome directive of the Central Committee. He is receiving from a trusted superior an order to go to another country and, in a designated hotel, at a designated hour, meet a man whose name he will never know, but who will give him a package whose contents he will never learn. Suddenly, there closes around the Communist a separating silence, and in that silence he hears screams. He hears them for the first time. For they do not merely reach his mind. They pierce beyond. They pierce to his soul. He says to himself: "Those are not the screams of man in agony. Those are the screams of a soul in agony." He hears them for the first time because a soul in extremity has communicated with that which alone can hear it—another human soul.

Why does the Communist ever hear them? Because in the end there persists in every man, however he may deny it, a scrap of soul. The Communist who suffers this singular experience then says to himself: "What is happening to me? I must be sick." If he does not instantly stifle that scrap of soul, he is lost. If he admits it for a moment, he has admitted that there is something greater than Reason, greater than the logic of mind, of politics, of history, of economics, which alone justifies the vision. If the party senses his weakness, and the party is peculiarly cunning at sensing such weakness, it will humiliate him, degrade him, condemn him, expel him. If it can, it will destroy him. And the party will be right. For he has betrayed that which alone justifies its faith—the vision of Almighty Man. He has brushed the only vision that has force against the vision of Almighty Mind. He stands before the fact of God.

The Communist Party is familiar with this experience to which its members are sometimes liable in prison, in illness, in indecision. It is recognized frankly as a sickness. There are ways of treating it—if it is confessed. It is when it is not confessed that the party, sensing a subtle crisis, turns upon it savagely. What ex-Communist has not suffered this experience in one form or another, to one degree or another? What he does about it depends on the individual man. That is why no ex-Communist dare answer for his sad fraternity the question: Why do men break with Communism? He can only answer the question: How did you break with Communism? My answer is: slowly, reluctantly, in agony.

Yet my break began long before I heard those screams. Perhaps it does for everyone. I do not know how far back it began. Avalanches gather force and crash, unheard, in men as in the mountains. But I date my break from a very casual happening. I was sitting in our apartment on St. Paul Street in Baltimore. It was shortly before we moved to Alger Hiss's apartment in Washington. My daughter was in her high chair. I was watching her eat. She was the most miraculous thing that had ever happened in my life. I liked to watch her even when she smeared porridge on her face or dropped it meditatively on the floor. My eye came to rest on the delicate convolutions of her ear—those intricate, perfect ears. The thought passed through my mind: "No, those ears were not created by any chance coming together of atoms in nature (the Communist view). They could have been created only by immense design." The thought was involuntary and unwanted. I crowded it out of my mind. But I never wholly forgot it or the occasion. I had to crowd it out of my mind. If I had completed it, I should have had to say: Design presupposes God. I did not then know that, at that moment, the finger of God was first laid upon my forehead.

One thing most ex-Communists could agree upon: They broke because they wanted to be free. They do not all mean the same thing by "free." Freedom is a need of the soul, and nothing else. It is in striving toward God that the soul strives continually after a condition of freedom. God alone is the inciter and guarantor of freedom. He is the only guarantor. External freedom is only an aspect of interior freedom. Political freedom, as the Western world has known it, is only a political reading of the Bible. Religion and freedom are indivisible. Without freedom the soul dies. Without the soul there is no justification for freedom. Necessity is the only ultimate justification known to the mind. Hence every sincere break with Communism is a religious experience, though the Communist fail to identify its true nature, though he fail to go to the end of the experience. His break is the political expression of the perpetual need of the soul whose first faint stirring he has felt within him, years, months or days before he breaks. A Communist breaks because he must choose at last between irreconcilable opposites—God or Man, Soul or Mind, Freedom or Communism.

Communism is what happens when, in the name of Mind, men free themselves from God. But its view of God, its knowledge of God, its experience of God, is what alone gives character to a society or a nation, and meaning to its destiny. Its culture, the voice of this character, is merely that view, knowledge, experience, of God, fixed by its most intense spirits in terms intelligible to the mass of men. There has never been a society or a nation without God. But history is cluttered with the wreckage of nations that became indifferent to God, and died.

The crisis of Communism exists to the degree in which it has failed to free the peoples that it rules from God. Nobody knows this better than the Communist Party of the Soviet Union. The crisis of the Western world exists to the degree in which it is indifferent to God. It exists to the degree in which the Western world actually shares Communism's materialist vision, is so dazzled by the logic of the materialist interpretation of history, politics and economics, that it fails to grasp that, for it, the only possible answer to the Communist challenge: Faith in God or Faith in Man? is the challenge: Faith in God.

Economics is not the central problem of this century. It is a relative problem which can be solved in relative ways. Faith is the central problem of this age. The Western world does not know it, but it already possesses the answer to this problem—but only provided that its faith in God and the freedom He enjoins is as great as Communism's faith in Man.

9   *A woman who was diagnosed as suffering from mental illness relates some of her rather unusual experiences.*

The cosmic crises

morag coate

I tended now when I thought about them—which was rarely—to interpret the content of my earlier illnesses in terms of the struggle against unseen powers. In my first illness I had been as it were captured and brought under control by the powers of light and forced to demonstrate, by my symbolic actions, a way of life acceptable to them. The second illness, from the one clue I had about its content, suggested also that I had been under the control of some power or person separate from me. I felt now much more strongly developed in myself and better able to preserve my individuality.

Not long after the incident of the milk and water, I was in bed for a few days with a virus infection. I spent my time daydreaming about the future, a luxury I had not allowed myself before. The small but seemingly supernatural occurrence had left me with a feeling that anything could happen now. Perhaps my earlier, unrealistic hopes were not inherently impossible after all. My daydreams were vivid and had a strong emotional content. I did not believe they gave me in any sense a preview of coming events, but I did begin to believe again that in one way or another much that I hoped for might prove possible. They absorbed me fully at the time, and they were subtly exhausting. When I returned to work I had a curious sense of remoteness from my surroundings; it was as though I were looking at life through the wrong end of a telescope. I dismissed this as a result of the minor physical illness and thought no more about it. Another four or five weeks went by before I started to lose contact with reality.

Suddenly a number of events took place which were of great significance. A submarine under the ice above the pole. Trapped miners seeking a way of escape. A moving and impressive burial at sea. A major earthquake in a part of the world that had specific spiritual associations for me. I knew without doubt what this meant; the liberation of hell was at hand. At the same time a spiritual migration of free souls was taking place. Earth was for them a temporary stopping-place. Like birds resting from their journey on a ship in mid-ocean, they came down and entered for a day into the bodies of small children who, in their youth and innocence, were not aware of them. No one else noticed, but I recognised them at once. I made no comment, there was no need; it was enough to know. By the following day they had left for their new destinations.

Also during this week a day was lost, or rather extracted unnoticed from our calendar, and used as a loop in time for the rescue of lost souls. It was cast round the outer limits of existence like a long fishing net, and then drawn in, bringing with it those who, for lack of any spiritual affinities, had drifted into the waste spaces of non-being.

Throughout the week I continued work as usual. The discipline of professional responsibility did not desert me when I became delusional: I had to wait until I was off duty before I could enter fully into the new life which had opened up for me. At midday on the Saturday I left my desk tidy and walked out through one of the university gardens where the earliest spring flowers were coming into bloom. The sun was shining and I had a sense of liberation and release. I was joined at once by an unseen companion and I decided to take him out to lunch. We went down the hill and into a restaurant that was well known to me. I was disconcerted to find that I was now invisible too; the waitress could not see me, and there was no hope of getting served. An observer would have commented that the waitress was extremely busy and I had not given her time to attend to me, but I knew better. She and others around her were not real people, they were animated fakes. As we went out again I realised how lucky we were that we had not been served; the food would have been spiritual poison to us. This region of the city had been transformed by a total removal of its spiritual component, and had become Vanity Fair. Luckily the district in which I lived was still intact, and the food in my own room was wholesome. My companion was somewhat upset and ashamed at what had happened to the main centre of the city, and so was I. During the afternoon he left me, as he had business elsewhere.

I had two unseen visitors that night in fairly quick succession. The first was the spirit of a man. He made love to me tenderly but briefly. His composition was of a different texture from mine and, like a wisp of cloud pressing against a fine-meshed screen, he passed straight through me and was gone.

The second visitor was my companion of the afternoon. A man, yet more than a man. When he made love to me it was with a vigour that fired my whole being. His composition was also different from mine, but in the opposite direction. His passion, untempered and unhumanised by flesh, left me inwardly a little burnt. We sat together afterwards in comfortable companionship for a time, but this relaxation was no more than a brief preparation for the grave and strenuous work we had to do.

The task before us was no less than to lift Christ down from the cross. Not the lifeless body on a wooden cross outside Jerusalem. This concerned the living person who had been re-crucified, and in a different way, through the influence of those of his own followers who, in imagery and worship, had concentrated their imagination on his physical sufferings and failed to grasp the mental and spiritual cost of the event. He had been lifted above life and immobilised in the posture in which so many of his worshippers wished to view him. What my companion had now to do, with my support, was very hard, but it was achieved. Afterwards there was a tremendous leap to be made across a gulf in which this earth was a stepping stone. Some great superhuman personage took part. He landed momentarily with one leg in the same place as one of mine, so that for a few seconds from mid-thigh downwards he shared my flesh. Then he was gone.

A few seconds later my right leg, which was the one that had been used, went into spasm. I thought quickly, and in the circumstances rather surprisingly, in terms of localised cerebral overstimulation; I lay down and called out, "Send for a doctor." I was confident of being heard by supernatural means. I lost consciousness and, when I came to, the spasm was relieved. Then it began again, even more severely, and this time there was no question of a neurological cause of the pain. I had been caught in the collision between two worlds, my leg was crushed between them and was being totally destroyed. For the first time in my life I screamed. I lost consciousness again, but just before doing so I saw as a kind of retinal after-image the shape of my severed leg in a phantasmagoric red colour; this image was being projected as a portent to other parts of the universe, where it caused much wonder and alarm.

When I recovered consciousness my leg was once more whole and undamaged. I was now alone, and busied myself in certain symbolic tasks I had to do. By washing off the stains on an ink bottle I ritually removed the guilt for a murder which had recently taken place. This murder, by an influence which had been projected into a contemporary psychopath, had released an impulse of retribution on Salome for the beheading of John the Baptist. The place in which it happened had, by a temporary displacement of space, been transferred to the room next to mine. I went in there later to make sure that all was well, and was reassured to hear the even breathing of a sleeping girl.

I went back into my own room and got into bed, but now I could not sleep, and this was dangerous for the room was filled with an unearthly light and my hand cast no shadow on the wall. The church spire which was a landmark from my window had disappeared, and time was passing at an altered speed. Time was stretched out like an elastic band, each minute of it was at once thinner and longer than usual. At last the stage was reached when external time ceased altogether and only I lived on. I could prove that by the fact that my watch stopped. I looked out of the window again and saw, rather blurred and low on the horizon, in a part of the sky where it had no right to be, the constellation of Orion. I knew then what had happened. I and my immediate physical surroundings had been projected to a far distant part of outer space. My room and part of the house were real, but the surroundings I could see outside the window, familiar except for the significant absence of the church spire, were an illusion. I was very far from home.

I had, as I realised, brought this on myself by my rash actions. I had defied and alienated the powers of light, and I had underrated the danger of coming under the influence of the powers of darkness. The particular focal nucleus of the powers of light which had, on earlier occasions, tried to subdue and convert me, now feared and distrusted me for two reasons. First because of my unrepentant view of the beauty and sacramental nature of sexual love, and secondly because of my recent activities in inviting the spirits of the dead to sup with me. It was reported of me, by some who had not been invited, that I had been performing a kind of black mass. Heaven now washed its hands of me and passed me over to the powers of darkness.

I had made allowance for the potential dangers arising from the warped or rejected creative spirits encapsulated in hell. I had ignored the activities of those who were just ordinarily bad for lack of any positive affiliations. From out of these a freelance group whose motive was greed and lust for power had heard I could work miracles and credited me with superhuman power. They believed that by inviting me to join with them they could use my powers for their own ends. It was they who had transferred me to outer space, and they expected me to know what to do next. When I realised this I was extremely angry; angry that they should credit me with superhuman powers, and furious that they could believe I would use such God-given power, if I had it, for their own selfish ends. My rage and rejection daunted them, and they withdrew their influence. I was left stuck far out in psychic space, beyond reach of the spiritual gravitational field of earth. I called in spirit to a friend on earth and this gave me a sense of orientation; I knew the direction of my home, but I could not make contact and I lacked any power to propel me back. I was frightened and alone.

The worst feature of the situation was that I was now lifeless but still active. I was cold, and I could not feel my pulse; that proved I was not normally alive. But I could not rest, I could not sleep and, since external time had stopped, I was likely to remain in this condition eternally, a solitary, animated corpse.

Now, increasingly, I became surrounded by a total spiritual

vacuum. I was cut off from all possibility of contact with any
living person. I became filled with absolute and overwhelming
terror.

It seemed that the highest concentration of emptiness was
here in the room with me, and my first panic reaction was to
want to jump out of the window. I checked myself by remember-
ing that everything outside was delusion. Better to remain here
at all costs. I fought back panic, but terror still remained. I
knelt down by my bed. There was no one to pray to; I was totally
cut off from God. The words I used were affirmation rather than
prayer. I said steadily, "I cannot believe that love is bad. I cannot believe that God is bad." I repeated the words over and over
again, and by degrees terror died down. I remained afraid, but it
was a manageable fear.

Some weeks earlier I had been making models of a crystal-
line structure that had rather curious mathematical properties.
This led to a sudden outburst of cerebral activity in which I
could visualise the square root of minus one, and I was able to
work out many relevant aspects of the interaction of psychic and
physical reality. The background to my thinking now was almost
equally complicated, and I could scarcely explain it all here even
if I could remember it in detail. But, taking many different
factors into account, I decided that my best hope was to see if at
a lower level and in a different direction it was still possible to
find a way out of the house that led back to reality. I therefore
got dressed and went downstairs. I discovered that it was not
possible to get out. My worst fears were confirmed; there was no
escape and consequently no possible end to consciousness in view.
But here in the last extremity a lingering faith that God could
reach me even though I was cut off from him awakened in me. I
lay down on the stone floor and called on God to receive my soul.
I fell into a deep and dreamless sleep.

No one out of a number who might have done so heard my
varied activities that night. I had used the telephone to help in
finding out whether time had really stopped. I had walked into
someone else's bedroom. I had knocked over a heavy chair on
one of the occasions when I fell down unconscious. I had once
given a loud scream. But no one heard me. Why? Perhaps be-

cause they were not intended to hear. So I reasoned to myself later when I thought of it. Meanwhile I found relief in sleep.

I have no idea how long I slept. The next thing I knew was when I was picked up and carried into a nearby room. I discovered to my horror that the surroundings were unfamiliar; I had left reality again. This was the right place but the wrong room. I had gone through the looking glass. A clock on the mantlepiece was turned against the wall and the works were facing towards me. This showed that the right time was on the outer side of the space I had moved into. A look at the newspaper beside me confirmed my fears. It showed an earlier date. In this place I would continue to move backwards in time, never again meeting my own friends. I would not make contact with the people who might surround me here. I would remain shut up within my private world. This was what it meant to be a soul lost in limbo. And this was what it meant to be insane. I could quite clearly visualise the practical implications of having gone insane in such a way. Since I was incapable of making human contacts, I would be put into a mental hospital and there end my days. But this would of course be done by strangers; I had lost my own world. And after I died the condition of being a lost soul in the grey loneliness of limbo would still remain. When I had become frightened on the previous night there had still been the lingering hope that something could be done. There was no hope now. I sat still in the apathy of despair, facing my dreadful future. It was the worst experience I have ever known.

Later in the day hope revived when I was moved back in what I sensed to be the direction of my own room. I kept my eyes tight closed, fearing to let the unreal world spread into the real one. When at last I dared to look about me, I felt a blissful relief. These were my own known surroundings; I was safe again.

10 Cory describes the self-concept of a homosexual as it is determined by society's prejudice and rejection.

The unrecognized minority

donald webster cory

In recent years the world has become extremely conscious of minority problems. Upon industry, government, and indeed upon society as a whole, there is a constant pressure to recognize the rights of minorities. Usually by biological accident, sometimes by intellectual choice, many people find themselves outside the pale of the mainstream of life, unable to enjoy the benefits of civilization side by side with their fellowmen. Their plight is recognized; one constantly hears that human rights must be granted, regardless of race, religion, color, or political creed. The attitude toward minorities has, in the opinion of many, become a touchstone by which the progressive character of an individual or a nation may be judged. Minority rights, many contend, have become the challenge of this century; they are regarded as the corner stone upon which democracy must build and flourish, or perish in the decades to come. The lack of recognition of the rights of dissident and nonconforming minorities is the most distinguishing characteristic of totalitarianism.

The struggle for advancement by groups that are denied their place in society at large takes place simultaneously on two levels. It is a struggle that is fought by those who, voluntarily or involuntarily, are in the ranks of the few. Almost without exception, they believe that they are deserving of full freedoms, and they strive to achieve them. They have an awareness of their

From *The Homosexual in America* by Donald Webster Cory. Copyright © 1951 by Donald Webster Cory. Used with permission of Chilton Book Company, Philadelphia and New York.

problems that follows them without cease; their escape is only occasional, momentary, and fleeting. They see life as divided into two seemingly hostile and irreconcilable camps; and seldom do they stop to inquire of themselves whether they display toward other minority groups the attitudes they demand be shown toward themselves. On occasion one discovers the rare individual of such stature that his attitude of deep sympathy for all human beings transcends his own identification with a group of people.

At the same time, the minority is not infrequently strengthened by the activities of some individuals from the dominant world who, whatever their motives might be, identify themselves with the aspirations of a group without being a member of the group. Their entire philosophy may be libertarian, their endorsement of the outcast may be prompted by personal, psychological, humanitarian, intellectual, or other experiences. But what matter the motive; history judges the deed. And history has taught them that the many cannot prosper while the few wither; that the majority cannot achieve a true happiness in a world in which a minority is deeply condemned.

Out of these majority-minority relationships grow literature protest, search for change. The more articulate describe what it means to live as a member of the minority—the blind alleys and the dead-ends . . . the discrimination . . . the sneer, the joke, the abusive language . . . the humiliation and self-doubt . . . the struggle to maintain self-respect and group pride. As these people describe and protest, their voices are complemented by those of the allies found in another world, people who can never fully know the psychological impact of a hostile culture on those whom they are aiding, but who are peculiarly well situated to further a cause without fully understanding it.

The minority question has been studied exhaustively in recent years. Attention has been focused on the Jewish people in Germany and elsewhere in the world, the Hindus and Moslems in India and Pakistan, the Catholics in Ulster and the Protestants in Italy, the Negroes in America. Nor are religion, race, and color the sole aspect of minority problems; the rights of Communists in the Western democracies are debated, and rights for non-Communists in the Eastern European states are demanded. The privileges of atheists on the one hand, or Jehovah's

Witnesses, on the other, fall within the scope of the study of minority problems.

It is my belief that another phase of the minority problem is demanding the attention of America. We who are homosexual constitute a minority that cannot accept the outlook, customs, and laws of the dominant group. We constitute a minority, and a unique one.

Some will protest against the classification of the homosexuals as a minority, on the grounds that the term usually encompasses ethnic groups, and that the latter constitute a number of people grouped together by act of accident of birth. Even the religious minorities are not exempt from the fact of being grouped in this manner, inasmuch as religious creeds are generally passed on from parents to children. However, such a concept of the minority, aside from the narrowness of the considerations, is significant only insofar as it emphasizes the involuntary and inescapable nature of group belonging. As I shall show in a section of this book devoted to the genesis of homosexuality, and as is conceded by psychiatrists, the fact of being homosexual, and therefore of belonging to a group, is as involuntary as if it were inborn, despite the fact that it is not inborn; and as I shall demonstrate in my discussion of therapy, the fact of retaining homosexual desires, whether one indulges or suppresses, and whether or not a bisexual adjustment is made, is virtually as ineradicable as if it involved the color of one's skin or the shape of one's eyes.

It goes without saying that there are some fundamental differences between homosexuals and the conventionally recognized minority groups. A minority, according to a rather narrow definition, would be any outnumbered people. But, in its broader connotations, a minority group must consist in the first place of people who have some important trait in common that not only unites them to each other, but differentiates them from the rest of society. Group psychology, writes Sigmund Freud, is "concerned with the individual man as a member of a race, of a nation, of a caste, of a profession, of an institution, or as a component part of a crowd of people who have been organised into a group at some particular time for some definite purpose."* From

* Sigmund Freud, *Group Psychology and the Analysis of the Ego*, London, International Psycho-analytical Press, 1922, p. 3.

this definition, it can be seen that not only Christians and Jews, Negroes and whites, constitute groups, but Communists are a group, deaf-mutes are a group, as are physicians and psychoanalysts. But a minority group, from a sociological viewpoint, must have another characteristic, and that is its lower or unequal status in society. The physicians would therefore not be a minority, in such a sense, and it is even possible for the minority group, as has been pointed out, to be a numerical majority, the classic example being the South African Negroes.

By such a definition, the homosexuals are a minority group, consisting of large numbers of people who belong, participate, and are constantly aware of something that binds them to others and separates them from the larger stream of life; yet a group without a spokesman, without a leader, without a publication, without an organization, without a philosophy of life, without an accepted justification for its own existence. In fact, there is surely no group of such size, and yet with so few who acknowledge that they belong. And, were it not for social pressure to acknowledge, or for biological ease of identification, would not other minorities likewise lose a large portion of their groups?

Many have written about this problem. There are hundreds of books: novels, sociological treatises, statistical studies, psychoanalytic critiques—some of them worthy contributions toward the building of a literature. Yet, with but one or two exceptions, no one has stopped to relate in simple terms, not couched in fiction, what it means to be a homosexual. Seldom has anyone ever told the sociologists, the legislators and judges, the novelists and psychiatrists—except in confidential conversations that can never become part of the public domain—what it feels like to be a homosexual, living with a constant awareness of the existence of something inescapable, and how this affects every aspect of life, here, today, now, in the middle years of the twentieth century in America.

What are the problems a homosexual might meet, the accommodations he makes, the compulsions he carries, the conflicts he seeks to untangle? What do we homosexuals think of the origins of our problem, of the search for an answer, of the laws and the blackmail, of the desirability of marriage, of the novels about our group? What sort of a philosophy of life are we seeking, do we find life hopeless, are we defeated and dejected, or is there an answer that some, or many, have found? Do we want to be what the world terms normal, have we made the effort, what is our experience when we try? Do we acknowledge our inclinations to family and friends, do we develop friendships outside our group, and what are the attitudes that we encounter?

Delving into these questions, I find that fundamental to all answers is an understanding that the dominant factor in my life, towering in importance above all others, is a consciousness that I am different. In one all-important respect, I am unlike the great mass of people always around me, and the knowledge of this fact is with me at all times, influencing profoundly my every thought, each minute activity, and all my aspirations. It is inescapable, not only this being different, but more than that, this constant awareness of a dissimilarity.

Sometimes, perhaps as I lie abed in the morning, fully awake but not yet ready to rise, or as I sit and relax in a soft chair in my home, and drop the newspaper to the floor and close my eyes, I am able to retreat into myself with only my own thoughts, and I am overcome by a peculiar wonderment. An insatiable curiosity grips me as I yearn to know what it would be like not to be a homosexual. My imagination wanders madly, and I conjure up images that are inspired by art, poetry, drama, fiction, cinema, and personal acquaintances. I bring into my fantasy the hetero-sexuals I know, in real life and make-believe, and I persevere in my efforts to identify myself with them. To add to the realistic aspects of the fantasy, I picture myself making condemnatory remarks and harsh judgments. But it's all in vain. It is outside the realm of my wildest flights of fancy. I am powerless even to capture a dream image of another world. If I were not what I am, what pursuits would occupy my pen, what problems would occupy my mind? I do not know, for a state of existence in which I would be like others is utterly beyond my conception.

To my heterosexual friends and readers, who find outside the realm of their comprehension the desires that I always carry within me, I can only state that I find their own sexual personal-ity just as much an enigma, just as foreign to myself, and beyond the powers of my imagination. To be transformed suddenly as if by magic into the body and consciousness of a heterosexual—

what would I think, know, feel, desire? My failure to be able to reply is more than an inability to imagine; it is a frightening fantasy from which I recoil.

I know that I cling to my entire personality, and that sexuality is basic in this personality and can never be relinquished. But sometimes I would wish to be normal—and I shall use this word in its usual connotation—just for a brief period. I would like to know the freedom from the anxiety of being the outcast; not merely to enjoy the pleasures of a relationship with the opposite sex, but to be free of the compulsive sexual urge that drives me toward my own sex. But, although I should like to experience such a freedom, it would be only to return to a gay world which I can never surrender.

Freedom—is this what I have been seeking? Is this what stops me for a moment from arising, as I hear the clock tick away on the dresser? Is all the past, I sometimes ask myself, a faraway dream? After all, I am a free individual, and at this moment no driving urge has me in its captive power. The body is momentarily void of yearning, has no conscious desire or anxiety. The homosexuality that has dominated it for so long seems to have departed during the turbulent unconsciousness of sleep. I am free of the bonds and the chains and the countless difficulties. I stretch my arms, push away the blankets, take another quick glance at the clock, and to myself I laugh. I cannot help but mock at my own folly, enmeshed in dreams and revelry as passing time bids me hurry to work. But with what clarity I recall the mind of a quarter of a century ago, the youth in his teens who would awaken with this new-found freedom. I would jump for joy, look with pride at myself, find a self-respect that had been lacking, and I would proceed to breakfast, my face radiant with smiles. A conscious feeling that I was not a homosexual would remain with me for perhaps a few hours or through the greater part of the day, until the inevitable doubts would assail me.

There was the occasion when I returned from a short winter vacation of skiing, tobogganing, and other delights. For five days my eighteen-year-old body had been consumed with athletic activities. Occasionally I would look at a friend and say to myself: what if he knew? Other than this question, sex was far from my thoughts. The first morning at home, I awoke, fresh and energetic and anxious for studies, and became aware of a curious exemption from any urge for a companion. A phrase came to mind: *adolescent tendencies*. Adolescence was now behind me, and with it I had left the secret thing. I smiled to myself and said, almost aloud, "I am a man."

The feeling that I was free—for so I termed it—was then rather frequent. That morning I felt particularly confident that it would not be transient. The cold has purged me of things sinful, I thought to myself. At breakfast I was remarkably comfortable with my family. How much more worthy of love I would become if I were really rid of this abnormality. After lunch I began to take seriously the free feeling. I passed the young men at college, and none excited me. I sat with students and teachers and looked particularly at the one whose presence had until that day been unpleasant because of the very fascination it held for me, but there was no evocation of feeling. The next day the freedom remained; it began to dominate my thoughts. Deliberately I put myself to test after test, but without arousal or desire. A curiosity came over me, at one point, to know just once again what the attraction to another male was like. The idea was eluding me, and I both feared and wished that it would never return.

A third day of a strange peacefulness, and I imagined myself disclosing the secret of the past to friends, teachers, psychiatrists. Imaginary conversations took place in my mind: I was relating my experiences to friends, and to a history teacher whom I had not seen for some time. Then, as I entered my home on the evening of the third day, I closed the door behind me, walked past the telephone, and stopped for a moment. My hand reached out and I knew that I wanted to call William, an acquaintance with whom I had had a recent intimate relationship. To tell him that I would be interested in seeing him no more, I said aloud, but my heart was now beating loudly, and I knew that it was a transparent deception. I paced up and down near the telephone, then proceeded, without making the call, to the kitchen, but I had lost my appetite. I awaited impatiently the end of the evening meal; then, excusing myself, I went to one of my hangouts. That night I found a companion much older than myself, and when I had left him I returned to seek another. Late in the night, alone in my own bed, I cried, but I had learned a cruel lesson, and one worth learning. No teacher but life itself could have convinced me that homosexual passions do not come and go at will, but cling relentlessly to the last breath of life. When I awaken today and feel devoid of the drive that has dominated my personality, I smile and merely await its inevitable return.

As I sit at a concert or engage volubly in a conversation in the office or at home, or as I look up from my newspaper and glance at the people occupying the seats of the bus, my mind will suddenly jump from the words, the thoughts, or the music around me, and with horrible impact I will hear, pounding within myself, the fateful words: *I am different.* I am different from all these people, and I must always be different from them. I do not belong to them, nor they to me. On my side of the chasm that separates me from the moving millions, I wonder who are my hidden companions. Is it a friend's secretary in an office, perhaps keeping a secret even more firmly than I imprison my own? Is it a married colleague or a cousin, here for an occasional evening, speaking in soft tones and well-enunciated words that lead me to suspect? Or the stranger sitting opposite me, engrossed in a book even as I am supposed to be in a newspaper? His eyes look up from the pages, and they meet my own, and because we retain each other's stare for a split second longer than one ought, I feel a sense of comradeship. To my mind, at least, if not to his, a bond of belonging has been established, although each of us goes his way, never to see the other again. Have I imparted to him, even as he has to me, imaginary pleasure; has he, like myself, received a feeling of mutual understanding?

I am different, I say to myself, but I know that my being different is not the same as that which members of other minorities feel. Are we not all different, a friend in puzzled sympathy asks one day. Is not each of us a part of some group, whether of religion or race or color, that does not keep step with the dominant majority? Do not the Jews, the Negroes, the foreign-born, the Southern Catholics, the atheists stop to state that they are different and that they must always be different from other peoples?

The analogy is weak. We homosexuals are a minority, but more than that, an intensified minority, with all of the problems that arise from being a separate group facing us that are faced by

other groups, and with a variety of important problems that are
unshared by most minorities. The ethnic groups can take refuge
in the comfort and pride of their own, in the warmth of family
and friends, in the acceptance of themselves among the most
enlightened people around them. But not the homosexuals.
Those closest to us, whose love we are in extreme need of, accept
us for what we are not. Constantly and unceasingly we carry a
mask, and without interruption we stand on guard lest our secret, which is our very essence, be betrayed.

Sometimes I find myself drawn as if into a net by the abuses
and sneers of the hostile world. I hear the vile jokes or the
calumnious remark, and must sit in silence, or even force a smile
as it were in approval. A passenger enters an elevator and remarks, "When I come out of a barber shop, I have a feeling I
smell like a fag. I better watch out or some goddam queer'll pick
me up on the way home." The operator laughs, and I find myself
forcing a smile, joining in the humiliating remark that is, un-
knowingly, directed against myself. And, leaving the elevator, I
resent neither the passenger nor the operator, but only myself,
for I had debased my own character by giving tacit consent and
even approval to the abuse of which I felt I was personally the
victim.

Where is your self-respect, where is your self-pride, I ask.
How do you dare to say that you are proud of what you are when
you allow the epithets of the enemy to go unanswered, when you
turn the other cheek out of cowardice and not Christianity, when
you even join—as so often you find yourself doing—the hostile
camp?

It is not only shame at my own debasement that demoralizes
me, but a great wave of self-doubt that is infinitely more difficult
to cope with. Am I genuinely as "good" as the next fellow? Is my
moral standard as high? Are my ethics—before my own self and
my own Maker—as defensible as those of others around me?

Or am I actually what they call me? Despite myself, for I
know that this urge is not of my creation and that I can neither
efface nor overcome it, am I a degenerate, immoral, and lecher-
ous character, a disgrace to the mother who bore me and to the
little girl and boy who call me Daddy?

Society has handed me a mask to wear, a ukase that it shall

never be lifted except in the presence of those who hide with me behind its protective shadows. Everywhere I go, at all times and before all sections of society, I pretend. As my being rebels against the hypocrisy that is forced upon me, I realize that its greatest repercussion has been the wave of self-doubt that I must harbor. Because I am unable to stand up before the world and acknowledge that I am what I am, because I carry around with me a fear and a shame, I find that I endanger my confidence in myself and in my way of living, and that this confidence is required for the enjoyment of life.

In fact, I must ask myself whether the life that I lead is an inferior one, and whether those who practice it are inferior people. Is there justification for the loathing with which mankind regards us? Nothing is more demoralizing than that I must even ask myself this question. And, though adamant, on an intellectual level, in my negative response, I find it difficult to reconcile self-pride with cowardice, abnegation, the wearing of the mask and the espousal of hypocrisy—in short, with an outward acceptance of the mores of the hostile society.

Retired into the intimacy of the homosexual circle, I find that it is only with the greatest of effort that an individual can acknowledge with words a tendency which he can so openly express in action. And when words are chosen, there will be euphemisms, a semantic choice of subtle synonyms that express the same thought, but with cushioned impact.

The trepidation to acknowledge extends even to the presence of those who have already discarded the mask. In the course of my studies I meet many individuals to whom I relate my own homosexual experiences, and although I am perfectly aware, not only by observation but by previous knowledge, that I am discussing these problems with people who share them, I find that I evoke intelligent participation in the conversation, a deepfelt understanding and sympathy, but seldom a frankness. Guarded is each word, and I look in vain for the admission. And why? Surely not out of fear, for there is no possible harm that I can do. Not out of lack of necessity, for how much more freely could the interchange of ideas take place if there were mutual confidence. In my opinion the individual is unable to bring himself, even in the presence of the most sympathetic ear, to say, "I am a homosexual," because of the impact that such a sentence has on himself, as a result of the total activity and attitudes of the hostile and dominant group.

It is not only out of fear of rejection by others, strong as that fear surely is, that homosexuals are stopped in the paths of self-expression; and it is not from fear of consequences, real as the latter may be. It is due to the fact that self-expression means self-acknowledgment, and this in turn requires a rejection of the opinions of those who despise.

The prejudice of the dominant group, seen everywhere and displayed in countless forms, is most demoralizing when we homosexuals realize to what extent we have accepted hostile attitudes as representing an approximation of the truth. Here and there, in a book, a sociological document, or a psychological treatise, there will be a justification, but it does not negate the overwhelming weight of antipathy. A person cannot live in an atmosphere of universal rejection, of widespread pretense, of a society that outlaws and banishes his activities and desires, of a social world that jokes and sneers at every turn, without fundamental influence on his personality.

That influence I find to be complex. First, there is what can be characterized as self-doubt, but this in turn evokes its own response, which comes out of the need for self-acceptance. The reaction against the world which insists that we are inferior beings is the search for a fallacy in that thinking. Some of us may take refuge in the involuntary nature of our predilections. Inferior or equal, whatever the verdict of the world may be, we are homosexuals in spite of ourselves. How, we ask ourselves in amazement, can a world condemn an individual for being what he was made to be? Despite the widespread view to the contrary, we homosexuals are utterly incapable of being other than what we are.

More than that, if we are to believe in ourselves, we must reject the entire theory of the inferiority status which the heterosexual world has imposed upon us. And therein we find a reaction common among people who live in a special minority category: we create a new set of beliefs to demonstrate that our gay world is actually a superior one. For some reason or other that few of us stop to investigate, we come to believe that homosexuals are usually of superior artistic and intellectual abilities. Everywhere we look, we seize upon outstanding examples of brilliant people, either in our own circles or in the public domain, who are gay, or are supposed to be gay. How is it, we ask ourselves, that our friends are always outstanding among their business associates; that members of our group frequently graduate from universities with the highest honors; that at least four of the giants of modern French literature were sexual inverts. The list could be continued, although it includes only those recognized; what of the many who have achieved success and have hidden their secret even from those who share their burden?

Whether or not there is a factual basis for this belief in our own superiority is of secondary importance. Whether illusion or reality, the belief exists, and it stems from a desperation, deeply imbedded in people who find themselves despised by the world, and who require a belief in themselves in order to bolster an ebbing confidence and enable themselves to function in society.

Thus the homosexuals constitute what can be termed the unrecognized minority. We are a group by reason of the fact that we have impulses in common that separate us from the larger mass of people. We are a minority, not only numerically, but also as a result of a caste-like status in society. As I shall demonstrate in these pages, our minority status is similar, in a variety of respects, to that of national, religious, and other ethnic groups: in the denial of civil liberties; in the legal, extra-legal, and quasi-legal discrimination; in the assignment of an inferior social position; in the exclusion from the mainstreams of life and culture; in the development of the protection and security of intragroup association; in the development of a special language and literature and a set of moral tenets within our group.

On the other hand, one great gap separates the homosexual minority from all others, and that is its lack of recognition, its lack of respectability in the eyes of the public, and even in the most advanced circles. It has become a sign of worthiness to take up the cudgels for almost any minority group, except the homosexuals. One is a "hero" if he espouses the cause of minorities, but is only a suspect if that minority is the homosexual group.

As a minority, we homosexuals are therefore caught in a particularly vicious circle. On the one hand, the shame of belonging and the social punishment of acknowledgment are so great that pretense is almost universal; on the other hand, only a leadership that would acknowledge would be able to break down the barriers of shame and resultant discrimination. Until the world is able to accept us on an equal basis as human beings entitled to the full rights of life, we are unlikely to have any great numbers willing to become martyrs by carrying the burden of the cross. But until we are willing to speak out openly and frankly in defense of our activities, and to identify ourselves with the millions pursuing these activities, we are unlikely to find the attitudes of the world undergoing any significant change.

11 *The author recounts his experiences of betrayal by his wife and of trying to act "normal" when being committed to a mental hospital.*

On entering a mental hospital

robert dahl

This Monday afternoon wore on . . . Marilyn had told me she'd be up to visit me at three-thirty. When four o'clock came I was worried. What had happened? She was never late for an appointment. During my stay in the receiving hospital, she hadn't missed one chance for a visit and always she'd been on time. Always she'd been early, waiting at the big entrance door, waiting for it to open, anxious not to miss a moment of our visit. But now she was a half-hour late. Something must have happened to her. . . . I thought of the horror she'd been through the last six months. And now this latest episode with me in a hospital again. How she must be worried about me. But where was she?

One thing I knew: If Marilyn could have been here by now, she would have been here. Something had happened to her. What was wrong with Marilyn that would keep her from visiting me at the time she'd promised? Something terrible must have happened to keep her away. What had happened to Marilyn?

I asked Sister Thérèse if I could use the phone. "I want to find out where my wife is. She should be here by now. I'm worried about her."

"There's a phone at the end of the hall," said Sister Thérèse.

I called home. There was no answer. I called the newspaper where she worked. They told me she'd taken the afternoon off. I called home again. There was no answer. I called the Douglases. Polly answered.

"Hello, Bob. How are you? How's the hospital treating you?"

"Polly, Marilyn was supposed to be up here to visit me forty-five minutes ago. Polly! Do you know where Marilyn is?"

"No, Bob, I don't. She hasn't been here. I know you must be upset, but she'll be along. Don't worry now."

"Polly, if she calls you, tell her to get on down here. I'm afraid something may have happened to her, Polly. Call me if she gets in touch with you."

Out of the corner of my eye, I caught a glimpse of two policemen emerging from an elevator at the other end of the hall. . . .

Now what would two uniformed policemen, with guns in their holsters, be doing up here in this hospital? Suddenly I knew.

"Polly, listen to this: A couple of cops just came on the floor and I think they've come to take me away. There's a sister up here in charge who's been on me about making too much noise and disturbing the other patients. I think she's called the police."

"Oh, Bob, no!"

"Polly, these two policemen, I've got a hunch they're up here for me. You've got to get hold of Marilyn and tell her what's going on. Polly, will you promise?"

"Yes, Bob, of course."

"Thank you."

"Good-by, Bob. I'll try to find Marilyn." Her voice came softly over the phone, hesitant: "Bob, please take care of yourself."

The two policemen—I'd caught them looking around and then looking toward me sitting at the phone at the far end of the hall from them. They turned and walked toward the center of the hall, toward Sister Thérèse's desk.

Watching them, into my mind there came a remembrance of my childhood and the thought: *"They" at last have come for you.* . . .

When I was just four years old I would play in my sand pile by myself and I would enact a fantasy with moldings of wet sand. I would build castles with tunneled entrances, and in these great castles I imagined there lived giants named "Human Beans." Inside the dark entrances of the castles I would imagine the giants were hiding, waiting for me, waiting to *get* me. These giant monsters became simply *They*. *They* were always waiting for me, waiting to *get* me. . . .

When I was little, I often had a dream—a nightmare. It consisted entirely of a spinning circle. When the dream began, when I would first see wide-eyed under my lids closed in sleep the circle, I would think: "Well, here is that circle again. Please don't let it grow this time. Please."

And I would tell the circle to go away and I would tell it to behave if it did have to stay. I would tell it that it just had to not start getting big. And then something would promise me, not a person, not a voice, but something, that this time the circle would grow no bigger—that it would stay, this time, just a harmless little spinning circle. Then, in my sleep, I would relax, and as I relaxed, the circle, as if it were taking advantage of my relaxation, would begin to spin faster and faster and grow bigger and bigger, increasing in size as it spun until at last there was no room for me and it—the circle was surrounding me, suffocating me, crowding me out of existence into oblivion. And then I would awake, certain in the brief moment between sleep and awakening, that if the circle had kept on spinning for just one more instant, I would have been swallowed up inside it and erased into a nothingness. And I would awake in my bed sweaty and filled with fright. . . .

As I moved away from the phone and toward the two policemen and Sister Thérèse, it was just as if I were in the grip of that child's nightmare of the circle. The circle was about to envelop me—*they* were about to get me. . . . And there was nothing I could do about it.

I was trapped.

I walked up to one of the policemen. They were sheriff's deputies.

I smiled at them. "You've come for me?"

"Yes," one of them said.

"I thought so."

"You'll come with us quietly?"

"What if I don't?"

"You wouldn't want to do anything you'll be sorry for later. We have to take you with us, but we're sure you'll come along now without causing any trouble."

"You're taking me to River's Edge?"

"Yes."

"I'm not going to fight you—I'll go along. But couldn't it wait for just a bit? I'm trying to reach my wife over the phone. I can't get hold of her this minute but it shouldn't take long."

"No. We have our orders and we have to be going now. We can't wait. We're sorry, but we have to be moving along."

They seemed nice enough. In different circumstances I would have liked to know them better. They were just carrying out their orders and neither of them seemed to be taking any joy in their duty. They were courteous and sympathetic. If they had been out of uniform, without the guns at their sides, I doubt if I'd have been afraid of them at all.

"I'll walk along with you," I said. "I won't cause you any trouble. But whoever is responsible for this—" I stared hard at Sister Thérèse—"I'm afraid she'll have trouble sleeping nights.

"God have mercy on you, Sister," I said. Sister Thérèse's mouth quivered a little, and she turned her head from me.

On the way to River's Edge in the sheriff's car, I talked to the two deputies. "Do I seem insane to you two?"

"No," one answered, "you seem all right to me."

"The thing that worries me is my wife. I can't figure out where she can be. I'm worried about how all this will hit her. She's had enough trouble lately."

"Your wife knows what's happened. I think she's the one who signed you in."

"You must be wrong," I said. "Marilyn wouldn't have done anything like that without at least talking to me about it first. She won't do anything that's important to the two of us without talking it over with me.

"It was that sister up there, the one in charge of the floor. She didn't understand some of the things I said." . . .

The sheriff's car wound its way through the grounds of the state hospital and up to the entrance. They escorted me inside.

"Good-by to you two and good luck," I said.

"Good-by. Good luck to you, fellow. . . ."

And now truly, my fears and nightmares were about to materialize. At last I was at River's Edge.

I was ushered into a great hall. Its walls were white plaster, its floor was concrete. The hall was so long the people at the other end were small dim figures in the gloomy light which filtered through its barred windows.

An attendant showed me into one of the many little rooms which led from the hall. "You'll sleep here tonight," he said. He ripped the bedding from the iron bed which was to be mine, felt the rubber pad on top of the mattress, and grinned at me. "I'll have to get you a fresh pad. The old man who was in this bed until a little while ago wet it."

"I don't need any pad," I said.

"I'll have to get one anyway. All the beds on this ward have pads in 'em. While I'm gone, you get out of your clothes."

"Why?"

"We have to mark your clothes. I'll bring you something to put on."

In a moment he was back with fresh sheeting, another rubber pad. He also carried a pair of white overalls. He threw them toward me.

"Put these on for now. And here's a pair of slippers."

Over my naked body I drew on the overalls. They were too small. The pants legs were above my ankles and when I pulled at the strap over my shoulder to fasten the overalls, the legs cut into my crotch.

Only one of the straps on the overalls had a button for fastening. The button was missing from the other. I tried pushing this strap through the buttonhole and tying it. But the strap wouldn't stay tied. When I straightened, the strain broke the buttonhole. The slippers were too big. I had to walk in a shuffle to keep them on my feet.

I walked down the hall. Midway down it, off to one side, there was a little room filled with charts and file cabinets and medical supplies. A young, white-coated man, another attendant, sat at the desk in the room, making out some papers.

"Pardon me," I said, "but can't you give me something to wear that'd fit me half decent?"

He looked up at me. "Let's see. You just came in?"

"Yes."

"Well, you'll just have to do the best you can with what you've got on until we open the storeroom in the morning. You can try to find something better then. Right now, we're too busy to look around in there trying to get you a perfect fit. . . . While you're here, I've got some questions to ask you."

He looked at me, pen poised over a form. "Your name?"

"Please help me, God! You drag me in here and you don't even know my name. Do you usually haul people into this place without even knowing who they are?"

The attendant winced. "Please answer these questions. They're just routine."

I howled with bitter laughter. "You haul people into this nuthouse and you don't even know who you've got when you net them! Are you an attendant here or are you a patient? You look, my friend, a little wild-eyed to me. What did you do? Attack an attendant and take his coat? Where, friend, is your identification?"

The attendant scowled. "If you're trying to be funny, it won't get you very far. What have we here? A comedian? Are you going to answer these questions or not? If not, we'll ask them later at your leisure—and it looks to me as if you're going to have plenty of that for a long time."

Suddenly I was conscious of a surge of fear, and I knew I should stop my attempts at wit. But I couldn't—not all at once. "It's strange you'd ask me if I'm a comedian. I am! I'm a clown! The clown of clowns. Don't you recognize me? My name is Bob."

"Bob what?"

"Why, Bob Hope, of course. Sometimes they say to me: 'You're Hopeless Bob!' But that's only a pun on my real name, Bob Hope."

The attendant wrote something on the form and said, "I'm going to give you one more chance. Maybe the reason we ask you your name is not because we don't know it, but maybe we want to find out if you do."

"It really is Bob Hope. I have another name, too, though, an assumed name—Bob Dahl. But there really is nobody named Bob Dahl. Bob Dahl is nobody, no heart, no mind."

"How tall are you?"

"Six feet."

"Weight?"

"One eighty-five."

. . . And so on, the attendant's pen scribbling busily the various statistical bits of information which identified me.

An older man, a doctor, came into the room. He was a heavy man of about forty. Around his waist his white shirt bulged and strained against rolls of fat beneath. His shirtsleeves were rolled. He came into the room walking swiftly.

"Boy! What a day!" he said to the attendant.

"Dr. Phillips—" the attendant flicked a finger my way— "here's the new patient."

"Are you in charge here?" I asked the doctor.

"Of this ward."

"Doctor, Dr. Phillips, I'm worried about my wife. I have to reach her! She was supposed to visit me this afternoon at the other hospital and she didn't show up and I tried to locate her by phone but I couldn't. Will you let me try to call her from here? She'll want to know about all this, and besides that I'm afraid something may have happened to her."

Dr. Phillips spoke in kind tones but firmly: "I'm sorry, Mr. Dahl—your first name's Bob, isn't it?"

"Yes."

"Bob, there's no phone on this ward which connects us with the outside, and we're too busy around here to send anybody with you to the phone up front. Anyhow, it's against the rules. You won't be able to have any contact with anyone from the outside for seven days."

"But, Doctor, I've got to talk to my wife!"

"Bob, believe me, your wife is all right. I've seen her and she knows all about this."

"What do you mean?"

"She consented that you be sent here."

"She betrayed me? She did this to me behind my back? She didn't even have the courage to talk to me about it face to face! Why? Doctor, why?"

Dr. Phillips looked at his watch. "I can give you just about ten minutes. I'm sorry it can't be more than that, but there's a lot to do around here right now. Sit down."

"Doctor," I said, "there's just one thing I want to know.

Why did she do this to me? And without talking to me? It wasn't
necessary to sic those two policemen on me! I wasn't violent!"

"That's just routine," said Dr. Phillips.

"Doctor, why am I here?"

"Please, I can hear you. Not so loud." He took a pack of
cigarettes out of his shirt pocket. "Like one?"

"Yes."

"Bob, I don't know all the reasons you're here. Some people,
including several doctors, thought you might be sick enough to
be hospitalized. Presently you're here for a week's observation.
You haven't been committed yet—and you won't be before the
end of that time."

"But, Doctor—I know maybe I'm sick. Maybe there's something really wrong with me. I know I'm different now from other
people, but that's only because I *want* to be. If I wanted to be
like other people, I could be. Maybe they think I'm sicker than I
am just because I'm not like everybody else any more. In any
case, there was no need to send me here! I could have had treatment under a private psychiatrist—if I am sick—and at the same
time I could have held down a job. I had a job offer just last
week."

"I don't know, Bob. Several people, including your wife,
thought you should come here for observation. Why don't you
tell me if you can think of any reason you should be here? Why
do you think you're here?"

"I'll tell you why I think I'm here! But that doesn't mean I
can tell you why I think I should be here. I think I'm here
because my wife is insane, because my friends are insane, because
certain doctors are insane!

"But first—about my wife—as far as I'm concerned I don't
know her any more. Tell Marilyn we've never known each other.
And tell her when I get out of here, if I ever do, I don't want to
be bothered by strangers—not by strange friends and certainly
not by a strange wife!

"Why am I here? I'll tell you why! Because some people
have been questioning my ability to think straight these last few
days and I have been questioning theirs. I suppose it was a question of who was right, them or me, and since there are more of
them than me, I guess they won."

Dr. Phillips said, "Now I want you to understand this. You are very fortunate you have good friends and a good wife. They made arrangements so you could stay at St. Francis until we could make arrangements for you here. And also, there was always the chance a good physical examination at St. Francis might uncover something. But it didn't and so here you are. You are very lucky. Ordinarily, under normal procedure, you'd have had to wait in jail until we could make room for you here. Sometimes people have to stay in jail nine or ten days before they are brought here."

"But, Doctor, what did I do? Why couldn't they talk to me about it? I probably would have come here voluntarily if I'd known they felt so strongly about it."

"People, I suppose—" Dr. Phillips smiled—"just didn't understand you. Didn't you tell a sister at the hospital you might jump out the window at any moment?"

"Yes. But I didn't mean I would. I was just trying to prove a point of logic."

Dr. Phillips looked at his watch.

"Doctor, before you go, one more question. Do you think I'm insane?"

"Insanity is just a legal term," said Dr. Phillips.

"Do you think I'm mentally ill?"

"Yes," said Dr. Phillips, "I think you are sick." He smiled at me—in kindness, in sympathy, with understanding. But I shuddered at his words, even though he added, as if to take the sting from them, "And I think you should stay with us for a while. But I believe it will be just for a while, not forever."

On my way out of the room the attendant looked at me and smiled. "Why did you say your name was Bob Hope?"

"Because I really am. I'm a clown. I have to be. Or else I'd cry myself to death."

"I see," said the attendant.

Beside the doorway leading to the hall, there was a small mirror. I hesitated before it, glanced into it. It seemed to me that my eyes were opened wider than usual. . . . *If you're ever going to get out of here, you're going to have to narrow those eyes. People can see clear through you, they're so wide open. You look like a maniac all right. Narrow the eyes. There, that's better, and you're going to have to quit talking so much. Only a lunatic tells people everything he knows. . . .*

Before I went to sleep that night, I prayed. But when I finished, I still felt alone and I was conscious of fear. Yet after a while, as I lay in bed, there came to me a sense of peace.

There was no door to my room and the hall outside was only dimly lighted. In the shadows the high walls surrounding me seemed unreal. Solid as they were, they seemed unreal, impermanent, a transient vision. I thought: I'll sleep, I'll close my eyes. And when I open them again, the walls—they'll have gone away. If not tonight, some time, some night, I'll close my eyes and the walls—they'll go away.

12 *A major literary figure takes note of his own mental breakdown.*

The crack-up

f. scott fitzgerald

February, 1936—Of course all life is a process of breaking down, but the blows that do the dramatic side of the work—the big sudden blows that come, or seem to come, from outside—the ones you remember and blame things on and, in moments of weakness, tell your friends about, don't show their effect all at once. There is another sort of blow that comes from within—that you don't feel until it's too late to do anything about it, until you realize with finality that in some regard you will never be as good a man again. The first sort of breakage seems to happen quick— the second kind happens almost without your knowing it but is realized suddenly indeed.

Before I go on with this short history, let me make a general observation—the test of a first-rate intelligence is the ability to hold two opposed ideas in the mind at the same time, and still retain the ability to function. One should, for example, be able to see that things are hopeless and yet be determined to make them otherwise. This philosophy fitted on to my early adult life, when I saw the improbable, the implausible, often the "impossible," come true. Life was something you dominated if you were any good. Life yielded easily to intelligence and effort, or to what proportion could be mustered of both. It seemed a romantic business to be a successful literary man—you were not ever going to be as famous as a movie star but what note you had was probably longer-lived—you were never going to have the power of a man of strong political or religious convictions but you were certainly more independent. Of course within the practice of your trade you were forever unsatisfied—but I, for one, would not have chosen any other.

As the twenties passed, with my own twenties marching a little ahead of them, my two juvenile regrets—at not being big enough (or good enough) to play football in college, and at not getting overseas during the war—resolved themselves into childish waking dreams of imaginary heroism that were good enough to go to sleep on in restless nights. The big problems of life seemed to solve themselves, and if the business of fixing them was difficult, it made one too tired to think of more general problems.

Life, ten years ago, was largely a personal matter. I must hold in balance the sense of the futility of effort and the sense of the necessity to struggle; the conviction of the inevitability of failure and still the determination to "succeed"—and, more than these, the contradiction between the dead hand of the past and the high intentions of the future. If I could do this through the common ills—domestic, professional and personal—then the ego would continue as an arrow shot from nothingness to nothingness with such force that only gravity would bring it to earth at last.

For seventeen years, with a year of deliberate loafing and resting out in the center—things went on like that, with a new chore only a nice prospect for the next day. I was living hard, too, but: "Up to forty-nine it'll be all right," I said. "I can count on that. For a man who's lived as I have, that's all you could ask."

—And then, ten years this side of forty-nine, I suddenly realized that I had prematurely cracked.

II

Now a man can crack in many ways—can crack in the head —in which case the power of decision is taken from you by others! or in the body, when one can but submit to the white hospital world; or in the nerves. William Seabrook in an unsympathetic book tells, with some pride and a movie ending, of

how he became a public charge. What led to his alcoholism or
was bound up with it, was a collapse of his nervous system.
Though the present writer was not so entangled—having at the
time not tasted so much as a glass of beer for six months—it was
his nervous reflexes that were giving way—too much anger and
too many tears.

Moreover, to go back to my thesis that life has a varying
offensive, the realization of having cracked was not simultaneous
with a blow, but with a reprieve.

Not long before, I had sat in the office of a great doctor and
listened to a grave sentence. With what, in retrospect, seems some
equanimity, I had gone on about my affairs in the city where I
was then living, not caring much, not thinking how much had
been left undone, or what would become of this and that responsibility, like people do in books; I was well insured and anyhow
I had been only a mediocre caretaker of most of the things left in
my hands, even of my talent.

But I had a strong sudden instinct that I must be alone. I
didn't want to see any people at all. I had seen so many people
all my life—I was an average mixer, but more than average in a
tendency to identify myself, my ideas, my destiny, with those of
all classes that I came in contact with. I was always saving or
being saved—in a single morning I would go through the emo
tions ascribable to Wellington at Waterloo. I lived in a world of
inscrutable hostiles and inalienable friends and supporters.

But now I wanted to be absolutely alone and so arranged a
certain insulation from ordinary cares.

It was not an unhappy time. I went away and there were
fewer people. I found I was good-and-tired. I could lie around
and was glad to, sleeping or dozing sometimes twenty hours a day
and in the intervals trying resolutely not to think—instead I
made lists—made lists and tore them up, hundreds of lists: of
cavalry leaders and football players and cities, and popular tunes
and pitchers, and happy times, and hobbies and houses lived in
and how many suits since I left the army and how many pairs of
shoes (I didn't count the suit I bought in Sorrento that shrunk,
nor the pumps and dress shirt and collar that I carried around
for years and never wore, because the pumps got damp and
grainy and the shirt and collar got yellow and starch-rotted).

And lists of women I'd liked, and of the times I had let myself be snubbed by people who had not been my betters in character or ability.

—And then suddenly, surprisingly, I got better.

—And cracked like an old plate as soon as I heard the news.

That is the real end of this story. What was to be done about it will have to rest in what used to be called the "womb of time." Suffice it to say that after about an hour of solitary pillow-hugging, I began to realize that for two years my life had been a drawing on resources that I did not possess, that I had been mortgaging myself physically and spiritually up to the hilt. What was the small gift of life given back in comparison to that?— when there had once been a pride of direction and a confidence in enduring independence.

I realized that in those two years, in order to preserve some-thing—an inner hush maybe, maybe not—I had weaned myself from all the things I used to love—that every act of life from the morning tooth-brush to the friend at dinner had become an effort. I saw that for a long time I had not liked people and things, but only followed the rickety old pretense of liking. I saw that even my love for those closest to me was become only an attempt to love, that my casual relations—with an editor, a to-bacco seller, the child of a friend, were only what I remembered I *should* do, from other days. All in the same month I became bitter about such things as the sound of the radio, the advertise-ments in the magazines, the screech of tracks, the dead silence of the country—contemptuous at human softness, immediately (if secretively) quarrelsome toward hardness—hating the night when I couldn't sleep and hating the day because it went toward night. I slept on the heart side now because I knew that the sooner I could tire that out, even a little, the sooner would come that blessed hour of nightmare which, like a catharsis, would enable me to better meet the new day.

There were certain spots, certain faces I could look at. Like most Middle Westerners, I have never had any but the vaguest race prejudices—I always had a secret yen for the lovely Scandi-navian blondes who sat on porches in St. Paul but hadn't emerged enough economically to be part of what was then society. They were too nice to be "chickens" and too quickly off the farmlands to seize a place in the sun, but I remember going round blocks to catch a single glimpse of shining hair—the bright shock of a girl I'd never know. This is urban, unpopular talk. It strays afield from the fact that in these latter days I couldn't stand the sight of Celts, English, Politicians, Strangers, Virginians, Negroes (light or dark), Hunting People, or retail clerks, and middlemen in general, all writers (I avoided writers very carefully because they can perpetuate trouble as no one else can)—and all the classes as classes and most of them as members of their class . . .

Trying to cling to something, I liked doctors and girl children up to the age of about thirteen and well-brought-up boy children from about eight years old on. I could have peace and happiness with these few categories of people. I forgot to add that I liked old men—men over seventy, sometimes over sixty if their faces looked seasoned. I liked Katharine Hepburn's face on the screen, no matter what was said about her pretentiousness, and Miriam Hopkins' face, and old friends if I only saw them once a year and could remember their ghosts.

All rather inhuman and undernourished, isn't it? Well, that, children, is the true sign of cracking up.

It is not a pretty picture. Inevitably it was carted here and there within its frame and exposed to various critics. One of them can only be described as a person whose life makes other people's lives seem like death—even this time when she was cast in the usually unappealing role of Job's comforter. In spite of the fact that this story is over, let me append our conversation as a sort of postscript:

"Instead of being so sorry for yourself, listen—" she said. (She always says "Listen," because she thinks while she talks— *really* thinks.) So she said: "Listen. Suppose this wasn't a crack in you—suppose it was a crack in the Grand Canyon."

"The crack's in me," I said heroically.

"Listen! The world only exists in your eyes—your conception of it. You can make it as big or as small as you want to. And you're trying to be a little puny individual. By God, if I ever cracked, I'd try to make the world crack with me. Listen! The world only exists through your apprehension of it, and so it's much better to say that it's not you that's cracked—it's the Grand Canyon."

"Baby et up all her Spinoza?"

"I don't know anything about Spinoza. I know—" She spoke, then, of old woes of her own, that seemed, in the telling, to have been more dolorous than mine, and how she had met them, over-ridden them, beaten them.

I felt a certain reaction to what she said, but I am a slow-thinking man, and it occurred to me simultaneously that of all the natural forces, vitality is the incommunicable one. In days when juice came into one as an article without duty, one tried to distribute it—but always without success; to further mix metaphors, vitality never "takes." You have it or you haven't it, like health or brown eyes or honor or a baritone voice. I might have asked some of it from her, neatly wrapped and ready for home cooking and digestion, but I could never have got it—not if I'd waited around for a thousand hours with the tin cup of self-pity. I could walk from her door, holding myself very carefully like cracked crockery, and go away into the world of bitterness, where I was making a home with such materials as are found there—and to quote to myself after I left her door:

"Ye are the salt of the earth. But if the salt hath lost its savour, wherewith shall it be salted?"

Matthew 5–13.

13   *A young Conscientious Objector describes the reactions of others to his decision not to enter military service.*

Diary of a C.O.

doug handler

September 18, 1961—Today I am eighteen years old. I went downtown to register at the draft board. We had a sort of mixup when they gave me a form where I thought they were trying to make me say I was a Conscientious Objector. But it turned out that they only wanted me to check off that I was *not* one. Other than that little incident, the whole registration was painless. Hell, I don't even really know what a Conscientious Objector is.

September 18, 1966—Mom called to wish me "Happy Birthday," but the pleasure of the day was somewhat dampened when Dean Gerbner announced that the final date for handing in my Master's Thesis title is two weeks from today. Read a disturbing article about guys who beat the draft by going to Canada. It seems the Canadians have no parallel law (draft) and so American dodgers can't be extradicted once they're up there. The article mentioned Arlo Tatum, the head of a Conscientious Objection counseling service right here in Philadelphia. I guess I'll go over there in a day or two. I want to get this C.O. information a little more clear in my mind. It does seem a little strange, though, that someone who was sure he couldn't kill would even sign up at all for C.O. Seems to me the only honest thing he could do would be to refuse the whole system, draft card, registration, classification, etc. But then, I guess if a guy really were

From *Moderator*, April, 1967. Copyrighted April, 1967 by the Moderator Publishing Company, Inc. Reprinted by permission of *Moderator*, 1738 Pine Street, Philadelphia, Pa. 19103.

sincere about it, he could want to make his feelings known and yet still want to stay within the law, too. I don't know . . .

October 10, 1966—The place is called Central Committee of Conscientious Objectors. The thing that amazes me is that they're so open about the problem of conscientious objection here. A Mr. Charles Shofer sat there and said he would not advise me to go to Canada because that was against the law, but that I should read the *Handbook for Conscientious Objectors* and answer the sample questionnaire because I may actually be a C.O. myself.

October 22, 1966—Being Jewish or, at least, being of Jewish origin, this Hitler-thing comes up much more often than it really ought to. People think I have a special bone to pick with Hitler. Now my mother does. She takes those six million deaths upon herself, each one, as a personal insult and she won't do business with the A & P because the butcher is German. But I don't really feel any more antagonistic towards Hitler than most non-Jewish Americans. The question came up though, would I have been a C.O. in the Second World War? The thing is, a C.O. is a C.O., not just for Viet Nam, but for every war. Now, I *can* react to Viet Nam. Here it is in the papers every day, on every newscast! I know people who are there, people who have been killed there. I *can* still take a stand on Viet Nam, I can object to it, because it's going on *now*. But when you bring up Hitler, well . . . I was born in 1943, went to school, college, I never heard one newscast involving Hitler, except maybe when the Nurenburg trials were going on. How am I supposed to know if I'd have fought Hitler? To tell the truth, I never even really thought about it too much.

November 3, 1966—Met an unbelievable person today. He was just visiting the Annenberg School, but he applied as a C.O. and he's no more religious than I am. He says that in 1965 the Supreme Court passed a landmark case, where they ruled it was unconstitutional to insist that a man must be religious in the conventional sense of the word in order to be a C.O. That if a man has a belief parallel in his life to the belief in God in the life of someone who has a conventional religious outlook and, if that belief prevents him from participating in wars, he could be a Conscientious Objector.

November 8, 1966—Today I finished *Catch-22* and I have no more doubts about being a C.O. I am one. I've thought about Hitler and the conclusion is just like Yossarian kept saying throughout the whole book. When he said, he didn't want to fly any more missions, they asked him, "What if everybody felt that way?" And he said, "Then wouldn't I be stupid not to think that way too?" And he's right and it's the same thing with Hitler. Do I object to the war with Hitler? How in God's name can I possibly have any second thoughts about it? Of *course* I object to the war with Hitler. I object to the Americans fighting him and I object to him fighting us. I object to the whole stinking bloody war and every other war before it and after it. Do I really object? Yes, I do. And I can show it by not participating in any myself. If I didn't really object to war, then I could allow myself to be drafted or I could enlist and I could try and beat my brains out beating sense into or beating life out of maniacs like Hitler. But I do object and what if everybody else felt that way? I'd say FINE. If all the German kids felt that way, Hitler wouldn't ever have gotten past Private First Class. In fact, if all the German kids felt that way, Hitler probably would have been a different guy because there wouldn't have been any army and there wouldn't be any armies or wars today. German kids aren't any different than I, except that they're just as proud of being Germans as I am of being American. And if they all felt the way I do about war, I'd say FINE.

November 9, 1966—Called Mom today to explain my "new" interest in Conscientious Objection. She was really shocked. At first, she just kept saying how could I be so stupid and then she kept insisting that she'd always thought she'd raised a nice Jewish boy instead of some Quaker. How do you ever explain little things like a 1965 Supreme Court decision to your Mother at a time like that, let alone your philosophy of life?

November 20, 1966—Talked to Mr. Shofer again today. He explained that your C.O. application is first reviewed by your local board. Of course, if they turn it down, you have the right to appeal, first to the State Appeal Board, which in turn gives the case over to the Justice Department for an investigation and final hearing. But it looks a little bit different to the local board than it does in a court of law. People like Mother are on the local board. "Now son, you're no Conscientious Objector. You're made out of the stuff all good soldiers are. You're just a little mixed up in your thinking, but boot camp'll straighten you out. We think you're basically a good fellow, which is why we want. . . ."

December 13, 1966—T. Oscar Smith. T. Oscar Smith, explained Mr. Shofer today, is why it's better if your local board sees fit to classify you a C.O. rather than having to rely upon the fairer Justice Deparment hearing. T. Oscar happens to be chief of the Conscientious Objector Division of the Justice Department. And he has it in his power to overrule the decision of every Justice Department hearing. Since January of this year, Smith has not permitted one hearing to recommend a C.O. classification. Mr. Shofer says he knows of forty to fifty cases since January in which Smith has ruled 1-A and none in which he has ruled for C.O.

December 25, 1966—Merry Christmas. I just had dinner at Caroline's house and her father said that Caroline was not going to be engaged to a Conscientious Objector and remain in his home. Caroline has chosen to remain in his home.

December 28, 1966—It's unstoppable now. I've mailed in form 150. I put the whole thing, the real form with my real answers on it, the list of people who know me, answers to all the questions, like why I didn't sign up for it when I was eighteen, the whole damn thing in a brown paper envelope and dropped it in the mail box. Of course Mother will be livid when I tell her. Father will say, "You know, you have just done something that may affect the future course of your whole life. I hope you realize that." Of course I realize *that,* Father. All through school and Scouts and suburbs, every one who has had any advice has said "Don't do anything that might affect the future course of your life." Well hot-damn, today I did something that's sure to affect the future course of my whole life, and as I crossed the street after leaving the post-office, I thought, what if a truck comes and hits me now, accidentally, then won't it be a waste all those years I never did anything to affect the course of my future life? However, a truck did not hit me and my next thought was whether or not people on draft boards understand that there can be a difference between what an 18 year old thinks about and what a 23 year old thinks about.

January 2, 1967—I told Alan Crop today that I'd put his name down as a reference on my application for C.O. Well I hadn't realized that Alan's uncle was on my draft board, but even if I had realized that, what I further didn't realize was that Alan doesn't *care* that he doesn't have to agree with me, that I merely want him to testify to the sincerity of my beliefs; Alan doesn't *care* about that. And on top of everything else, he doesn't want me to work for him, even during vacations, anymore.

January 10, 1967—Well, now it's all official and I'm signed up as a C.O. and it occurs to me, "What am I doing here?" I mean, maybe I'm just fooling myself with all this stuff. Maybe all I do need is a little boot camp, some indoctrination, and then I'll be able to fire a gun with the best of 'em. Maybe I'm just an enormous chicken-shit. How am I ever supposed to know for sure? How does anybody ever know?

February 3, 1967—Well my personal hearing with my draft board is next month, but today I realized I don't really know whether or not I can convince them. I am a C.O. in my own mind. But can I convince someone else of that fact? I would think that just the fact that I've applied, put my name on paper and said, "I am a C.O.", would be enough to convince anybody. But, no, I have to convince some guys first and then they judge whether or not they think I am. How do you explain to a guy who was born poor in 1900, served for five years in World War I, again in World War II, lost a son in the Korean War, while working his way up to where he now owns a clothing chain and is one of the most respected residents of Winnetka, Illinois, how do you explain to this guy that Life is more important than War and that you'd prefer to serve your country working on the City

Welfare Board or for the County Mental Hospital? Is he going to think I'm slightly off when I walk in there, before I even open my mouth? What's he going to think when I start explaining everything? Can I justify my position? Just because I will have an M.A. in Communications in June, to go with my B.A. in Math, just because this means the Army wouldn't put me anywhere near the front lines, just because I *know* I could get a soft job in the Army, with my background, just because I know all this and I'm *still* applying for a C.O., would my local board really realize. . . .

14 *An alcoholic traces the stages by which he became a problem drinker.*

Becoming an alcoholic

henry beetle hough

The way to alcoholism is not across a bridge or through a portal marked with warning signs and illuminated with flood-lights; it lies across a shadow line that is crossed in heavy dark-ness, at night, and in obscure cloud and haze.

I know now that my pleasantly controlled social drinking developed into alcoholism as subtly and unnoticeably as some case of diabetes creeps into the life of a victim of this disease.

But certainly there must be signs? Yes, there are signs, but usually they are not of a spectacular sort. They are slight changes of viewpoint and of behavior that the drinker can explain away and usually conceal from those around him. Some of these had already become part of my experience, and it is time to tell about them.

SNEAKED DRINKS

I don't remember the first time. I cannot even guess when the first time was. But I do recall that when I was mixing silver fizzes or highballs or gimlets in the kitchen, a period came when I would sneak one or two in order to be that much ahead of the crowd, or even ahead of Alice, if we were alone.

It was a simple transition from merely tasting a drink to be sure it would greet the palate well, to tossing off one or two for my own hasty indulgence. If I didn't have a head start, my feeling was that I would be laboring under a handicap. Or perhaps I didn't have any feeling as definite as that—perhaps it was that I just wanted the liquor, and there it was.

Once having had the experience of this head start, I wanted it whenever opportunity offered. There was no thought of turning back. I had made a permanent departure so far as drinking was concerned.

The really significant aspect of what may seem trivial was that to sneak drinks ahead of time was not like me. I was not selfish about things, and it was always instinctive and natural for me to follow the practices of courtesy. Here, then, was an instance, even if a slight one, in which alcohol was causing a deviation from my normal behavior.

And I was already committed to concealment that would naturally lead to lying.

LYING ABOUT THE NUMBER

All these things started innocently.

"Look at Gus," somebody said. "He's on his fourth."

"I should say not," said Gus. "You're counting the one I brought in for Elsie."

"What difference does it make? It's a poor night when you don't have a fourth."

"That's so," Gus replied, "and I want it understood that the fourth is still ahead of me, see?"

Persiflage about the number of drinks ran like that, and somebody looked at me and said, "How many has old Pete had?"

And I, embarrassed under Alice's eyes, held up two fingers and said, "Only two." I laughed as I said it, and this wasn't a lie. It was part of the conventional discourse of drinking.

But pretty soon the jocose evasion, or the pretended forgetfulness, or the mock protestations were all turning into deliberate deceit. At first I would usually admit to Alice the next morning just what the extent of my drinking had been. Sometimes her comments were caustic, but it was a long time before we had real quarrels about liquor. I believe one reason real quarrels were postponed was because I stopped being frank.

In the background of my mind I classed this sort of lying along with the social deceits and so-called white lies that are familiar to all the human race, but I was utterly wrong in so doing. Alcoholic lying belongs in a category of its own.

I had not gone far as yet, and I can still believe that my earlier lies were fairly innocent—but they were tainted with alcohol. They did not begin and end in themselves, for they were the first expressions of alcoholic thinking and the alcoholic turn of mind. Honestly confronted and described, they were symptoms.

HAIR OF THE DOG

Long, long before Alice became troubled and critical, I had discovered the value of the classic "hair of the dog that bit you." The drink in the morning that restored, the drink in the morning that was necessary to minister to a bad feeling—here was a formula of renewal.

Hangovers became, though still regrettable, a necessary part of a drinking man's experience. Something had to be done about them. The drink in the morning was the best answer.

Many people who are not alcoholics take drinks in the morning—sometimes—but nevertheless drinking in the morning is one of the primary badges of alcoholism. Here is a danger signal glowing bright red and visible from afar, by night or by day. If a man drinks in the morning as a means of recovery from his drinking the night before, it is possible to make a prediction concerning him that will not be far wrong.

BUT I CAN QUIT WHEN I LIKE

Evasion and vacillation are conspicuous in all human behavior and it is hard to recognize them as especially important in relation to drinking. The woman who departs from her diet is not much different from the man who yields to the temptation of one more highball. We are all human.

The first time doesn't count. It isn't as bad as it seems. I'll pull myself up a bit. If I want to, I can quit right now.

It is in respect to this last that the drinker and the incipient

alcoholic have their strongest argument, for when they say they
can quit, the chances are that they are telling the literal truth.

*It's easy to stop a man's drinking. You can stop it by locking
him up. He can stop it, and generally does, for a week or a
month or even longer. All alcoholics stop drinking—most of
them stop repeatedly. The stopping is as common a symptom as
the drinking. The problem is to remain stopped.*

I remember how I used to quit drinking. Alice was pleased
with me and I was pleased with myself. I could stop when I
wanted to—therefore I had proposed a test and met it satisfac-
torily—everything was under control. So I thought, but as a matter of cold fact, I had met no test at all and had no reliable
inkling whatever as to the extent of my control. Because, having
stopped for a while, I invariably began again.

Alice knew even less than I about the danger signals and
about my relationship to alcohol, for the reason that I, like most
drinkers, kept my experience as completely as possible secret to
myself. If a suspicion arose that liquor might be playing too large
a part in my life, I had only myself to satisfy, and I was easily
convinced by rationalizations and evasions that would not have
gone over with Alice if she had been possessed of full information. I let her into my problem—and I denied then that it was a
problem—only when there was some outward slip—such as having to be put to bed, or missing time at the office or an engage-
ment with a client.

The awkwardness of the overt occasion was that it had to be
explained to someone else, and with reasoning of a sounder sort
than I used on myself. But even here the rationalization was
usually successful in the end. I was plausible and my stories were
plausible, because alcoholism was still a mere hazy ghost of a
threat, nothing that was likely to happen to *me;* and because I
was bright enough and resourceful enough to tell plausible
stories. The alcoholic is likely to be an intellectually able and
articulate person. Even if he is not possessed of a formal education, he has a native dynamism that spills over.

All this I put down here, *before any of the major develop-
ments of my alcoholism,* because it is precisely at this phase, in
advance of serious trouble, that danger signals may be of use;
and because it is significant that early changes in habit and view-

point may find an ultimate development and explanation in terms of alcoholism. The fact that, at the moment, there need be no such inevitable chain of cause and effect, of beginning and end, is far less important than the fact that there very well may be. In my own case, as I shall proceed to show, there was what now appears an inevitable sequence. But I was not looking for danger signals, and if anyone had called them to my attention I would not have observed them.

One reason for this, of course, was that I refused utterly to recognize anything in common between myself, who had been drunk many times, and other men whom I had seen drunk. Even at the stage of which I am now writing, I might well have remembered the drunks I had seen as a boy, and compared my situation to theirs. The young man wearing pointed shoes in the park, who so frightened the tailor's wife—surely I might have felt now some stirring of an alcoholic bond between him and me. But no, not at this time or later, not until much, much later when all had been painfully laid bare, did I discover any relationship running from me to the alcoholic kinship of the world at large.

If I had been able to suspect such a kinship through some secret process of intuition, I would have denied it and refused to acknowledge it to myself. For I was different.

I might get drunk at times, but still I was different.

My own case was distinct and special.

The drinker never sees himself as others see him, and the deliberate mental twist or evasion that enables himself to preserve his confidence in his own difference, and his own independence of general weaknesses and defeats, is capable of being enlarged and distorted as alcoholic thinking replaces the normal processes of which he was once capable. Once you surrender realistic thinking, it is hard to get back. . . .

GUILT

The stranger in my house was not the substance known as alcohol but a fantasy that I myself brought into existence chiefly through a sense of guilt. Guilt led to deceit, but Alice could be deceived only part of the time and ultimately not at all.

The sense of guilt did not make its appearance abruptly

on a particular day that can be identified and recalled but, like so many other elements in the pattern of alcoholism, subtly and by almost indistinguishable degrees.

I don't remember that Alice ever demanded, as the wives of drinkers are supposed to do, "Where were you last night?" Or: "Drunk again today, weren't you?" Or: "Where did you go after you left the office?" She did say sometimes: "Say, how many drinks have you had, anyway?" I began lying to her when a tugging sensation of guilt made me ashamed to tell the truth.

But the questioning was most often in her eyes, and this was how it happened more and more. She was not looking for an answer from me. She was seeking the answer for herself. She could tell what shape I was in. She could estimate pretty closely the extent of my drinking, though not so closely as she thought. I contrived ways of preventing her from knowing.

One Washington's Birthday I crawled out of bed with all the grumbling misery of a hangover. The night before, in anticipation of a day of idleness and no responsibilities, I had stayed up late drinking B. & B., benedictine and brandy, with a group of our friends. Nothing was easier for me to drink through a sociable evening but the after-effect was bad. Morning brought the need for a good stiff whisky as soon as possible, and I slipped downstairs and got one, or two, and experienced the anticipated revival—as if disintegration had been avoided by a narrow margin.

I covered my tracks well and was sure that Alice knew nothing about the morning drinks; but later in the day she called to me, "Pete, what happened to that bottle of rye in the cupboard?"

"How should I know?" I snapped back.

"Now if you don't, who does?"

"So you're checking up on me," I said with a good deal of resentment.

"I am not," said Alice, without losing her good nature. She could be exasperatingly patient. "I had to get the cooking sherry, which meant moving the bottle of rye, and how could I help noticing that something had happened to it since yesterday? Why the mystery? If you gave somebody a drink or if you had a drink or two yourself, why not say so?"

But she wasn't being frank, for she knew why I didn't want

to say so. I didn't want to admit sneaking the drinks that morning, along with the disclosure that was necessarily involved. Alice knew what it meant when I needed this quick prescription for a hangover. I was guilty and therefore guiltily anxious to cover up.

After that I made it a matter of custom to keep an extra bottle or two in the cellar, the attic, or the garage—any place where Alice would not come across them. I varied the repository because this seemed the smart thing to do. I couldn't be cornered again. I wouldn't be answerable to Alice for every drink I took, or in a situation which gave her a chance to cross-question me.

The unseen stranger was by no means a constant presence in our household, for some years at least, because alcohol, though I no longer controlled my drinking, was still subordinate. There were long periods when I drank little or not at all. We had our first baby. My older son may now consider himself an eye-witness, though not for a long time aware of the one special difference between his home surrounding and another's. We pursued our life together, and it seemed a natural, settled sort of thing that would grow and develop as year succeeded year. Alice and I talked of plans for the future and looked ahead to a promise that, though obscure, seemed full of pleasant possibilities and sure to be faithfully performed.

We thought of ourselves as normal. We lived in a state of order in a civilized time, with the evidences of a vigorous, healthy, successful American way of life around us. We were part of a wonderful system, as one branch of mathematics is part of a complete and ordered whole; but, since our plane was organic, the branches of our system were more vitally and usefully related. We would naturally share in the happiness and success of the whole.

In some such way as this, I think, any family looks at others, at the segment of society round about, and gains the same assurance that one may gain from looking at a reflection in a mirror. But each outlooking family selects the most desirable aspects it can see and, from these, forms a rationalized and idealized image that it chooses to accept as its own. So easily an assurance is accepted that may be cruelly false and, where alcoholism is concerned, is sure to be false. . . .

"I can stop drinking any time I want to."

Who is this speaking? It is I. Perhaps it is some man from next door, or a stranger met on the train, saying my words. It is almost any alcoholic, or any person in danger of alcoholism. Famous, famous words. Let my sons learn now how old and worn they are, how often hollow.

As I have said before, they express a genuine truth. But one trouble is that to speak them is not much different from saying, "I can't stop drinking unless I want to."

Do I want to? Do you want to, my chance acquaintance, or my friend? Will my sons want to, at some future time? It may be helpful to consider the question even now. Does any drinker who enjoys alcoholic liquor want to stop enjoying it? Of course not!

"Wanting to" is the catch.

I wanted to stop drinking. I wanted to stay sober and make a good husband and father. I wanted to be clear-headed and to do the best work of which I was capable.

All this, in general terms, was vivid and unqualified. But it did not prevent me, at some given moment, from needing a drink.

I want to stay sober but I need a drink.

The contradiction that appears in these twin statements is one that requires thought. So long as I have the craving, the feeling of need, I do not really want to stop drinking—not at the given moment. What I need, I want, for wanting is surely inseparable from needing. I want a drink now, because I need it.

At the same time I still want to stop drinking, but this is a more general and remoter aim with a little less urgency in the "wanting."

The stopping can always wait a while longer. It is an ideal, long range program. The need is immediate, a thing of the moment, NOW, as jangling nerves and sick cells of my body insist.

I have always planned to call upon my willpower. I have thought of the will as a kind of bulldozer to be brought in when I really make up my mind to overcome all obstacles. *When I really make up my mind*—when will that time come? Long before then I am discovering that willpower is much more effective for accomplishing what I want than for accomplishing what I do not want.

The will helps, obviously, to subordinate various lesser desires and to push through the attainment of a greater gain in the long run. But can it ever help us to do the thing, socially permissible, which we just plainly and in all honesty do not want to do?

In terms of alcoholism, at least, there is only one answer.

Yet, once again, I stopped drinking—for a while. This act of decision and of abnegation somewhat restored my self-esteem and brought an appearance of happiness to my home, but this time did not deceive Alice nor exorcise her haunting insecurity. She must have known by now that she was married to an alcoholic husband, though I doubt if her loyalty would have allowed her to admit it in plain terms. A woman married to an alcoholic husband never knows what will happen.

In reflecting upon my circumstances, it seemed to me that I had let alcohol get the best of me, and that I should knock off entirely until I could be sure of handling it better. I must have a holiday of a sort and after a while I could make a fresh, intelligently-considered thing of normal drinking. I would be like other men who drank and got by, apparently with ease.

I was aware, you see, of a physical craving for alcohol. I had trained the cells of my body to expect it, I had accustomed them to make the most of a larger and larger quantity, without many interruptions in the supply. If alcohol was habit-forming—and the smoking of cigarettes, the eating of candy, even taking a nap at noon are also habit-forming—then I had slipped into the groove too far and would have to declare some revision.

I was aware of this, for even my ingenuities of self-deceit could not disguise a conclusion so obvious to Alice and everyone else who knew me well. I could hardly be the one person to ignore what others showed me they recognized clearly.

I was not aware, however, that my bodily craving for alcohol was less important in the long run than another reliance I had come to place in it. I wasn't the fellow I wanted to be unless I could make myself so with timely doses of liquor. I had used alcohol to build up a relationship with the life of which I wanted to be a part. Physical gratification was nothing as compared to the use of alcohol for this self-administered act of creation.

It was as simple as that, though I did not know it then or for a long time. When I reassured myself that I had no concealed drive for revenge upon either of my parents, or for escape from any fantasy of long ago, or any of the other psychic forces of the underground that I had heard about second or third hand, my reassurance was complete—but wholly groundless. For me to be an alcoholic by psychic conditioning, it was not necessary to find any such dramatic mutilation from long ago.

It was necessary only for me to have placed reliance upon alcohol for adjustment to and in the competition of the world.

Liquor helped establish me with the people I must know. It protected me from unpleasant reminders. It softened anxieties. It helped me to a better opinion of myself. It seemed to give me the ability to work more effectively and longer. It was the difference between a well-rounded life and the narrow, specialized life of tensions and pressure to which otherwise I was committed.

Without liquor I was like a tightly coiled spring from which any impact or even any stir of air could evoke shrill twanging sounds.

With the mysterious power of alcohol I had tried and was still trying to make myself a man of charm, wit, and urbanity, a man of prowess in professional life, a man not troubled by nerves, a man who would never be tempted to look back over his shoulder.

So when I stopped drinking and admitted that I missed the physical gratification, I was also experiencing this other deprivation. I was prevented from being the man I had made of myself, the man I thought I wanted to be.

It was inevitable that I should soon start drinking again, for a little while without alcohol has a wonderful way of wiping out apprehension. Liquor may have the best of other men, but I see perfectly how I can and will control it. The new page has been turned.

But I did not begin this time with Alice's consent. For a while I drank only when she was not around and when I thought she would not know. I drank moderately and decently and assured myself there was every reason to expect no more trouble. I had learned my lesson and, as an intelligent man, applied its obvious conclusions.

When Alice did find out, she made no scene; she had suspected for some time what was going on.

"If you are going to take a drink," she said, "you don't have to hide it from me. You don't, do you? I don't want you to."

"I've just been proving to myself that I can handle it," I said. "I know now that I've got it licked. I'll never go off the deep end again."

She accepted my confidence at its face value, for how could she doubt when I so obviously believed? Perhaps she too believed for a while.

But within a month I had bottles concealed in the cellar, the attic, the car, the garage—one or all at different times—and within two months came a Monday morning when I was not fit to go to the office. I was without a drink that Monday morning, for Alice was watching me and I could not get to my liquor supply.

"How long are you going to go on like this?" she asked.

I swore. I threw myself into a tantrum. What sort of perfection did she think she had married? What was she accusing me of? Should I feel like a sinner because I had accumulated a little hangover? How would she feel if I kept watching her like a plainclothesman, begrudging her every drink and making her feel that liquor should be measured by the drop? On I went, yackety-yacketing, almost convincing myself that it was Alice's fault my mouth tasted so badly, my head ached, and I could not remember what I had done the night before.

That Monday passed, but by now the relationship between Alice and me had changed completely and permanently. Even when our lives seemed normal, there was the stranger in our house, the unspoken awareness between us. She knew there would be a next time. She knew she must have a reserve of independence and leadership. She knew she must prepare to be responsible for the boys if need be.

To the extent that I recognized her attitude, I resented it. She had no right to be superior. Something about her seemed pushing me all the time. Pushing, watching, suspecting. When I wasn't guilty, she could make me feel guilty, and at such times I was sorry for myself.

We exposed our raw nerves to each other. We quarreled more and more. I knew that liquor was at the bottom of everything that didn't go well, but I had no intention of cutting it out again. Why should I? I was handling it all right.

When my sons suspected the truth, when they began to compare the life of their home with others, when they not only suspected but *knew,* they alone can say. I shall not ask them now. But as they read these words, they will piece together meanings that first were vague shadows long ago. They knew something for a long time, then they knew all. . . .

SMALL VOICE

One summer evening, not early, not late, but when the dusk was beginning to gather, I walked toward my house in the New Jersey suburb with considerable uneasiness. I had made several stops on my way from the office and I knew I was not in good shape. For this I suffered a sense of guilt, yet I had stopped short of drunkenness and considerably short of starting off on a spree, and for this I suffered a sense of dissatisfaction and persecution. I was irritable. I was mean.

If good luck held, Alice wouldn't be at home. This was her day for a meeting and tea of some kind, and those things broke up late. Sometimes she fixed supper for the boys ahead of time and left something for me, and didn't get back until almost bedtime.

At first I thought I would take my chances and walk right up to the front door—but Alice might be home and I didn't relish the idea of confronting her. Maybe it would be better to skirmish around back and ease into the house. At least I could see how things were, fix myself up a little, and maybe contrive to face Alice on ground of my own choosing.

"I didn't hear you come in," she might say, without even looking at me carefully. "How were things in the city?"

And I would say, "Not bad, not bad at all. What's for a guy who's hungry?"

The light touch often worked. So I walked in by the side of the hedge that separated our yard from the next. I covered the most exposed area and was soon under the shelter of deep shadow; but in this darkness my foot struck against a child's wagon or some other object, and I tripped over into the hedge, sprawling. If I had been really steady, I probably wouldn't have tripped. As I remained for a measurable span of time, entrapped in privet, I made out two small boys crouching a short distance away. They were playing in their own yard and I had probably scared them.

But the fright was soon over. One of the kids said to the other, "It's only Gussie's old man."

Gussie is reading these words now. He is my youngest son. Perhaps he has not come across the old nickname for a long time—at one period of his life he was called this after a character in a comic strip.

I extricated myself from the hedge and went into the house by the back door. No one was home. It turned out later that Alice had skipped the meeting and tea and had taken the boys to the early show of some educational movie.

Alone in the hollow shell of a house I gave way to bitter emotion. Tears ran down my cheeks. "It's only Gussie's old man." What would those kids say to Gussie tomorrow? What would he say to them? Was I so much of an unreliable character that anything could be expected of me? Other fathers remained upright, but I stumbled into hedges. Why not face it—I arrived home half slewed over and staggering. Why wouldn't children notice it even more readily than anyone else?

I know now that my tears were alcoholic. It was thoroughly in alcoholic character to go through all this emotion without any idea of doing anything to remedy the original situation. . . .

I did not drink for a considerable time. I forgot or suppressed the revelation that I might be (after all, it was never certain in my own mind) what is known as a periodic, a drinker who goes back to the bottle as certainly as a homing pigeon to its loft. I began to feel well, at least physically.

You don't keep pushing against something when there is really nothing there to push. You don't put forth effort when obviously no effort is required. So it was with my dramatic resolution to exert my willpower: at first I derived some satisfaction from rolling the bulldozer along the ramparts and observing that all was clear. But I wasn't even tempted to drink, and the parade of needless force seemed foolish. After a while I forgot about it.

I assumed that a drinkless state was going to be natural to me, for a long, long time, if not forever. I had learned my lesson.

But the time came, and I now have no distinct recollection of just when it was, that I craved a drink. The physical sickness and misery were long gone. At first I wanted a drink without really being aware of the craving. I wanted to be let off the hard driver's seat of my job. I wasn't sleeping well. I was restless.

"How did things go at the office?" Alice asked.

"It's a rat race," I said.

She looked at me with that secret, observing quality in her gaze. She looked at me often that way.

"A rat race," I said. "But don't worry. I'm not going out and get pickled."

"I didn't think you were."

"You looked at me that way," I told her.

Alice didn't understand—so I had often told myself. She had her feminine intuition about many things, but she couldn't know what went on inside a man. I resented the responsibility and authority that had, through the years, passed from me to her because of alcohol. I couldn't be whittled down any more. Just because of what was past, she had no right to expect that the future was going to be the same . . .

"Don't worry," I said. "I'll be home early."

I was home early.

Alice watched me and I knew she was watching me. Certainly she was justified, and I couldn't deny that, but a man doesn't want to be watched all the time. And when I had said the job was a rat race, I had meant just that.

There were words that you used, and everyone knew what they meant. A lot of city people never had seen the wire spring from a bale of hay when it was cut, but they said themselves that things had "gone haywire" and the expression was commoner than most phrases deriving from their own experience. A "rat race" was not a competition between rats in a cage, but it was the way we lived and worked and tore ourselves to pieces with haste, anxiety, frustration, and uncompleted tasks or effort that fell short always and had to be renewed. Our personal affairs and our civilization were a rat race, and every day things went haywire.

I wanted a drink but I did not take one. There were plenty of chances but I just didn't. I wouldn't.

When I wanted to and didn't, I felt unsatisfied but reassured. The old willpower was working. Yet why should I keep myself forever away from the satisfaction of a single drink? It wasn't the use of alcohol that was bad, it was the abuse. I had abused it and had suffered and had come out a wiser man.

But one drink—why wasn't I entitled to it after so long? As a boy and as a younger man I had begun drinking at will and stopped at will, and wasn't that the real function of willpower?

Still I didn't take the drink.

Not for a day after that thought crossed my mind, or two days, or three days. But the next week I did. Then it seemed that I had been anticipating that drink for a long time, as if it were a Miltonian "far off divine event" toward which my destiny moved. Not consciously but deep inside I had waited and looked forward and shaped the expectancy of all my body cells for the alcohol that was coming.

The drink was like arriving home after a long and difficult journey at sea or in desert country. It was like the completion of a rhyme. It was like an appointment kept suddenly after the opening of sealed orders. Alice had known about the orders but I had kept them sealed from myself.

The first drink, however, was incomplete as it always has been and always will be for an alcoholic.

When you start something, it isn't always desire that is the important factor. You can get along, and often do, with too little sleep and partial satisfaction of hunger. You break off a pleasant social talk in order to get to work on time. But the first drink is a process begun and not finished. It lacks the completion that is somehow as inevitable as the progression of a chemical reaction in nature.

I took that first drink after leaving the office half an hour early in the afternoon. Without explaining the matter to myself, I had even allowed in advance for the extra time.

At nine o'clock, in a high state of intoxication, I engaged a room in a small hotel because it wasn't possible to go home that night. I tried to get Alice by telephone but she didn't answer. She didn't need to hear from me—she already knew. She had called my office to find out when I left, and the rest was perfectly clear. She had stayed alone often enough because of my drunkenness, but this time she hadn't wanted to, so she had taken the boys and gone to a friend's house for the night. What had she told the boys? They may remember, as they read these lines. I guess she hadn't had to explain much. They knew as well as she.

I did not go home until the third day.

It wasn't the same story. It never was quite the same, for although the basic circumstances were present—the sickness of body and spirit, the unbearable racking and torment of nerves, the self-reproach—there was always something new. This time the new and bitter element was the realization—why had I not grasped it before?—that Alice would never again place real confidence or dependence in or upon me.

I was marked. I had marked myself. Now she could not even pretend convincingly to believe my protestations.

"I know you mean what you say," she told me after the crisis was over, "but you can't help yourself."

"I can't help myself?"

"No."

Implausible as this may seem, the idea was a new one to me. I was hurt and disturbed that Alice should believe it. The fact that she did believe it made it something to be reckoned with, almost as if it were true. But it couldn't be true . . . and then I ran through the old familiar routine. I am, after all, an intelligent man. I am perfectly capable of regulating my own conduct.

Alice might have said, though she didn't, *"Intelligence has nothing to do with it."*

Willpower has nothing to do with it.

To come to this conclusion earlier is one of the important challenges for those around an alcoholic as for an alcoholic himself. The act of drinking, which seems voluntary and for so many men and women is voluntary, becomes quite otherwise for the alcoholic. It is compulsive. One might well say, "The poor guy can't help it."

Drinking originates in forces as beyond conscious control, though different in kind, as the symptoms of scarlet fever.

It is a gift of the human mind to be able to learn by experience; but there are hidden drives behind many actions, and these hidden drives are not taught by experience or anything else. In one sense the alcoholic is aware of the lessons to be drawn from his life, but at the same time there are strange and sometimes fantastic forces that bid him ignore or deny what should be obvious. He is under this inner compulsion to go on repeating a cycle he can change only if he himself is changed.

Ben Jonson wrote of "the wild anarchy of drink," and so far as the human will and intelligence are concerned it is, for the alcoholic, the wildest of anarchies. Yet beyond his will it follows a familiar routine like the typical fever chart of an illness.

Thus come about the almost endless repetitions in an ever-descending course. Thus I found the repetitions in my own alcoholic life, and that is why I make record of them here.

Repetition is the essence of alcoholism. The expectation of reform or improvement, in the absence of some major change in the alcoholic's personality, is unlikely. Ordinary rules don't apply. The matter is almost always beyond reasoning.

It happens. It will happen again.

Over and over, under circumstances essentially the same though outwardly different, I made my protestations, denials, and assurances to Alice. At the times I made them, they were true. My penitence, self-accusation, and firm determination to free myself from alcohol were all real. Yet often I did have some reservations or at least awareness of extenuating circumstances that I knew it would be impossible to communicate to any other person, even to Alice. No one, outside this identical experience, can understand the quality and nature of the ordeal an alcoholic undergoes.

Alice was sympathetic. She wanted to understand. But words do not communicate the nature of a man's maladjustment and need when the very routine of life and work has become a discipline, the nerves jangle and shriek, the flesh and blood rebel. There is no adequate analogy. And to understand how these frictions, tensions, and clashes prevail over the rational behavior so natural to other human beings is harder when the break to alcohol seems to occur sometimes so suddenly, without resistance or warning. The pattern is not plain under observation, or it has twists and deviations.

15 *Psilocybin is derived from a mushroom known to Mexican Indians as* teonanacatl, *"the flesh of God." Jones describes the effects of this hallucinogen upon himself and a companion.*

"Up" on psilocybin

richard jones

A friend and I decided to set aside a Saturday night early in July for an experiment with psilocybin. We met after work and drove to my home in the country where we knew we would not be disturbed.

The psilocybin came in sugar lumps in doses of 2.5 milligrams, the lumps stained yellow with food coloring for easy identification. While I boiled water for coffee, my friend Mike put a record on the hi-fi. When the coffee was ready, I took it into the living room on a tray and asked, "One lump or two?"

"Two." We had previously decided that 5 milligrams would be suitable. We finished the coffee, swirling the dregs to avoid losing any of the drug and settled back to await signs of intoxication. After half an hour I began to feel unduly nervous, and I recognized this as a common first symptom. Mike claimed he noticed nothing unusual in himself. A few minutes later, however, I saw that he was twitching his feet and mentioned this to him.

"It's just the coffee," he said. "It keys me up. I don't usually drink it." He added suspiciously, "I don't think you put anything in my cup—are you trying to play some kind of joke on me?"

I saw that his hostility was growing and knew it to be induced by the drug. In order to change the subject, I suggested to

From *The Harvard Review*, 1 (Summer, 1963). Reprinted by permission of *The Harvard Review*.

Mike that he glance around the room to see if things looked different to him. He followed my suggestion, letting his gaze linger on a pair of brass andirons. From his extraordinarily intent concentration on these, I sensed he was coming under the full effects of psilocybin.

We next tried looking around at pictures on the wall and magazines on a coffee table. The red fringe of *Time* seemed to me to be glowing warmly. A lamp next to the record player caused a reflection on the surface of the turning disc that seemed to glisten with an intense light. These visual oddities held tremendous fascination for me; I knew I was "going up." Mike evidently was, too, for without cause we both began smiling.

Over the mantel there was a portrait of some great-grand-relative who had frowned down on the living room for years and whom Mike and I had nicknamed Ugly Nell. Suddenly, Mike said gravely, "Quick, look at Ugly Nell—she just winked."

I looked up at the old girl to find her smiling broadly. Mike had already gone into peals of laughter over this hallucination, and in a few moments I was also laughing hysterically. We kept pointing at the portrait, laughing so hard that we fell onto the floor. It took great will power to calm ourselves down and sit quietly listening to the rich sounds of the stylus swishing back and forth near the center of the record. When I rose to turn the player off, Mike commented, "Good, there's too much going on now anyway." He was silent for a moment, then continued, "I haven't laughed so hard in years; was it the drug?"

"Yes," I answered, "it often happens when psilocybin begins to take effect." As I said this, I noticed I had to make a great effort to speak in sentences. The problem was that my thoughts were coming too fast for me to express them. I also noticed that Mike hadn't paid the slightest attention to my reply but instead had been judiciously fingering a leather cigarette box. "Leather," he said, and then again, "Leather."

Mike then became interested in the objects on the coffee table, and I lit a cigarette, watching the smoke make eddies between my fingers and form patterns against the green background of the wall. Something red in a bookcase suddenly caught my eye, and as I looked up at it, it seemed to come closer to me.

With the idea that we should eat in order to experience

heightened sense of taste, I pointed toward the kitchen and mumbled something about food. Mike understood perfectly and accompanied me into the next room. When I opened the door of the freezer, I had a strong temptation to run my fingers over everything inside and feel different textures of the frozen foods. Instead, I took out two TV dinners and peeled the foil coverings back. We both had great fun feeling the fried chicken inside, for it was at once greasy, crisp, and frozen, and we could feel these qualities separately as well as all at once. I then bit into a pea with my front teeth, pressing the halves to the roof of my mouth. I could taste the ice and the pea as distinct properties and also noticed a great change in taste and texture as the pea thawed. Mike then tried one. "It tastes green," he said.

I tested another. "Yes, green, too."

After nibbling at peas for a while, we went to the refrigerator to see what else we could uncover. I found an egg, a white egg, round at both ends, though one end felt rounder than the other. Touching it, I could feel the cold of the shell, and as I rubbed it warm, I could clearly feel the very granular texture with my fingertips and the roundness with my palm. It seemed all an egg should be: perfectly regular. "The egg of eggs," I said, handing it to Mike. He examined it carefully, first with his fingers and hand, then with his eyes, and finally with his tongue. Ten minutes later he agreed: "Yes, the egg of eggs. From the chicken of chickens." He next took a brown egg from the shelf, turned it over quickly, and presented it to me shaking his head. "Imperfect." I examined it, finding it long, uneven, and coarse. "A bad egg," I decided.

We had by now lost all sense of time (which is only a measure of man's normal incapacity to deal with the present; under psilocybin, we were more than able to deal with it). We had also developed a great desire to leave the house and drive to a nearby beach club in order to watch people while under the effects of the drug. It took us a full fifteen minutes to walk as many yards to the car. We were barefoot, and the grass was cold with dew; it "felt" fresh, even through the calloused soles of our feet. A flagstone walk seemed wonderfully smooth while gravel in the driveway was sharp but warm. The tender parts of our feet had become unusually sensitive to all of these textures.

I drove, or rather put the car in drive and steered. Mike became intrigued by the running lights on boats in the bay, but we had to hurry on in order to catch the end of a party at the beach house. The people there would not be in the same timeless state we were enjoying. On arriving, we got out of the car and were delighted by the sound of the car doors closing. We tried opening them and closing them repeatedly, listening to differences in tone. We could sense security in the sound.

As we stood in the parking lot, feeling details of the ground with our feet and watching colored lights strung around a porch fifty yards away, we held a remarkable dialogue:

MIKE: (*very seriously, pointing to a spot with his voice*) Shells.

I: Clams.

MIKE: The (*pause*) gulls left them.

I: Dropped them.

MIKE: To break.

I: Food.

MIKE: Warm, still.

I: Yes, from day.

MIKE: Holds heat.

I: Of course, blacktop.

MIKE: Lights alive—green and red.

I: The yellow (*pointing with arm*).

With such short phrases we indicated sensations and thoughts as soon as they occurred. Just brief hints at ideas enabled us to understand each other fully.

I walked very slowly savoring the feel of the round white stones embedded in the tar, the stones cool, the tar still warm from the afternoon sun. We had decided to say we were drunk if anyone questioned our strange behavior. To be sure, the first person who saw us walking with such concentration up the porch steps (wood with distinctly granular sand on it) cried out, "Here come the drunken lifeguards."

From our separate world, we watched these people who could not possibly understand how we felt. Whenever they would try to talk to me, I immediately felt bored and looked away. Nothing these outsiders said was meaningful; they all seemed slow-witted and simple-minded to us. Those among them who were perfectly sober found it even more difficult to understand us and our peculiar condensed conversation.

We moved toward the plates of crackers and bowls of dips. Mike tasted one, and with his finger still in his mouth said, "Cheese." Taking a cracker and dipping it into another dip, I replied, "This!" Mike imitated my action and shouted, "With Frito." I can't remember how long we kept this up, but eventually the manager's wife started to eye us suspiciously. "You two birds must be high as kites," she said.

"Vodka," I explained, trying to sound like a cossack, but this little deception merely set Mike and me off into a laughter that was almost as hard as that for Nell earlier in the evening.

By the time we got home and had settled back to listen to Berlioz's *Symphonie Fantastique*, we were slowly "coming down," yet listening to music was still a unique experience. The sound surrounds you—you virtually drown in it. It becomes a physical sensation, almost as tactile as taking a bath, and different sounds seem to have different textures: you can feel the high notes just as you can normally feel the bass. Your listening mind seems to be working so fast that you can fully comprehend each single sound before the next one comes along.

Later, after the symphony, when the effects had diminished to the point that we could express our thoughts before they got away from us, we discussed our experiences while they were still fresh in our minds. Mike told me that he had felt his thoughts were going so fast that he could fit a complete train of thought between two notes of music. Talking, he said, was impossible earlier in the evening because he couldn't slow his mind down enough to finish a sentence once he had started it. I replied that I learned to control my consciousness under the drug by focusing it on only those sensations I chose to the exclusion of all others. In this way I could perform necessary actions such as driving, cooking, asking directions of people, and so on.

Our contacts with normal people convinced us that our feelings of heightened awareness were no illusion. Our minds actually were keener and more active than theirs. One might imagine this phenomenon of "expanded consciousness" more easily by considering a scale of mental activity ranging from one to one hundred, with 75 representing the mean normal activity. Some persons, through accidents of body chemistry, fall higher or lower on that scale; the higher one is, the more of his world he is aware of. A person under psilocybin has a rating considerably above 75;

it seemed to us that our consciousness (particularly, our ability to receive sense impressions) was raised as much above normal as a normal person's is above that of an idiot or drunk.

Despite an acute problem of communication, this heightened consciousness seemed to us a distinct improvement over what we were used to. Even the communication difficulties were partially solved by means of our condensed dialogue (which might have worked because we were simply reporting sensations to each other—sensations we had experienced together). Yet we both felt that persons under the drug could discipline their thoughts in such a way as to be able to communicate. This would still only be between two people on the same level of consciousness. Our contacts with others at the beach club showed us the impossibility of establishing any kind of rapport between persons on widely different levels. The man on the upper level can, with effort, make himself understood to the man below him by consciously limiting his own perceptions, but in the other direction, there is no chance of understanding.

At the end of our session, we both felt that a new world had been opened to us—but a world that was still our own. Psilocybin had merely enabled us to see ordinary things more clearly and more intensely. The subjective change was purely internal: a change in our point of view and in the extent to which we could focus our awareness on selected objects. It seemed to us very likely that we could attain a similar state permanently by training our minds; psilocybin was an easy, artificial means of reaching it briefly.

16   *This selection attempts to provide some assurances*
for women who are reluctant to become nudists.

A mother speaks of nudism

ruth kirk

I think that as a rule the husband first becomes interested in
nudism. The wife generally holds back a little and sometimes
quite a bit. It is easier for the male to throw off his so-called
modesty, and shyness. He is a little more used to seeing others of
his own sex in the nude—in sports, on the job, etc. I think that
women are reared more guardedly and instilled much more with
the idea of the shame of exposing the nude body. We have so
many inhibitions and complexes to get rid of. Both men and
women.

Nudism usually starts at home. First the husband grows lax
in dress—he runs around in shorts for a while before dressing—
or from bath to bedroom with nothing on—or maybe he sits and
reads the paper a while that way. The children start to copy
him—they just naturally like to go nude anyway. You fuss at
your husband for setting the example—it just isn't decent to let
the children see you that way; you fuss at the children to put
their clothes on. He likes the freedom of movement without
clothes and knows the children do too, and tells you to let them
alone and let them enjoy themselves. He coaxes you to try it. But
you are horrified—the children will lose respect for their mother
if they see her running around like that. And besides, what
would the neighbors think? But after a while you catch yourself
going from the bathroom to the bedroom quickly to get something you forgot or you dash to answer the telephone in the nude
and one of the children catches you. And the child doesn't seem

Reprinted by permission of The American Sunbathing Association, Inc.

to be horrified at all—you are the one horrified and ashamed of your nude body. But still—you don't think it is right for decent people to act that way—the body is sinful and shameful and should be kept covered so as not to excite thoughts or give the children "ideas."

Then one night your husband brings home a nudist magazine he has seen on the news stand. You refuse to look at it. That filthy thing—imagine bringing that into the home where the children might see those nasty pictures. You are indignant at the whole matter and refuse to have anything to do with it. Your husband reads the articles and tells you about one or two of them. About what a nudist camp is and the activities that go on there. How healthy it is for children—the outdoor living. Out of curiosity, one day when you are alone, you pick up the magazine and leaf through the pages. You see the posed pictures of the beautiful girls. You don't like them. Then after a while you look at the articles and glance through two or three of them. They do sound interesting, yes, but—you wonder what kind of people are those nudists, anyway. Sunworshippers? Exhibitionists? Fanatics of some sort? Some kind of religious cult? Why do they have to take all their clothes off to get the benefit of the sunlight, why not leave some little thing on to cover up their nakedness?

Your husband continues to discuss the subject occasionally. Finally you realize his seriousness and you sit down with him and discuss the matter of taking your family to a nudist camp. Your mental attitude has to go through quite a change. In order for you to make your first visit to a nudist camp a lot of the inhibitions and complexes you have carefully nurtured all these years have to be cast out; the false modesty you have been taught; the shame complex; the idea that you have a body that is sinful and shameful and it is obscene to show certain parts of it in public—especially in front of the opposite sex. Most of us have been brought up very strict morally, and nudism seems to be absolutely against everything we have been taught as a child. And then there are the children—supposing they told the neighbors—or their school chums—or Aunt Sally or Uncle Fred—what would you do?

And there is also a very personal fear—your figure isn't as pretty as those girls in the magazines. Supposing you went there and your husband saw someone prettier than you. Or perhaps you have a surgical scar—it would look so awful. And besides you would lose all your femininity and allure for your husband. You know the old saying, "Familiarity breeds contempt."

Your husband can see the benefits to be gained for his family. And as he becomes more insistent, you finally give in and say, well, all right, just this once. He writes to the local club, whose name and address is in the magazine, and finds out where their camp is and gets permission to visit. You pack a picnic lunch, load the children into the car and are on your way. You have varied feelings of fear, curiosity and bravado. You don't know what to expect. Is it really a place to take your children? What will they see there? You round a bend in the road, go through a gate, and suddenly you are there. You see a nude man chopping wood. There is a spirited game of volley ball going on. People down by the pool—children running back and forth, playing, swinging on the swings and hardly anyone even turns his head as you drive in. You sit in the car a minute, taking it all in. Before you can make up your mind to get out of the car you are greeted cordially by one of the members and invited to get out and walk around the camp and see what is there. You are taken here and there and introduced to some of the members. Without apparently looking, you see all kinds of people: short, tall, slim, stout, all sorts of figures, both male and female, some with fine tans and some white and some pink with sunburn. You look at the inviting pool, the green lawn and the sun is warm. The children are tugging at your hand, begging to go in the pool, and can't we take our clothes off, Mommy? And suddenly you feel so conspicuous with your clothes on and you want to enjoy the sunshine and fresh air with the relaxed freedom these other people seem to have. You go to your car and disrobe, and the first step has been taken. The biggest step.

As time goes on, you find all your fears disspelled. As for your figure, you find there are some who look better than you do and some look worse. You have learned that physical limitations go unnoticed; they are entirely commonplace. You find that it is the individual, the personality that is important. You think of the different ones, not of their physical defects or beauty, but of their individuality—the effect that person has had on you. Their body is unimportant. You find that the moral standard is **very** high in a nudist camp. There is no liquor allowed, either on the premises or in the individual. There are no smutty stories told—no over display of affection—folks conduct themselves the same as on any public beach—only their conduct is better. You find there is no sex stimulation brought on by lack of clothing of anyone present. There is almost always a game of some kind going on—volley ball is the universal nudist sport; there is usually work to be done to improve or beautify the grounds.

Another thing, you find that the freedom of nudism intensifies the beauty of your marital relations. Your fears on that score were entirely unfounded.

As for the children—they are so healthy living in the fresh air and the sunlight this way—learning new and interesting things about the outdoors. They do not have the ingrained inhibitions you have had to overcome. To go without clothes is a perfectly natural thing for them. It is easy for them to understand that here they can go nude but in town they can't because everyone doesn't do it as they do at camp. And that is all the explanation they need. They look at you strangely if you try to bring out the shame of showing your body in public. You find in the future that your nudist life has made the answering of the children's questions in regard to growing up and adulthood and their sexual problems much easier. They do not have the curiosity about the opposite sex other children have. They have seen and understand the differences in the human figure and explaining the functions of the different parts of the body is simple. They are easier in their attitudes toward other children. I do not mean freer—I mean easier. They do not have the shyness that other children have because of curiosity. They have a poise, a sureness—an attractive freshness—a wholesomeness—that comes from knowing they have a healthy body and a healthy mind, which is more important. They are not interested in sneaking down on burlesque row or reading books that have to be sneaked behind the barn or looking at obscene pictures. The facts of life are known to them and there is no vicarious thrill in these things. From my own experience—my fifteen year old boy came home to me one day and told me that some of the boys in his class had climbed up on the wall to peek in the windows of the girls' room so they could see the girls. I asked him if he did and he say why should he—he knew what girls looked like. He was disgusted with such behavior and said if they were all nudists that sort of thing could not happen. There is no record of a juvenile delinquent from a nudist family.

As time goes on, you will spend as much time as you can at the nudist camp because it is an inexpensive outing—the children love it—and it is something your whole family can take part in. No more husband going off fishing or golfing or something else, while you and the children stay home on Sundays. Now, everyone eagerly goes to the "country" for the day or the weekend. And that is because you have found the greatest thing for all—the thing that makes us nudists for the rest of our lives and makes us wish we had not wasted so many years accepting it. That is the freedom—*the utter freedom*. As I said before, in order to take the first step, you have already cast out some inhibitions and old conventionalities. And you get rid of more and more as you go along. You remember wondering why nudists have to take everything off—why not leave something on? You have found out why—because you have overcome the shame of the body—of certain parts of the body. You have found that one part is as beautiful as the other and each has its own natural function to do. There is nothing to be hidden—no reason for wearing "some little thing." Actually, now, you feel it is indecent and obscenely suggestive to cover parts of the body. You feel it is wrong for clothes to be worn for the purpose of concealment. Better that they be worn because of the inclement weather or because of the job being done or some other such reason. You have learned the thrill of the sunlight and the air and the breezes on your nude body—the smoothness with which your body glides through the rippling water.

You have come to the point where you can hardly wait for the weekends to come around so you can go to camp and take off the clothes you have to wear all week in town because you have learned that the act of taking off your clothes and cleansing your body in the clean air includes cleansing your mind of all the nervous tensions and cares and worries that beset you daily at home; and you find utter relaxation. Absolute, utterly free rest and relaxation. And you go home rejuvenated not only in body but in mind. You get the feeling as you stand by your car and disrobe, that with your clothes you strip off the ugly, dirty world and here alone is peace and brotherhood with your fellow man. Here you find friendly, cordial people, broad of mind, tolerant, respectful of persons.

This is not something that happens immediately. For some, the transition to true nudism is quick. For others it takes quite a while. For some, it is easy to take their clothes off—but not so easy to take their minds off, so to speak—to take off the false veneer of conventionalities; to overcome the petty jealousies and possessiveness between husband and wife; the lustful thoughts towards others; the false shame of the body that is evidenced in these things. And when you do finally reach the understanding of the philosophy of nudism, you find your horizons unlimited, a great peace of mind, a richness in your enjoyment of life. You have found that freedom. And you bless the day you agreed to go to the nudist camp.

17 *A heroin addict discusses some aspects of his experiential world: narcotics, hospitals, police, overdoses, and girls.*

Danny Stern

jeremy larner

ralph tefferteller

I'm twenty-three years old and I've been on narcotics for about six years. It was in vogue at the time; everybody was doing it. There were four or five of us; one boy had been doing it for quite a while and said, would you like to try? This was at a sweet sixteen party at the Clinton Plaza. To prove a lot of fallacies wrong, it was heroin and it was a mainline shot from the very first. The boy who'd been taking narcotics staked everybody to a free shot, and administered it and made a big adventure out of it. He said that we could try it once and not get addicted, which I can say, so many years later, was the truth. He explained that you can steal and carry on all kinds of perverted things to get it, but at the time you're not concerned about what's going to happen later; it's what's going to happen now and the feeling you're going to achieve. And the feeling was so overpowering that it clouds your mind to any idea of going to jail, breaking society's rules, stealing or anything like it. You don't believe it.

Of the kids who took a shot at that party, all of us became addicts—only one didn't. He was what we considered a weekender. He partied and partied until he finally got married and settled down. Then he felt that it was passé; it was out of style, and he quit. Of the five who took shots, four of us are still addicts

From *The Addict in the Street* by Jeremy Larner and Ralph Tefferteller. Copyright © 1964 by Grove Press, Inc. Reprinted by permission of Grove Press, Inc. and Penguin Books Ltd.

today, that still keep in touch and see each other, and try and play this big game of not getting caught by the police.

I just came back last November from doing a hitch at Elmira. It was June 26, 1957; I was out with a boy and we decided to buy some narcotics up in Harlem. We took a fix, I was feeling kind of good, there was nothing to do, we were just walking around enjoying the sensation, and we decided to take a taxi ride home, all the way back to Queens. We took the taxi without the driver. We took people around, and we pretended that we were hacking this cab. We didn't take any of the money—just a weekend prank. I was sent to Elmira for zip-five and I did forty-eight months. And upon my getting out, the first thing I did, the first day, was look to secure some narcotics. To see if, was this forty-eight months worth it? And now that I took that fix, I feel that no amount of keeping anyone incapacitated will cure it—if you want to do it, you will do it.

I wouldn't consider myself honestly a criminal. This was done in a clouded mind, as a prank. It was an out-and-out robbery, grand larceny, but I don't think that I'm a criminal at heart. I'm disturbed to a degree, because I like narcotics and I wouldn't want anyone to sway me from the thought of narcotics. But I was subjected to perverts, wise guys, guys that had much more time than me. They send a guy that has zip-five—that's a maximum of five years—in with a guy that has twenty to life. And that boy who has twenty to life, he's lost hope to a certain degree. He doesn't care how much aggravation he causes you while you're there. You run into so much difficulty; you have to be a fighter and you have to fight back. And it makes you hard. You come out, you resent people, and you just want to go into a shell. And that's only another reason I went back to narcotics. I forget the past. I don't want to remember that forty-eight months; it was the most horrible forty-eight months in my life. I don't think anything could have done as much harm as Elmira. I don't feel narcotics has done any greater harm to me.

It taught me things that I didn't have any need to learn, like how to steal a car. It graduated me into the higher crime bracket. It gave me telephone numbers of people to look up when I got out, more connections, more criminal activity. Narcotics is very easy to get, once you're in Elmira. You can get synthetic drugs.

It's very easy to go to the hospital and get seconal or miltown or tranquilizers of all sorts. Dorazine, paraldehyde, chloral hydrate . . . I could go on and name more. Heroin, I will concede, is very hard to get in, but there have been cases where it has been gotten in. It's rough treatment; you're not treated like a human being, you're treated like an animal. And the only thing that you can do when you're treated like an animal is fight back. And there's no weapon. There's no weapon that a young boy that wants to help himself can fight back with other than his hands and his feet. They say, and I believe this, that the only person you hurt when you fight is yourself. But you're too blind to it, you can't see it.

The whole subject of narcotics has been gone at the wrong way. Everybody says you're a criminal. Basically I think that a narcotics addict, if he's under the influence of narcotics, will not bother anyone. If he's not under the influence of narcotics, and he's trying to secure his fix, he *will* bother you, to a certain degree. But it's not because he wants to bother you; he's not a violent individual. It isn't as bad as this gang warfare, believe me. They're out there causing trouble just for the sake of trouble. For the sole enjoyment of aggravating people, picking on somebody. We're doing it for a reason. We need narcotics, that's all.

After speaking to numerous addicts in the jail at Elmira, in The Tombs, and in the street, I find this: that when the dope addict needs money, he doesn't want to hurt anybody; he just wants the money. He will take your money and run. He's meek. He's the meekest of all people there is, because he's sick. Everybody says he's a killer, but he won't kill you. He's afraid. If you scare him, he might do it out of fear and not even know what he's doing. But that's not his goal. I've went on numerous things to get money, and I knew in my heart I didn't want to hurt anybody. And thank God, to this day I haven't hurt anybody.

An addict is very yellow. Once he's hooked, he's very afraid of withdrawal. So what he does, he steals from people he knows will not send him to jail. That takes in your own immediate family, your mom and pop's friends. People that like you, that you know will try and help you and say, well, it was a mistake. That is the first step in stealing for a narcotics addict.

Second step is boosting. That's going into a department store and walking out with two pair of pants. It's easy, it's tempting, and you learn very easy. Once you do it and get away with it, there's no stopping you from coming back and doing it a second or third time.

The third way is selling fake narcotics to other addicts, to fool them. In other words, you take a cellophane bag and fill it up with any white powder that looks like heroin. And when you see a sick addict that comes strutting down pounding the pavement begging for a fix, you sell him this. It's very cutthroat, you rob from one another. There's no honor among dope addicts.

Or you tell a fellow you're a gopher. You know the pusher and you'll gopher narcotics. The addict is from another neighborhood, but he knows you and he doesn't know the pusher. So you promise him: give me your ten-fifteen-twenty and I'll go look for the pusher for you. As soon as I score the dope, I'll bring it back to you. What happens then is you take his money and you buy the dope, but you never bring it back to him. You take it yourself. It's too overpowering. It's like being very sick, and a doctor says one shot of penicillin cures you. It's the same thing. Narcotics is mental; it's physical. One shot cures you.

You see, it works like this. Every boy in his teens, in his growing years, idolizes somebody—usually a tough guy. It's like the kids today watching TV—they idolize the Capones, and the Roaring Twenties, and the Untouchables. They're all glorious, picturesque characters. In my stages of growing up, there were certain boys in the neighborhood that were the big shots, the strong arm; everybody respected them. Now, we realize it's a false respect. At the time, I wanted to be so much like him. And when I realized he was taking dope, I said, well, if it's good for him it's good for me; he's the big shot. Now, today, when I see this boy, I know he's not a big shot.

But what I try and do is, being I'm taking narcotics, I try to keep it to a minimum, where I can control it. I don't ever want narcotics to control me again. And I feel that if it's done rationally, with a realistic mind, to a certain degree you can control it. Unless it takes over your body. Mentally, if you're strong and have a good will power, you can control it to a degree.

When it really comes down to it basically, everybody wants

to be recognized. Everybody. Now these boys that stick with it—
the reason they stick with it is narcotics brought them a new way
of life. It's an adventure. Let's face it: if narcotics was easy to
come by, there wouldn't be half as many addicts. To take narcotics right now, it is cloak-and-dagger, it's spy work, it's something out of television, believe me. You have to walk the street,
you have to secure a pusher, you have to locate the money to buy
this narcotics, you have to check in dark hallways, on roofs, go
through cellars, all this running about, all the time keeping one
eye out for the police.

All this. This is an adventure for a young man. And when
you finally get your narcotics back to your pad where you can use
it, you say to yourself: man, I did it, I beat the fuzz. I made the
scene. And you feel relieved.

Then the second stage is to take it. And that clouds your
mind. You feel content just to sit there and not be annoyed and
let the world go by. Just leave me alone, I'm happy the way I
am.

When people see these glorious characters like Buggsy Siegal
walking around with Rolls Royces and diamond stickpins and
bodyguards and throwing money around with all these fine-look-
ing broads on their arm, it gets you wondering. I know myself,
I'm from a pretty well-to-do family, I have never been in want of
anything in my whole life, except narcotics. Anything I asked for,
I got. I had broken rules—when I was sixteen, I had secured an
automobile. Through a forged birth certificate. It wasn't completely legal, but I drove around. I was a big shot in the neighborhood. Everybody looked up to me. There goes Danny in his
big Buick convertible!

Everybody wants to be recognized. And to be recognized as
an Al Capone, it's a great thing for these people. It gives them a
chance. I have a cousin who's been to college six years; he's
gonna be a psychiatrist. I talk to him; I think I'm of an intelligence to understand some of the things he tries to explain to me.
And right now I'm a common laborer—I'm a painter by trade, I
paint apartments in housing projects. And I make $127 a week,
union scale. I'm bringing home more money right now than my
cousin who works for the Board of Education as a clinical psychologist! Those are the things that warp the youth today; that's

what's warping me. This false sense of values—everybody has a price. That's what children are taught today.

Recently in the papers there's seventeen boys from well-to-do families in Queens arrested for 500 burglaries and fencing. Now these boys were offered help by a psychiatrist. Now I know this case personally; I know all the defendants in this case. I know all the parents. To my knowledge, this is a shyster move on the part of the families, pooling their funds to secure this psychiatrist, who's head of a clinic in Forest Hills. He is probably going to say all these boys are mentally disturbed, and offer for a dismissal of the case, pending that they have psychiatric treatment. Which will last for approximately a week. I have had the same circumstances for myself. I've had a shyster psychiatrist say that I was not well, and after everything was dropped he declared me sane again. And the probation officer dropped the case. That's what the youth today learns. How do they expect them, when they send them to institutions to be helped for narcotics, to be helped?

When you get in the hospital the first thing they do is give you sedation, they put you to sleep, they keep you in a state of complete obliviousness for a week. And then they tell you you're cured of your narcotics habit, go home. When you go home you're not really cured; all you do is tell all the boys in the neighborhood about, man, what a hospital this hospital was! I went up there and ate steak, and lamb chops, and milk! Which some of these boys don't eat when they're home. They're getting it the first time in the hospital, and talking about, man, free dope! This isn't solving the problem. There has to be another way to do it.

It got to the point once where I wanted to quit. I'd gotten to the stage where I felt I would go out and commit a robbery of some type. I knew I was on the verge of violating a law. So I went to my parents and asked help. I explained the situation, I was a dope addict. At first everybody got excited and nobody knew how to handle it, so I tried to help. I explained to them that there's only one right way to do it, and that's cold turkey. I explained that I would like everything removed from my bedroom. My father and my uncle and two cousins much older than I came in a bare room—all it was was a nine by twelve room, with nothing in it, a bare floor. I was told I could secrete on the floor, I could vomit—anything I wanted to do. Just stay in here. And I asked them to please not let me out for at least four days, and if possible to keep me there a week. This went on for five days. They stayed there around the clock. They changed shifts like changing of the guard at Buckingham Palace. And I kicked my habit.

But I found one thing. What that did was open a door to me. You see, kicking the first time is the hard one. I didn't know what to expect; I heard so much about it. You die, you're in agony, you suffer, you carry on something terrible. I admit it: I carried on something terrible, I suffered, I vomited, I threw up, I sweated, I chilled—I did everything that all addicts do when they kick. And I had been on some strong narcotics at the time.

But—it's like a kid. When you take a kid, and he beats you up all your life, you're afraid of him. And when you beat up this kid, you flex your muscles every time you see him. Because finally you beat him. And it's the same thing. I had feared withdrawal so bad that when I finally accomplished complete withdrawal— conquered the physical aspects of it—I felt very good and I was flexing my muscles. I was ripe right then to get addicted again. Because I knew, well, I know what it is to kick now, and I think it's possible. The human mind is an irrational mind at times like that. You say well, I got it beaten. I won, I'm not dead. I can take another beating, it won't kill me. And that's the way I looked at it.

I stayed off it approximately a month. And I was running around with the same boys. It was a test of will power to myself. I did this on my own. I hung out with my old cronies, I carried on all the scenes they made: I went to the dances—they blew pot, I refused; they shot up heroin, I refused. I refused everything for one month, and at the end of the month I said to myself, Danny, you have the will power. Now it's up to you. If you want to do it, go ahead. But in my heart I knew that anytime I wanted to, I could stop.

Physically, I find now that it's impossible. Eventually, you do get hooked. You get hooked physically. Mentally, the aspect may take twenty-thirty years; you may never get cured. The mental outlook is a very hard subject to go into. But to institutionalize people is very wrong in a narcotics problem. It won't help them. It only makes them bitter.

I don't want to condemn Riverside, I've never been there. I

have been to Lexington, Kentucky, at the federal hospital. And I found that, speaking to people about Riverside, it's a home away from home. The boys say, look, man, let me get high. Let me catch a habit. Who cares? What's the consequences? If worst comes to worst, they send me up to North Brother Island, I kick my habit, I eat good, I come out sixty-five pounds heavier, I look like a million dollars with a sun tan, and everything is great. I'm healthy again, and I'm ripe to start again. This is what it is: it's a big merry-go-round.

The boys don't want to get off. It's like a child with sex. You ask a little boy what he's gonna do. Go out and play with the girls? No no no, I wanna play with the boys, I don't want to be with the girls. But when he comes into his teens and he finally has an experience with a girl, sexually, all he does now when he sees girls with big fannies, he's out after girls and running after girls. He's had his taste. It's the same thing with narcotics. Once you have your taste, you just keep running and running and running.

I have a cousin that had been an addict since 1949. He got out of Lexington, Kentucky, in February. He got married. He died two months later, in April, in Miami Beach, Florida, of an overdose of narcotics. Now this is in my own family. I should sit down and feel terrible about it, because we were very close. We were more or less junkies-under-the-skin, so to speak. But I know that he played the game, and he paid. Because he played wrong. The idea is to be careful. I'm careful now. I don't want to hurt anybody; I don't want to hurt myself. I just want to achieve the better things I can out of life.

Today, the world is in such a turmoil that the pressure on youth, and the people not understanding us, it's just terrible. The boys have nothing to do; they're bored with themselves. You take a boy nineteen years old. His friend has a car so he buys a car. And the first thing you know the car gets him in trouble. He's joy-riding all hours of the night, drinking beer. It's the same thing. Some boys find that narcotics is a lot cleaner and easier than alcohol, because if you take whisky you have to drink for hours. Whereas if you take narcotics you feel the effect within a few seconds. That's the easy way.

I've taken about six overdoses. One overdose I've taken was

on Rivington and Avenue D. I was out for thirteen hours; I thought I died. But when I woke up, came to, and all these boys was there, I really felt indebted to these fellows for not leaving, for sticking to me for thirteen hours. Now thirteen hours when you say it in numbers is nothing. But in reality, when you're unconscious from an overdose of narcotics, it's a lifetime. I died and was born again in that time. And I feel that I owe these boys something.

I was on a landing in a hallway, one landing down from the roof. I was injected with salt into my veins—I don't know if that has any effect at all, to be honest—and rubbing and massaging, trying to keep the blood circulating through my body. They inject the salt water with the same needle they use the heroin with. It's just that to call up an ambulance and to say there's somebody up here took an overdose of narcotics, we know the treatment that's gonna happen. The ambulance takes three hours to get there. The police come, they'll beat your brains in. They're liable to find you and say they found dope in your pocket. Which we know isn't true. If a dope addict is unconscious from an overdose, there's nothing in his pockets. Because addicts today do not take off by themselves. Everybody wants somebody there, just in case, because there's been an epidemic of bad narcotics. And everybody's afraid.

I took an overdose, and upon being out and coming to, I felt that this was it. I was quitting. But when you go out, everything is so white and pure. The world goes by. You don't care about anything, you have no worries. You're not thinking about Mom paying the telephone bill or your wife being sick. Everything is so great. I want to do everything for everybody. I may act a little spooky and groggy, and appear to be not in my senses, but really I'm in my senses, more so than a lot of people believe. Nothing goes past your hearing; everything is extra-sensitive as far as your hearing goes. The only thing that's numb is your thinking mind. You can't think abstractly, you can't think of the future. You just think for now.

About cops and bribery, I wouldn't like to talk about what other boys tell me, because I don't hold too much to a narcotic addict's word; a lot of it is fantasy. I will say this has happened to me. There is a neighborhood cop, he knows what I'm up to, he

knows I'm an addict, he knows that I do things in the neighborhood concerning drugs. He watches me every time he sees me;
he'll tail me for hours. Twice he stopped me. And I was sick both
times, in dire need of a fix. And he looked in my pocket, and
there, sure enough, he found an eighth of heroin. Which I know
was not there, because I know at the time he "found" it, my goal
was to secure narcotics. The agent had put it there, and he
threatened me.

Another time I was stopped in a brand-new car. It was my
own, I had bought it from my hard-earned money. It had nothing to do with narcotics; I have never peddled narcotics to that
extent. I have peddled narcotics among my own friends, in my
immediate club. If I had bought $40 worth, I could afford to sell
$20 to my friends, and save them a trip up to Harlem. But what
happened was I got stopped, and at this time I had about $300 in
my pocket. A narcotics agent took the $300 and said it was money
I had earned pushing dope. He refused to give it back, and said
if I put up a big stink I'd find myself in the seventh precinct. So,
of course, being a narcotic addict and not wanting to be arrested,
I gave him the money and never said anything about it. Because
my word is nothing. I'm the bad guy.

This one policeman told me, he said, look, Danny, you just
come home. I have this circular, I got the wire on you, you're
here, I know what you're up to. You're still an addict, you're still
associating with the same people. I'm gonna catch you. It'll take
me a week or two, and you bastard, if I don't catch you, I'm
gonna frame you. You're going back anyway. So get out of the
neighborhood; don't get into trouble.

Now things like that, where there were no grounds for it. . . .
All right, I admit, I might have had narcotics hidden on me. But
he didn't find them. That does not give him the grounds to call
me guilty. He's supposed to call me innocent till I'm proven
guilty.

This Harry Anslinger, the head of the Federal Narcotics
Commission. I had two of his agents come down to the precinct
and question me when I was arrested. They offered me a deal:
they told me if I gave names and places, I would go home on a
state robbery charge. It just shows you how the two agencies work
hand in hand. The federal agent promised that if they had the
names, he could sway the state into dropping the robbery

charges. It doesn't give a guy the sense of values that he's supposed to have. It shows you that there's graft and corruption.

Two fellows get arrested; one fellow has $800 in his pocket. Who goes away? Of course, the boy that had no money. The boy that had the $800, he doesn't go to jail; he gets a boot in the pants and get home, and don't let me see you in the neighborhood. This has been going on, but nobody believes it. It's the same cry all the time: aah, he's a junkie! He's looking for a way out, so he's making the police a patsy. But it isn't so.

The police, they're undermanned. They're going about apprehending narcotics addicts. They should leave the darn addict alone. Don't get the addict, he's helpless. Get the pusher. Not the pusher that's selling it so he could get a fix. He's not really a pusher. He buys ten dollars' worth of narcotics and takes an eighth and cuts it into two sixteenths. He sells you a sixteenth for ten dollars, so he gets his fix free. He's not a pusher; it's the guy dealing in the ounces—$350 an ounce, $475 an ounce—these are the businessmen. They don't take narcotics themselves, but they sell it. They beg you to sell it for them.

It's not like it used to be. They give drugs on consignment these days. It's been offered to me on numerous occasions—take three ounces of pure heroin. It's not pure—it would come out about eighty-six per cent on a police meter. Anyway, I could get a good grade of heroin—three ounces for $750. That's the bargain for buying the three ounces in a batch. Now I can bag this up into five-dollar bags, and I can turn over exactly 340 percent over the price I pay. So even a small nobody, a nothing like me, a street dope addict, if I had the initial money, I can have that big car and those three-hundred-dollar suits and all those pretty girls and the money to burn. But the consequences are great.

You're working with neighborhood police, who know who's doing what, but don't say anything because it's bigger than them. They can't fight it. They're joining it. They'd rather accept the fifty dollars under the table to forget this bar and forget that there's junkies hanging out in the bar. They're not in there to arrest them. They know where they hang out; they're there all the time. We're not stupid, we know their cars. We know twenty minutes before they're in the neighborhood that they're coming, so when they get there they don't find anything. But I give them credit for the arrests they do make, if they're honest arrests. Because the dope addict will fight back; he fears going to the city jail, because that means kicking cold turkey right there.

From meeting them and seeing them, I'd say that out of every ten dope addicts, three are girls. Girls are a big factor in making boys dope addicts, believe it or not. Let's face it. You take a quiet guy, a little backward and shy, the potential raper, the guy that has trouble getting a girlfriend. He's slow and awkward with girls; he doesn't know the female sex. He's the type of fellow that will snatch a little girl in the street and rape her. Or force a lady to do things that are perverted. You take a guy like that, and you get one of these real, so-called "hip chicks," a swinger that knows the score. She's a hustler, she's been around, she turns tricks. She'll do anything for a buck to secure her fix. She has an outlet. It's easier for a girl to secure a habit and to keep it under control, because all she has to do is lay down on the bed and there's ten dollars. She can put any price she wants on that, see? Because she's a woman, and men will buy women. Those girls take a plain ordinary joe that doesn't know too much, and they say, look honey, you can sleep with me and live with me and I'll take care of you. They give this guy his first taste of sex. And believe me, he's at their beck and call. They'll make him anything they want to make him. They'll make him a dope addict, eventually. Girls are the biggest factor in making dope addicts.

My sex drive, before narcotics, was so great that upon having intercourse with a girl, I would achieve my climax almost immediately. And I noticed something. That upon taking narcotics, it killed my sex drive. But on drugs, I was able to have sex for three-four hours at a time. Which made me feel superior over the girl. The girl was always begging me to stop, she couldn't take it, when it used to be the other way around, when I used to tell this girl, you're wearing me out, honey. I never reach a climax when I'm under the influence of narcotics, but mentally, I feel that I can satisfy the woman I'm with.

Any girl that has sexual intercourse with a dope addict will never be satisfied by a normal person. Because there are very few normal human beings on this earth that can have a sexual intercourse for three-four hours, without achieving a climax. It's almost an impossibility. Heroin will help you achieve that effect.

And you'd be surprised the effects when you have a few girls running after you, talking about your powers as a lady's man. It does something to your ego, and your super-ego, and you get all excited and you go out and you do sillier things to prove it.

I don't know the figures on narcotics addiction in New York City, but I will say that of the narcotic addicts that I know personally, I found that eight out of ten have never been arrested and are not known addicts. So therefore, whatever figures the state and the federal might have, the number of addicts is actually five times larger than that. You have a minority who get the blame for everything.

My parents were very hurt by my addiction, because I never asked for anything in my life that I didn't get it. They're trying to trust me now, 'cause I'm fresh home from Elmira Reformatory, but other than that. . . . There's the sneaky look at my armpit, to see if I have any new marks. It's where ya goin?—it's eleven o'clock! I'm a boy of twenty-four and that bothers me, that annoys me. I'm not a baby, I want to be a man. I feel I'm strong enough to take care of myself right now, even though I use narcotics. I use narcotics that I feel I have control over. I've proved it to myself on numerous occasions. When narcotics have gotten the best of me, I went into seclusion for a few weeks, staying away from the neighborhood and my old friends.

But it's not that taking a boy out of his environment will keep him from using narcotics. That's wrong. I lived on the East Side all my life. While using narcotics I have met boys from Queens, Brooklyn, Bronx. . . . Now, no matter where I go, I can pick out a dope addict. You can take me to a strange neighborhood where I've never been, with people I don't even know, put one dope addict in the crowd, give me twenty minutes and I'll pick him out. It's like a brother club. One junkie knows another junkie. You smell each other.

It's not a matter of take him away. I was taken away. They moved me to Queens, in one of the most exclusive parts of Jamaica, Long Island. And I find narcotics addicts. I might not find the type of narcotic addict I find on the East Side now, because of the big migration of Puerto Rican and Negro into the neighborhood. The older addicts are Irish, Jewish and Italian. But I find dope addicts. If I don't find a C.P.A. that's a dope addict, I find a lawyer, I find a sculptor, I find them all over.

These are the lucky few. They have never been to court, so they're not considered addicts, they're not statistics. But they do exist.

Living out in Jamaica Estates, I migrate to Harlem to get my narcotics. Harlem is the center-point for narcotics in the New York area. From 100th Street to 140th Street is narcotics row. Narcotics can be got very easy, it's not too much trouble, most of the policemen are paid off, and the ones that aren't—they're not out for the big people. The big people pay too much. The big people are covered. When they do a business that turns in twenty thousand dollars a week, they're not letting a little patrolman—a nothing that makes $5,800 a year—arrest them. They pay him. They give him a thousand dollars. A thousand dollars is gold to this officer, I don't care who he is. It's very tempting.

I have worked for this lady up in Harlem, around the corner from the Park Palace. I have been there one night when there was a raid. I was up there for the purpose of securing one-quarter of an ounce of heroin. I wasn't up there to buy weight, so-called, ounces. As a personal favor from this girl to me, she was giving me a quarter of pure heroin. It was a raid. The cops came in, money was passed, the cops walked out. Nobody was arrested. When I came downstairs I seen what they did. They had arrested two junkies on the street—street junkies. Poor, helpless creatures. They didn't arrest her. She's probably still in circulation to this day. Because she pays, and she pays big and to the right people.

I feel that if they legalized narcotics to a certain degree, that would kill half of the narcotics problem. If you look at the crime statistics in New York City, they say that crime is up 50 per cent. And the crimes are committed by dope addicts. We don't have a big crime rate in New York City, we definitely do not—it's the dope addict, the guy who boosts a pocketbook from an open car, he takes a camera or he goes in a candy store and boosts a box of candy—or something. This is what makes a big crime rate. Of every five thousand burglaries, all but three hundred are by dope addicts that couldn't help themselves.

If they had some sort of system where narcotics could be administered free of charge, or for costs, it would kill the black-market trade. We're not strong enough to kill it otherwise; it's run by a lot of people with a lot of money that runs into millions and billions, and they're not letting anybody push them out. They like money. They smuggle in dope on planes and on boats —with their merchant marine friends that I know bring stuff in.

Now you open up a clinic and you take away the main incentives of a dope addict. You take away the adventure in it. There's no more adventure; it becomes hospitalization. Dope addicts thrive on this adventure of running around and going to buy it and getting off without getting caught. And then sitting and being with all the boys and *talking* about how it felt. That would be taken away. There wouldn't be all this scariness, and all the worries. It wouldn't get to the point where you would get addicted—and even if you did get addicted, it could be controlled to a degree. If a dope addict can be maintained so that he will not get sick, he will not commit a crime. He will be content not to be sick.

What they do is they make it hard for the dope addict to get dope, they make the prices go up and the business illicit, and the addict has to steal. He has to do something to keep up with it.

So I feel they should have some sort of a clinic, where you can come in and get fingerprinted if you want to be a known addict. Let it be known! If you want to be an addict, don't be ashamed of it. Take your card, go in, get your thing to keep you happy. It would kill the crime and they'd live a happy life.

There would be a few that would want more than whatever the clinic would be administering. If the clinic was giving just enough to keep them satisfied and not on cloud nine, they'd want a little extra so they could get up to cloud nine. That kind of illicit drug trade you can't stop. But taking the adventure away would kill a lot of the drugs. It would stop a lot of these young schoolboys that are ripe for picking. There wouldn't be anything interesting to them; it would be just a bore.

Take any kid. You just walk up and say, you want to be a junkie? I'll get you a fix. But you gotta go down to Joe's Hospital with me. He wouldn't want it. What is it to walk into a hospital? It's a cold institution where somebody sticks a needle in your arm, you get a fix and you go back. They don't want that.

The teenagers today are standing on the street corners and

sitting in the luncheonettes. They're talking baloney. *Nothing* to talk about—they're beat for conversation. They're not intellectuals. They ain't even pseudo-intellectuals. They just stand there. And when somebody offers them a cloak-and-dagger game, it's like taking a kid and giving him cowboys-and-Indians, or let's-play-soldier. They enjoy it. It gives them something to do, it keeps their mind occupied.

How to beat the cop on the beat? How to beat the narcotic agent who's sneaking up on you in the hallway? You think at the time that your mind is working. Your mind isn't working—I know that now. But I feel that I can't be helped, because I have found in drugs something to keep me calm, collected. I'm happy with the knowledge I have; I think I can make my way in the world. But I want to be an honest citizen. I don't want to hurt people, I don't want to bother anybody. I'm just content—like somebody comes home and has his five beers, I want to come home and be able to smoke marijuana, take a shot of dope.

I find marijuana never to be habit-forming. I feel that the only reason they don't legalize marijuana is that the liquor industry and the A.B.C. [Alcoholic Beverage Control Board] would go crazy. Let's figure it out. Take a couple, they go into a bar. It takes eight dollars to drink before they feel a little giddy. Where marijuana, with sixteen cents for one stick, puts you in the same state as twenty dollars' worth of liquor. And it has no after effects. I've had two occasions to drink—once I drank rye and once I drank scotch. And I had some head in the morning; I had a hangover, I was sick, I was nauseous—all the works. I smoked three sticks of marijuana, I was loaded all night, I woke up in the morning and never even knew I did it. Everything was good.

Marijuana made my senses more alert—more so than heroin. Heroin calms me down, more like a tranquilizer. Whereas marijuana made me lively, like whisky. It made me a little boisterous. Everything is funny, whole world is a big joke.

And I feel the only reason they never make it legal is the A.B.C. My ideas may be warped, I grant you that. I need help, I know I need help. I want to help myself; I eventually will, in time. But fighting people with a lot of money, you can't.

18 *A consideration of human evolution as it is to be affected by the "consciousness-expanding" drugs.*

The politics of consciousness expansion

timothy leary
richard alpert

EXPANSION-CONTRACTION. The tension between the flowing process and the fixed structure.

Inorganic processes: The expanding gaseous cloud whirls into temporary patterned structures. The structures always changing, hurtling towards eventual entropy.

Organic processes: Watery, electro-biochemical globules cluster into cells. Cells cluster into temporary hardened forms (vegetative or animal), themselves always changing, eventually returning to the entropic.

Social processes: The free expansive vision is molded into the institutional. Hardly has the institutional mortar set before there is a new cortical upheaval, an explosive, often ecstatic or prophetic revelation. The prophet is promptly jailed. A hundred years later his followers are jailing the next visionary.

One is led naively to exclaim: Will man never learn the lesson of cyclical process? Must we continue to jail, execute, exile our ecstatic visionaries, and then enshrine them as tomorrow's heroes?

Naive question, which fails to appreciate the necessary tension of the expansion-contraction play. Membrane contracts. Life force bursts membrane. Establishment controls vision. Vision bursts establishment.

From *The Harvard Review*, 1 (Summer, 1963). Reprinted by permission of *The Harvard Review*.

The expansion process in physics and biology is described in evolutionary terms.

The expansion process in human affairs is defined in terms of the word "freedom."

We measure social evolution in terms of increased freedom—external or internal. Freedom to step out of the tribal game and move to construct a new social form. Freedom to move in space. Freedom to experience. Freedom to explore.

Society needs educated priest-scholars to provide structure—the intellectual muscle, bone and skin to keep things together. The university is the Establishment's apparatus for training consciousness-contractors. The intellectual ministry of defense. Defense against vision. This statement is not pejorative but a fact about evolutionary function. We need stability. We need expansion. The far-out visionary. The academic council which sits in learned judgment on Socrates, Galileo, Bacon, Columbus, Thoreau. The protagonists in these dramas are neither good nor evil. No villains, no heroes. They just are. What will be the next step in biological and social evolution? Here are two clues. (1) You are more likely to find the evolutionary agents closer to jail than to the professor's chair. (2) Look to that social freedom most abused, most magically, irrationally feared, by society. Exactly that freedom which *you,* the intellectual, the liberal, would deny to others. Good. Now you are getting close.

The administration always recognizes intuitively the next evolutionary step that will leave it behind. To cast this drama in terms of saints and pharisees is entertaining, but outmoded.

The drama is genetic. Neurophysiological.

So spare us, please, the adolescent heroics of Beethoven—Shakespeare.

Where, then, will the next evolutionary step occur? Within the human cortex. We *know,* yes we *know,* that science has produced methods for dramatically altering and expanding human awareness and potentialities. The uncharted realm lies behind your own forehead. Internal geography. Internal politics. Internal control. Internal freedom.

The nervous system can be changed, integrated, recircuited, expanded in its function. These possibilities naturally threaten every branch of the Establishment. The dangers of external change appear to frighten us less than the peril of internal change. LSD is more frightening than the Bomb!

There are two obvious avenues toward this next stage of human evolution. (1) Biochemical methods of freeing the nervous system, slowed down by heavy learned concepts and starved of tryptamine.*

We are, in a real sense, prisoners of our cognitive concepts and strategies. Passed on from generation to generation. The cognitive continuity of history. And the stuff of it is words. Our current reliance upon substantive and "closing-off" concepts will be the amused wonder of coming generations. We must entertain non-verbal methods of communication if we are to free our nervous system from the tyranny of the stifling simplicity of words.

(2) Biochemical methods of increasing cortical efficiency. "Biochemicals" in the human body, in plants, and in drugs. There exist in nature hundreds of botanical species with psychedelic ("mind-opening") powers. There exists around the indole circle a wide variety of psychedelic compounds. Cortical vitamins.

The existence of these substances has been known for thousands of years, but has been maintained as a well-guarded secret. The scarcity of botanical supply. Now, in 1963, the mind-opening substances (e.g., mescaline, LSD, psilocybin) are available for the first time in limitless, mass-produced quantities. What a threat! What a challenge! What a widespread menace!

The danger, of course, is not physical. A recent editorial in the *Medical Tribune* (March 18, 1963) clearly recognizes the physiological safety of consciousness-expanding drugs. Nor is the danger psychological. In studies reported by Ditman, McGlothlin, Leary, Savage, up to 90 percent of subjects taking these drugs in supportive environments testify enthusiastically.

The danger is not physical or psychological, but social-political. Make no mistake: the effect of consciousness-expanding drugs will be to transform our concepts of human nature, of human potentialities, of existence. The game is about to be changed, ladies and gentlemen. Man is about to make use of that fabulous electrical network he carries around in his skull. Present

---

* Tryptamine refers to chemicals found naturally in the body, in certain botanical species, and now produced synthetically. Tryptamines alter, probably speed up, synaptic function.

social establishments had better be prepared for the change. Our favorite concepts are standing in the way of a floodtide, two billion years building up. The verbal dam is collapsing. Head for the hills, or prepare your intellectual craft to flow with the current.

Let's try a metaphor. The social situation in respect to consciousness-expanding drugs is very similar to that faced sixty years ago by those crackpot visionaries who were playing around with the horseless carriage. Of course, the automobile is external child's play compared to the unleashing of cortical energy, but the social dilemma is similar.

The claim was made in 1900 that the motor carriage, accelerated to speeds several times that of the horsedrawn vehicle, would revolutionize society. Impossible to conceptualize because in 1900 we possessed no concepts for these possibilities. But we always have the standard objections to the non-conceptual. First of all, we object to the dangers: high speeds will snap nervous minds, gas fumes are fatal, the noise will prevent cows from giving milk, horses will run away, criminals will exploit the automobile.

Then the puritanical objection: people will use cars for pleasure, for kicks.

Then we question the utility: what can we do with speedy carriages? There are no men to repair them. There are no roads, few bridges. There are no skilled operators. The supply of fuel is small. Who will sell you gas?

Then we raise the problem of control: who should be allowed to own and operate these powerful and dangerous instruments? Perhaps they should be restricted to the government elite, to the military, to the medical profession.

But why do we want cars anyway? What is wrong with the good old buggy? What will happen to coachmen, blacksmiths, carriagemakers?

The automotive visionary of 1900 could have pointed out that his skeptical opponent had no concepts, no social structures to implement these possibilities. Remember, if one talks about experiences and prospects for which the listener has no concepts, then he is defined (at best) as a mystic. Our automotive mystic 60 years ago would have asserted the need for a new language, new social forms, and would have predicted that our largest national industry would inevitably develop out of this vision.

Can you imagine a language without such words as convertible, tudor sedan, General Motors, U.A.W., Standard Oil, superhighway, parking ticket, traffic court? These most commonplace terms in our present culture were mystical images three generations ago.

In totalitarian states, the use and control of instruments for external freedom—the automobile, the private airplane—are reserved for the government bureaucracy and the professional elite. Even in democracies, the traditional means for expanding or contracting consciousness (internal freedom) such as the printing press, the radio transmitter, the motion picture, are restricted by law and remain under government control.

Now consider consciousness-expanding drugs in 1963. No language. No trained operators. Lots of blacksmiths whose monopoly is threatened. A few people who do see an inevitable development of a new language, a transfiguration of every one of our social forms. And these few, of course, the ones who have taken the internal voyage.

It is possible that in 20 years our psychological and experiential language (pitifully small in English) will have multiplied to cover realms of experience and forms of thinking now unknown. In 20 years, every social institution will have been transformed by the new insights provided by consciousness-expanding experiences. Many new social institutions will have developed to handle the expressions of the potentiated nervous system.

The political issue involves control: "automobile" means that the free citizen moves *his* own car in external space. Internal automobile. Auto-administration. The freedom and control of one's experiential machinery. Licensing will be necessary. You must be trained to operate.* You must demonstrate your proficiency to handle consciousness-expanding drugs without danger to yourself or the public. The Fifth Freedom—the freedom to

---

* To bring the discussion from the verbal-controversial down to the more practical: a psychedelic "driving school" will open in Mexico on May 1, 1963, in a panoramic Mexican village, Zihuatanejo. There, during the next 22 months, manuals, chemicals, and guides will be available for training those who want proficiency in consciousness expansion.

expand your own consciousness—cannot be denied without due
cause.

A final hint to those who have ears to hear. The open cortex
produces an ecstatic state. The nervous system operating free of
learned abstraction is a completely adequate, completely efficient,
ecstatic organ. To deny this is to rank man's learned tribal concepts above two billion years' endowment. An irreverent act.
Trust your inherent machinery. Be entertained by the social
game you play. Remember, man's natural state is ecstatic wonder, ecstatic intuition, ecstatic accurate movement. Don't settle
for less.

19 *In her memoirs, Nell Kimball describes her high-class sporting house on Basin Street in New Orleans around the turn of the century.*

Sportin' house

stephen longstreet

You can say you never saw better people any place in town. I had put in a lot of Venice glass over the gas jets and drapes of blood-red velvet reaching to the floor and had eight girls I had picked out myself, some from as far as San Francisco, and two high yellows I called Spanish, and nobody gave a damn what they were after they went upstairs for wick dipping.

Furnishing a sporting house, and I did over three of them before I retired in 1917, called for some sense and a lot of feeling for the customer's comfort, habits and little tricks. I used only the best food and had a cook, Laccy Belle, who was with me for twenty-two years. She did all the marketing, and two darkies carried home the stuff fresh as she bought it. Lacey Belle could cook French, and she could cook Jim Brady style or American, but I never served any guests poor food or food badly cooked. Girls and gentlemen ate the best. The silver and the dishes were heavy and good. Wine came in dirty bottles with the right labels for the Johns who knew what they wanted. But for those who didn't, I had a lot of fancy bottles which we refilled from time to time with red wine and white wine from a Cajun farmer's barrels. Whiskey was the best Kentucky bourbon, and my handyman and coachman, Harry, could mix gin-fizz, tom-collins, horse's necks—all the things some sport called for to show off he'd been to Saratoga or Churchill Downs or Hot Springs.

157

Linen is a big item, and a house can go busted if that isn't watched, counted, marked, and sent to the best wash-tub mammy in town who had the top whorehouse trade. I always changed linen after every customer, but some houses did it only every day, and the cribs they just had a gray sheet on a pallet and maybe never changed it, just threw it away when nobody would lie down on it.

I never had no truck with the idea whores had hearts of gold, and I never turned a girl down because she was rabbity and jumpy, what they later called neurotic. They made the best whores sometimes. If a madame can't handle girls, she's better out of the business. The girls make or break a house, and they need a solid hand. You had to watch out for Lesbians among them, and while I didn't mind the girls doing a bit of chumming and doubling up, if I found a dildoe, I knew it had gone too far. Girls that become libertines with each other don't satisfy the johns because they are involved with themselves.

I had a lot of girls who were mulatto, what they call *metisse*, *negrillonne*, and from Brazil *caboclo* and *mulato*. If they couldn't pass as Spanish I'd turn them over to a madame that ran a nigger house. I never ran anything but a white whorehouse with a little color, you might say, for flavor. I was firm but I got no pleasure from making their life mean—as one or two madames did.

I'd punish the girls with fines, and if they got real out of line I'd have Harry work them over, but not bruise them. This may sound mean and cruel, I suppose, but they were often wild girls, a bit batty upstairs, who could do harm if they went off the deep end. And once a house gets a reputation as having girls who don't act right with the customers you might just as well close up and turn out the red light in the front of the place and throw away the key.

I paid the girls one third of what they earned and never held back, and I didn't shark them with interest on loans I made them, or get them on drugs or have them mulcted by fancy men like some houses did. I never cottoned to the sweet daddies that attached themselves to a girl's earnings.

The girls got their money and they could do what they wanted with it. They were charged for meals, linen, room, and if they weren't fall-down drunks, I threw in the likker free. A drunk is no good as a whore. You can't hide her breath, and she doesn't do her work in style. Hookers are mean but sentimental. They cry over dogs, kittens, kids, novels, sad songs. I never cared much for a girl who came to work in a house because it was fun for her. There was a screw loose somewheres. I remember a Jew girl from a good family who was the wildest thing in the act ever to hit Basin Street. She lasted two months, tried to kill a John with a chair, and hung herself that night in the attic.

I never knew many whores to hold on to any money. But there was a half Indian girl from Oklahoma who went back and married a farm boy who became a big oil man and later a U.S. congressman.

I always ran a tight house the way a good captain runs a tight ship. Mornings a house was like a tomb. The girls sleeping and Harry hosing down the plant boxes and sidewalks, the shutters up. Inside Lacey Belle and two maids were cleaning up the cigar trays, sweeping, dusting, rubbing out the wet glass stains and sorting out the linen. There was no use making any dinner because it wasn't until two o'clock that some of the girls would yell down to the maids to shake their black ass and bring up coffee. The girls were pretty weak stomached till the coffee came. And I had to watch the lushes didn't get any likker.

I insisted everybody be down at four o'clock for supper. And I made them wash, do their hair before they came down, and wear clean robes or peignoirs. I saw they had a good meal. No ladee da ing. A gumbo or okra soup, steak, potatoes, turkey, white meat of chicken, a river catfish fried golden, apple pie and lots of stewed fruit. One of the problems with whores is constipation. I insisted they stay regular and used cascara and rubarb. At first most didn't like the daily bath I made them take, but I didn't put in all that plumbing for just show. And after a while perfume doesn't hide the human being under it. Bidets were new to a lot of them, and one Kansas farm girl used it as foot bath till I took her in hand. Coming from the corn-husk and catalogue belt she had never seen toilet paper either.

I didn't let the girls out much, but each got a day off, and the Catholic whores were usually very pious and went to mass. You could tell when they'd been to confession. They were all wide-eyed and polite and enjoying a state of grace. I didn't let them have crucifixes in their room on the wall. One of our best customers was a very wonderful Jew gentleman who used to send each girl a basketful of wine bottles every Christmas. He later owned a string of movie places and he always sent me a season pass.

Till nine in the evening the girls sat and smoked, did their hair over, lied to each other, bragged, looked over the magazines —they hardly ever read a newspaper till the funnies were popular.

They were always borrowing from each other and in debt to Suroyin, the old Greek bundle peddler who sold them robes, dresses, underwear and shoes against future payment. The girls who had a fancy man had to keep him happy with clothes and gambling money and bail money to get him out of jail for a slashing or a little robbery. I didn't allow the fancy men in the place, but once a month they could come to dinner on a Sunday.

Nine o'clock the three darkies would start the music in the front parlor, and the piano player would be noodling on the baby grand in the back parlor, which was the parlor for the big muckamucks, the city hall boys, the state capitol gents, the better family folk, out-of-town actors. (John Barrymore's father left a top hat I kept around for a year.)

A stray customer would maybe show around ten and ask for a girl. If he looked a bit out of place, I'd say, "I'm sorry, we're closed by a death in the family." The sports didn't start coming in till after a late supper near ten. I'd ring a bell for one of the nigger maids to ask some of the girls to come down. I *never* called out, "Company, girls," or as some did, "Gentleman callers, ladies." I let the maid usher the girls in.

By midnight the place on a good night would have a dozen to twenty men in both parlors, the girls circulating and the maids passing out drinks. I used high class nigger help, and the girls would not jump at being pinched in the derriere or boobs, but beyond that I'd move in and say we catered to gentlemen and I was sure he was one. No one well bred would talk back to that.

Most of the girls were dressed in evening gowns I had approved of. They had the damndest taste for frou-frou and feathers. I didn't allow much piling up of hair with rats or pads unless they had a customer who was all for hair. Some of the girls dressed as jockeys in tight white pants, caps and patent leather boots or as school girls in buckle shoes, big blue hair bows.

I always liked trade that was steady and came back and could find a way to feel at home away from home, you might say. An old client and his visitors were welcome, and any passing prizefighter (white), actor, senator or judge. I didn't care much for just trade off the street, and in good times I discouraged it.

The girls got cold tea in their drinks, but every fifth round I'd give them a belt of rye. Champagne was a bullseye for them, and they'd save their corks. They got a dollar a cork. I didn't like loud girls or bold girls. But I always kept a self-starter around, a girl who worked on shy Johns, or adolescents down from college getting their cherry copped. She had to make the advances but not frighten them off. A house that got a rumor going against it as a place where shyness or impotence couldn't be brought round, lost a good part of its special trade.

By two in the morning the rooms were all occupied and I'd be drinking with the waiting customers, and the girls would sort of slide downstairs again, their faces refreshed and their hair combed. I'd make introductions and manage at the same time to get the fee, if I hadn't gotten it in advance. And I'd see the departing guest to the door, being sure all likker and breakage was paid for. Some of the old trade I remember, a magistrate, a court judge, used to kiss me on the cheek goodnight and give me a pat on the fanny.

I had a housekeeper—usually an old dyke—and she kept order upstairs and took care of the linens. By three the crowd business was petering off. The all-night tricks, Johns who stayed the night, were tucked away, and on the third floor there might be a show going on, two or three of the girls doing a dance, a bit outré, just enough to set up the clients who could join in as a group or a solo. Unless a special guest asked for a little voodoo, I hardly went in for group orgies.

The girls down in the parlors sat around listening to the piano player finger a cakewalk, or the band do Stephen Foster. Around four o'clock they went up to bed; the most rabbity I gave a hooker of gin. By five unless there was a big all night ball in town, or a special boat was in and people were making the rounds of the town, I had the light turned out downstairs. Harry got the doors locked. I hardly ever opened the door to knocking, and the cop on the beat would come along and tell them to shove off.

I never counted the take till the next day—I was that bushed—but soaked my feet in hot water and one of the maids would rub my neck while I got out of my corset and into bed with a cup of hot milk and nutmeg. I was a poor sleeper as I got older, and sometimes I'd take one of the maids to bed with me and we'd just talk lazy, gab with a night-light burning, talk about the Johns, the family life the maid came from, and when the girl saw I was real woozy she'd get out of bed and I'd cork off and have a sleep until ten or eleven in the morning when I'd hear the girls coming downstairs, or Harry moving around with the big watchdog we kept by the stable, or outside testing shutters, and I'd come awake, and then it was goodbye Charlie to sleep.

Some of the madames sniffed cocaine, but my tensions were usually under control and I'd just lay there—half out—until morning light came in through the shutters, just a line of light.

I always had plenty to do, getting the police and city hall cut of the take put in envelopes, inspecting the laundry with the housekeeper, the cleaning bills, replacing busted chairs, lamps, linens. The house in the morning was still a bit strong. Body powder, Lysol, dead cigars, the woman smell of it always heavy, and spilled likker. After awhile to me a house wasn't a good house unless it had that musk smell in the morning. Lacey Belle, the cook, and me would drink our coffee in the kitchen, all the girls sleeping, and I'd read the paper and see who was at the good hotels and make bets with Lacey as to who would show up that night.

That's pretty much the average day in any house I ran. And mostly they were good and like that, and not like the whorehouses in the books and plays and later the movies. There never was a real sporting house in any of them, just men's ideas of them, the average John's idea of people they didn't know a goddamn thing about, except the dreams we were supposed to make real for them.

20

The author, once a female impersonator and later a male madam, comments on some heterosexuals and the harassment of homosexuals.

Some comments on being homosexual

kenneth marlowe

In my private life most of my friendships are with heterosexuals and they do not fear or shun me.

Many a wife is married to a homosexual and doesn't know it. And sometimes neither does *he!* Most men have done something homosexual in their lives. But *few* will admit the fact until they've accepted their homosexuality.

Kinsey put the rate of homosexual incidence quite high. And all the critics howled "Foul!" But if the rate isn't as high as that why did so many married men with children come seeking my "call boys"?

Of course, as soon as women have the ring in men's noses, they let go of the waistline, the sweet tone, and the lovely appearance fades. They're so involved with family, and children, friends and obligations, they treat their husbands like just another thing that has to be handled through their day. They should study the geisha girl, and perhaps their husbands would stay home more nights.

I've had so many married men tell me they can't stand looking at their wives that I wish I'd kept count. But men felt they weren't cheating on their wives when they're with my boys, or another man. The psychology of our American adult morality says it is "wrong" only if he has his sex with another woman,

From *Mr. Madam* by Kenneth Marlowe, published by Paperback Library, Inc., 1965. Copyright 1964 by Sherbourne Press. Reprinted by permission of Sherbourne Press.

prostitute or otherwise. When he's with the boys he's not cheating. But *he sure as hell is getting his satisfaction!*

Beware of those who talk too strongly against homosexuals or the women who yell too loudly—you should check out *their* husbands—because they must have something in their own lives to hide. They are usually associated close enough with the subject or they're too frightened, or too uneducated to know what to do about it, in their own lives.

The public is still carried along on such ancient myths that it's pathetic. Generally, homosexuals *don't* rape three year olds— boys or girls, nor do they kill people, nor do they give off a disease by being in the same room with *normal* people. Most publicized rape cases have been proven to be committed by heterosexuals. Homosexuals aren't lepers, you know. We're people.

There are no stereotypes among homosexuals just as there are none in any other area of sex. But realizing the human factor, it's understandable that the public thinks "homosexuals" seduce children.

When I waltzed down the street or sat in a movie theatre, tricked up and down the Y halls or anywhere else, *I didn't force any man to bed.* He came of his own free will. I was just available.

A *real* "straight" heterosexual wouldn't *see* me standing there on the corner or, if he did, would ignore me. Men never climb into the feathers with you unless they *want* to do so. *It is impossible to entice any adult individual into a homosexual act unless he consents.*

Being around homosexuals doesn't affect heterosexual men *if* they are *sure of themselves.* Homosexuals don't concern themselves with men who are obviously not interested.

The only men I ever found afraid of homosexuals were those who *were* unsure of themselves, who were afraid of their own state of masculinity, and feared they might *lose* it.

Borderline cases are the *haters.* They do the most yelling about and against overt homosexuals.

Heterosexuals who have to get their *kicks* by going out to "beat up queers" are the ones who are *kidding themselves.* They talk about it boldly because they have to "prove" *they* aren't homosexuals.

Homosexuals are a minority group who are denied their human rights!

The public, usually with the aid of front page newspaper publicity, confuses and links mentally deficients who commit sex crimes with all homosexuals. *Most* homosexuals are *not* sex criminals except in the eyes of the law because laws are antiquatedly against morals, which should be intelligently relegated back to the province of religion and medicine.

American police departments make a big show of "wiping out" the homosexual element in their cities because it gives them great amounts of publicity and certainly makes them *look busy* to the Public Eye. And crime is often left unsolved because they're so busy with the morals of men who don't bother *other men who are not responsive.*

Vice squad officers are another breed. They certainly are "interested" in their work! Too many of them are *enjoying* the sexual favors of their entrapments *before* they get around to make the arrests. You'll never, however, find *those* statistics available. Nobody seems to have kept them!

One of our largest west coast cities does a huge business in homosexual entrapment. Annually, the city reaps enough from aggressive Vice Squad entrapments to enrich the coffers by half a million dollars in fines. And that's big business. It pays a lot of salaries. And the whole dirty method should be shocking. It is. But the only shocking the city promotes is convincing the citizenry a lot of homosexuals are dangerous. They neglect to inform them that these same homosexuals are very profitably used.

When entrapped, each homosexual pays an average fine of $300 . . . for, inviting someone for a "cup of coffee." Or accepting an encouraging come-on, only to find bitter results rather than emotional pleasure.

If homosexuals ever organized, banding together for mutual protection and rights, like other minorities, they could exist without bondage as long as they publicly behaved themselves as thinking adults.

21
A jazz musician finds that his performance becomes a little different under the influence of marihuana.

Becoming a viper

milton "mezz" mezzrow

bernard wolfe

It was that flashy, sawed-off runt of a jockey named Patrick who made a viper out of me after Leon Rappolo failed. Back in the Arrowhead Inn, where I first met Patrick, he told me he was going to New Orleans and would be back one day with some marihuana, real golden-leaf. He asked me did I want some of the stuff, and coming up tough I said sure, bring me some, I'd like to try it. When Patrick marched into the Martinique one night I began to look for the nearest exit, but it was too late. "Hi ya, boy," he said with a grin bigger than he was hisself, "let's you and me go to the can, I got something for you." That men's room might have been a death-house, the way I kept curving away from it, but this muta-mad Tom Thumb latched on to me like a ball-and-chain and steered me straight inside.

As soon as we were alone he pulled out a gang of cigarettes and handed them to me. They were as fat as ordinary cigarettes but were rolled in brown wheatstraw paper. We both lit up and I got halfway through mine, hoping they would break the news to mother gently, before he stopped me. "Hey," he said, "take it easy, kid. You want to knock yourself out?"

I didn't feel a thing and I told him so. "Do you know one thing?" he said. "You ain't even smokin' it right. You got to hold that muggle so that it barely touches your lips, see, then draw in

air around it. Say *tfff, tfff,* only breathe in when you say it. Then
don't blow it out right away, you got to give the stuff a chance."
He had a tricky look in his eye that I didn't go for at all. The last
time I saw that kind of look it was on a district attorney's mug,
and it caused me a lot of inconvenience.

After I finished the weed I went back to the bandstand.
Everything seemed normal and I began to play as usual. I passed
a stick of gauge around for the other boys to smoke, and we
started a set.

The first thing I noticed was that I began to hear my saxo-
phone as though it was inside my head, but I couldn't hear much
of the band in back of me, although I knew they were there. All
the other instruments sounded like they were way off in the
distance; I got the same sensation you'd get if you stuffed your
ears with cotton and talked out loud. Then I began to feel the
vibrations of the reed much more pronounced against my lip,
and my head buzzed like a loudspeaker. I found I was slurring
much better and putting just the right feeling into my phrases—I
was really coming on. All the notes came easing out of my horn
like they'd already been made up, greased and stuffed into the
bell, so all I had to do was blow a little and send them on their
way, one right after the other, never missing, never behind time,
all without an ounce of effort. The phrases seemed to have more
continuity to them and I was sticking to the theme without ever
going tangent. I felt I could go on playing for years without
running out of ideas and energy. There wasn't any struggle; it
was all made-to-order and suddenly there wasn't a sour note or a
discord in the world that could bother me. I began to feel very
happy and sure of myself. With my loaded horn I could take all
the fist-swinging, evil things in the world and bring them together in perfect harmony, spreading peace and joy and relaxation to all the keyed-up and punchy people everywhere. I began
to preach my millenniums on my horn, leading all the sinners on
to glory.

The other guys in the band were giggling and making
cracks, but I couldn't talk with my mouthpiece between my lips,
so I closed my eyes and drifted out to the audience with my
music. The people were going crazy over the subtle changes in
our playing; they couldn't dig what was happening but some

kind of electricity was crackling in the air and it made them all glow and jump. Every so often I opened my eyes and found myself looking straight into a girl's face right in front of the bandstand, swinging there like a pendulum. She was an attractive, rose-complexioned chick, with wind-blown honey-colored hair, and her flushed face was all twisted up with glee. That convulsed face of hers stirred up big waves of laughter in my stomach, waves that kept breaking loose and spreading up to my head, shaking my whole frame. I had to close my eyes fast to keep from exploding with the joy.

It's a funny thing about marihuana—when you first begin smoking it you see things in a wonderful soothing, easygoing new light. All of a sudden the world is stripped of its dirty gray shrouds and becomes one big bellyful of giggles, a spherical laugh, bathed in brilliant, sparkling colors that hit you like a heatwave. Nothing leaves you cold any more; there's a humorous tickle and great meaning in the least little thing, the twitch of somebody's little finger or the click of a beer glass. All your pores open like funnels, your nerve-ends stretch their mouths wide, hungry and thirsty for new sights and sounds and sensations; and every sensation, when it comes, is the most exciting one you've ever had. You can't get enough of anything—you want to gobble up the whole goddamned universe just for an appetizer. Them first kicks are a killer, Jim.

Suppose you're the critical and analytical type, always ripping things to pieces, tearing the covers off and being disgusted by what you find under the sheet. Well, under the influence of muta you don't lose your surgical touch exactly, but you don't come up evil and grimy about it. You still see what you saw before but in a different, more tolerant way, through rose-colored glasses, and things that would have irritated you before just tickle you. Everything is good for a laugh; the wrinkles get ironed out of your face and you forget what a frown is, you just want to hold on to your belly and roar till the tears come. Some women especially, instead of being nasty and mean just go off bellowing until hysteria comes on. All the larceny kind of dissolves out of them—they relax and grin from ear to ear, and get right on the ground floor with you. Maybe no power on earth can work out a lasting armistice in that eternal battle of the sexes, but muggles are the one thing I know that can even bring about an overnight order to "Cease firing."

Tea puts a musician in a real masterly sphere, and that's why so many jazzmen have used it. You look down on the other members of the band like an old mother hen surveying her brood of chicks; if one of them hits a sour note or comes up with a bad modulation, you just smile tolerantly and figure, oh well, he'll learn, it'll be better next time, give the guy a chance. Pretty soon you find yourself helping him out, trying to put him on the right track. The most terrific thing is this, that all the while you're playing, really getting off, your own accompaniment keeps flashing through your head, just like you were a one-man band. You hear the basic tones of the theme and keep up your pattern of improvisation without ever getting tangled up, giving out with a uniform sequence all the way. Nothing can mess you up. You hear everything at once and you hear it right. When you get that feeling of power and sureness, you're in a solid groove.

You know how jittery, got-to-be-moving people in the city always get up in the subway train two minutes before they arrive at the station? Their nerves are on edge; they're watching the clock, thinking about schedules, full of that high-powered mile-a-minute jive. Well, when you've picked up on some gauge that clock just stretches its arms, yawns, and dozes off. The whole world slows down and gets drowsy. You wait until the train stops dead and the doors slide open, then you get up and stroll out in slow motion, like a sleepwalker with a long night ahead of him and no appointments to keep. You've got all the time in the world. What's the rush, buddy? Take-it-easy, that's the play, it's bound to sweeten it all the way.

I kept on blowing, with my eyes glued shut, and then a strange thing happened. All of a sudden somebody was screaming in a choked, high-pitched voice, like she was being strangled, "Stop it, you're killing me! Stop! I can't stand it!" When I opened my eyes it seemed like all the people on the dance floor were melted down into one solid, mesmerized mass; it was an overstuffed sardine-can of an audience, packed in an olive-oil trance. The people were all pasted together, looking up at the band with hypnotic eyes and swaying—at first I saw just a lot of shining eyes bobbing lazily on top of a rolling sea of flesh. But off to one side there was discord, breaking the spell. An entertainer, one of the girls who did a couple of vocals and specialized in a suggestive dance routine, was having a ball all to herself. She had cut loose from her partner and was throwing herself around like a snake with the hives. The rhythm really had this queen; her eyes almost jumped out of their sockets and the cords in her neck stood out stiff and hard like ropes. What she was doing with the rest of her anatomy isn't discussed in mixed company.

"Don't do that!" she yelled. "Don't do that to me!" When she wasn't shouting her head off she just moaned way down in her soundbox, like an owl gargling.

Then with one flying leap she sailed up on the bandstand, pulled her dress up to her neck, and began to dance. I don't know if dance is the right word for what she did—she didn't move her feet hardly at all, although she moved practically everything else. She went through her whole routine, bumps and grinds and shakes and breaks, making up new twists as she went along, and I mean twists. A bandstand was sure the wrong place to do what she was trying to do that night. All the time she kept screaming, "Cut it out! It's murder!" but her body wasn't saying no.

It was a frantic scene, like a nightmare walking, and it got wilder because all the excitement made us come on like gangbusters to accompany this palsy-bug routine. Patrick and his gang of vipers were getting their kicks—the gauge they picked up on was really in there, and it had them treetop tall, mellow as a cello. Monkey Pollack stood in the back, moving a little less than a petrified tree, only his big lips shaking like meatballs with the chills, and the Ragtime Cowboy Jew was staring through the clouds of smoke as though he was watching a coyote do a toe-dance. That girl must have been powered with Diesel engines, the way she kept on going. The sweat was rolling down her screwed-up face like her pores were faucets, leaving streaks of mascara in the thick rouge. She would have made a scarecrow do a nip-up and a flip.

The tension kept puffing up like an overstuffed balloon, and finally it broke. There was the sharp crack of pistol shots ringing through the sweat and strain. Fear clamped down over the sea of faces like a mask, and the swaying suddenly stopped.

It was only Mac, our gunplayful cowboy bartender. Whenever he got worked up he would whip out his pistols and fire at the ceiling, catching the breaks in our music. The excitement that night was too much for him and to ease his nerves he was taking potshots at the electric bulbs, with a slap-happy grin on his kisser. Every time he pulled the trigger another Mazda crossed the Great Divide—he may have been punchy but his trigger finger didn't know about it.

The girl collapsed then, as though somebody had yanked the backbone right out of her body. She fell to the floor like a hunk of putty and lay in a heap, quivering and making those funny noises way down in her throat. They carried her upstairs and put her to bed, and I guess she woke up about six weeks later. Music sure hath charms, all right, but what it does to the savage breast isn't always according to the books.

The bandstand was only a foot high but when I went to step down it took me a year to find the floor, it seemed so far away. I was sailing through the clouds, flapping my free-wheeling wings, and leaving the stand was like stepping off into space. Twelve months later my foot struck solid ground with a jolt, but the other one stayed up there on those lovely soft clouds, and I almost fell flat on my face. There was a roar of laughter from Patrick's table and I began to feel self-conscious and nauseous at the same time. I flew to the men's room and got there just in time. Patrick came in and started to laugh at me.

"What's the matter, kid?" he said. "You not feeling so good?" At that moment I was up in a plane, soaring around the sky, with a buzz-saw in my head. Up and around we went, saying nuts to Newton and all his fancy laws of gravitation, but suddenly we went into a nosedive and I came down to earth, sock. Ouch. My head went spattering off in more directions than a hand grenade. Patrick put a cold towel to my temples and I snapped out of it. After sitting down for a while I was all right.

When I went back to the stand I still heard all my music amplified, as though my ear was built right into the horn. The evening rolled away before I knew it. When the entertainers sang I accompanied them on the piano, and from the way they kept glancing up at me I could tell they felt the harmonies I was inventing behind them without any effort at all. The notes kept sliding out of my horn like bubbles in seltzer water. My control over the vibrations of my tones was perfect, and I got a terrific lift from the richness of the music, the bigness of it. The notes eased out like lava running down a mountain, slow and sure and steaming. It was good.

The Muslim program

muhammad speaks

WHAT THE MUSLIMS BELIEVE

1. *WE BELIEVE in the One God Whose proper Name is Allah.*
2. *WE BELIEVE in the Holy Qur-an and in the Scriptures of all the Prophets of God.*
3. *WE BELIEVE in the truth of the Bible, but we believe that it has been tampered with and must be reinterpreted so that mankind will not be snared by the falsehoods that have been added to it.*
4. WE BELIEVE in Allah's Prophets and the Scriptures they brought to the people.
5. WE BELIEVE in the resurrection of the dead—not in physical resurrection—but in mental resurrection. We believe that the so-called Negroes are most in need of mental resurrection; therefore, they will be resurrected first.

     Furthermore, we believe we are the people of God's choice, as it has been written, that God would choose the rejected and the despised. We can find no other persons fitting this description in these last days more than the so-called Negroes in America. We believe in the resurrection of the righteous.
6. WE BELIEVE in the judgement; we believe this first judgement will take place as God revealed, in America . . .
7. WE BELIEVE this is the time in history for the separation of the so-called Negroes and the so-called white

Reprinted by permission of *Muhammad Speaks.*

Americans. We believe the black man should be freed in name as well as in fact. By this we mean that he should be freed from the names imposed upon him by his former slave masters. Names which identified him as being the slave master's slave. We believe that if we are free indeed, we should go in our own people's names—the black peoples of the earth.

8. WE BELIEVE in justice for all, whether in God or not; we believe as others, that we are due equal justice as human beings. We believe in equality—as a nation—of equals. We do not believe that we are equal with our slave masters in the status of "freed slaves."

   We recognize and respect American citizens as independent peoples and we respect their laws which govern this nation.

9. *WE BELIEVE that the offer of integration is hypocritical and is made by those who are trying to deceive the black peoples into believing that their 400-year-old open enemies of freedom, justice, and equality are, all of a sudden, their "friends." Furthermore, we believe that such deception is intended to prevent black people from realizing that the time in history has arrived for the separation from the whites of this nation.*

   If the white people are truthful about their professed friendship toward the so-called Negro, they can prove it by dividing up America with their slaves.

   We do not believe that America will ever be able to furnish enough jobs for her own millions of unemployed, in addition to jobs for the 20,000,000 black people as well.

10. WE BELIEVE that we who declared ourselves to be righteous Muslims, should not participate in wars which take the lives of humans. We do not believe this nation should force us to take part in such wars, for we have nothing to gain from it unless America agrees to give us the necessary territory wherein we may have something to fight for.

11. WE BELIEVE our women should be respected and protected as the women of other nationalities are respected and protected.

12. *WE BELIEVE that Allah (God) appeared in the Person*

*of Master W. Fard Muhammad, July, 1930; the long-
awaited "Messiah" of the Christians and the "Mahdi" of
the Muslims.*

*We believe further and lastly that Allah is God and
besides HIM there is no God and He will bring about a
universal government of peace wherein we all can live in
peace together.*

WHAT THE MUSLIMS WANT

*This is the question asked most frequently by both the
whites and the blacks. The answers to this question I shall state
as simply as possible.*

1. We want freedom. We want a full and complete freedom.

*2. We want justice. Equal justice under the law. We want
justice applied equally to all, regardless of creed or class or color.*

3. We want equality of opportunity. We want equal membership in society with the best in civilized society.

*4. We want our people in America whose parents or grandparents were descendants from slaves, to be allowed to establish a
separate state or territory of their own—either on this continent
or elsewhere. We believe that our former slave masters are obligated to provide such land and that the area must be fertile and
minerally rich. We believe that our former slave masters are
obligated to maintain and supply our needs in this separate territory for the next 20 to 25 years—until we are able to produce
and supply our own needs.*

*Since we cannot get along with them in peace and equality,
after giving them 400 years of our sweat and blood and receiving
in return some of the worst treatment human beings have ever
experienced, we believe our contributions to this land and the
suffering forced upon us by white America, justifies our demand
for complete separation in a state or territory of our own.*

5. We want freedom for all Believers of Islam now held in
federal prisons. We want freedom for all black men and women
now under death sentence in innumerable prisons in the North
as well as the South.

We want every black man and woman to have the freedom

to accept or reject being separated from the slave master's children and establish a land of their own.

We know that the above plan for the solution of the black and white conflict is the best and only answer to the problem between two people.

6. We want an immediate end to the police brutality and mob attacks against the so-called Negro throughout the United States.

We believe that the Federal government should intercede to see that black men and women tried in white courts receive justice in accordance with the laws of the land—or allow us to build a new nation for ourselves, dedicated to justice, freedom and liberty.

7. As long as we are not allowed to establish a state or territory of our own, we demand not only equal justice under the laws of the United States, but equal employment opportunities —NOW!

We do not believe that after 400 years of free or nearly free labor, sweat and blood, which has helped America become rich and powerful, that so many thousands of black people should have to subsist on relief, charity or live in poor houses.

8. We want the government of the United States to exempt our people from ALL taxation as long as we are deprived of equal justice under the laws of the land.

9. We want equal education—but separate schools up to 16 for boys and 18 for girls on the condition that the girls be sent to women's colleges and universities. We want all black children educated, taught and trained by their own teachers.

Under such schooling system we believe we will make a better nation of people. The United States government should provide, free, all necessary text books and equipment, schools and college buildings. The Muslim teachers shall be left free to teach and train their people in the way of righteousness, decency and self respect.

10. We believe that intermarriage or race mixing should be prohibited. We want the religion of Islam taught without hinderance or suppression.

These are some of the things that we, the Muslims, want for our people in North America.

23

An English career criminal discusses the philosophy of his occupation.

On being a criminal

tony parker

robert allerton

My first question is this: If you were to describe yourself in one word, would the description invariably be 'A criminal'?

Yes, definitely. That's what I am, I never think of myself in any other way.

And have you any intention of changing, of going straight or reforming?

None whatsoever. There's one thing, though, I'd like to make clear right at the start—and that is, I don't want to try and pass myself off as a 'master criminal' or anything like that. I'm not. I've had successes and failures in life like everyone else, and I'm nothing out of the ordinary as far as criminals go. I don't consider myself cleverer than most, or even cleverer than the police, for example: sometimes I have been, and quite obviously sometimes not. On the whole I'd say I was just the ordinary run of professional criminal, similar to—well, let's say to a bank clerk from Surbiton in the straight world. But having said that, still definitely 'a criminal', yes.

And would you say your earnings were comparable with those of a Surbiton bank clerk?

I don't know what he'd earn—quite honestly, I don't know how much I've made in my time either, because I haven't kept accounts to show to the income tax. My earnings have usually

From *The Courage of His Convictions* by Tony Parker and Robert Allerton. Copyright 1962 by Tony Parker. Reprinted by permission of Hutchinson & Co., Ltd.

been large sums of money spread over short periods of time—both in the getting and the spending. I've gone into a club, a gambling place, not once but many times, with two or three hundred quid in my pocket—and come out with exactly nothing. One time a girl took sixty quid out of my pocket and I never even noticed it'd gone until somebody told me months afterwards she'd had it. And at other times I've had only about fourpence in the world. It's so irregular, you see, it's difficult to say just how much I have had from crime. I should say that if I worked it all out with pencil and paper, relying on my memory which is faulty at the best of times, and then dividing the whole lot by ten or twelve for the number of years I've been at it seriously . . . well, it'd come out at about £2000 or £2500 a year, perhaps a little bit more. We'd better change that first idea to a bank *manager* from Surbiton, I suppose, hadn't we? Still, the point's the same: that sort of figure, which is as near as I can get on a calculation, is not a tremendously rich living from crime or anything else, is it? Especially when you take into account how quick I spend it when I've got it. All the same, I don't know of a straight job I could do that'd bring me in that yearly income.

Is there any particular form of crime, or criminal activity, which you wouldn't commit?

A year or two ago I used to think I'd never go in for drug trafficking, but now I'm not so sure about that. I've never actually done it yet, but as I get older I seem to be losing my inhibitions, I don't feel as strongly about it as I used to. There's only one thing I still feel I could never do, and that's poncing. To me it's the worst thing of the lot, I'd never stoop to it—or at least I hope I wouldn't. Maybe I'm old-fashioned, or sentimental about women or something—but I just can't stomach the idea of poncing at all. I've nothing but contempt, real, deep contempt, for ponces.

There's no other limit you'd set yourself?

No. I'll go as far as necessary, whatever it is.

What does that mean, exactly?

What it says. If it was ever necessary to kill somebody, well, I'd go up to and including that. I'd kill somebody in a fit of temper, I'm quite capable of that—or if they were trying to stop me getting something I'd really made up my mind to have. Or if they were holding me down, and there was so much at stake that I'd just got to get away. But I think most people have it in them to do murder at some time in their lives, under certain circumstances.

The thing which I find most difficult to understand about you is that you're apparently quite undeterred by your repeated prison sentences. You've now reached the stage, with your record, that when you're caught next time it's more than likely you'll get about eight years' preventive detention. I don't understand how you can be prepared to face that.

I'm not prepared. This is the thing which people like you can never grasp. I'm no more 'prepared' to do eight years' P.D. than you're prepared to knock somebody down in your car tomorrow. I don't think too much about the one more than you do about the other. It's an ever-present risk but one doesn't dwell on it—do you see what I mean?

I've always got this thing in my mind, and so have most other criminals like me—'it won't be this time that I'll get caught'. Prison only becomes the dominant thought when you're actually back in the prison cell—or no, to be realistic, perhaps a bit before that, when you're actually in the arms of a police officer, although even then you've still got some hope you might not end up in the nick.

Occasionally I get the vague idea that if men who'd been in prison were to go back and contemplate the prison wall from outside, just before they set out on a job, they mightn't do it. But it wouldn't work. You see, three days after you've come out of prison, however long the sentence, you've forgotten all about it. You've forgotten the caged-up feeling, the monotonous food, the smell of latrines, the piggishness of the screws, the soul-destroying torture of visiting-boxes with your friends having to shout a conversation with you through plate-glass—it's all gone, soon after you come out, and you do everything you can to make it go, too.

Then one day one of your mates comes along and says: 'I've heard of a peter wants blowing, it's got two grand in it, you want to come in on it and make one?' So you knock down the amount by 50 percent because people exaggerate, and you think: 'Well, at least I'll have a look at it, there's no harm in that.'

So he takes you along to look at the set-up, you weigh it up and work it out, and you think: 'Well, this is an absolute doddle, it can't miss; yes, of course I'll do it.' So you say to your mate: 'O.K., sure I'll come in, when do we start?' It doesn't even occur to you that there's even a chance you might get nicked, it all looks so easy. And where's your 'prepared' gone then?

I don't want to do eight years, no—but if I have to I have to, and that's all there is to it. If you're a criminal, what's the alternative to the risk of going to prison? Coal-miners don't spend their time worrying about the risk they might get killed by a fall at the coal-face either. Prison's an occupational risk, that's all—and one I'm quite prepared to take. I'll willingly gamble away a third of my life in prison, so long as I can live the way I want for the other two-thirds. After all, it's my life, and that's how I feel about it. The alternative—the prospect of vegetating the rest of my life away in a steady job, catching the 8.13 to work in the morning, and the 5.50 back again at night, all for ten or fifteen quid a week—now that really does terrify me, far more than the thought of a few years in the nick.

You don't think, then, that there's anything wrong in not working for your living?

But I do work for my living. Most crime—unless it's the senseless, petty-thieving sort—is quite hard work, you know. Planning a job, working out all the details of the best way to do it—and then carrying it out, under a lot of nervous strain and tension—and having to run round afterwards, if it's goods, fencing the stuff, getting a good price for it, delivering it to the fence, and so on—all this needs a lot of thinking and effort and concentration. It certainly is 'work', don't kid yourself about that.

But anyway this whole point's not all that simple. A lot of other people don't 'work' for their living, in the way you mean—but nobody goes on at them like they do at criminals. Quite a large proportion of the 'upper classes', for instance. You can see them any day round Piccadilly, Vigo Street, Savile Row—nattily dressed half-wits who've never done a stroke of work in their lives, popping in and out of Fortnum's or Scott's, spending all their time trying to get rid of the money their fathers and grandfathers and great-grandfathers left them. And usually it's that sort who get fiercest about people like me, saying we ought to be caned and whipped and flogged because we never do an honest day's work.

I can steal from people like that without the faintest compunction at all, in fact I'm delighted to do it. I remember once screwing the town house of the Duke of . . . well, I'd better not say who, because I didn't get caught for it. The inside of the house was the most beautiful place I've ever been in in my life—gorgeous curtains and furnishings, antique furniture, silver bowls and vases all over the place, exquisite miniatures on the walls—it was a fabulous place. My only regret was I hadn't got a furniture van so I could strip it from top to bottom. His Lordship I suppose was up in Scotland shooting wild birds, or some other civilized hobby, and his house was just standing unused until he chose to come back and live in it again.

I remember after I'd come out I passed an old man in rags, standing on the street-corner scraping at a violin to try and earn himself a few coppers, and I thought: 'You mug, why don't you go in there and at least get yourself a good sleep in one of his Lordship's unused beds for a night.'

All the things that were in that house, all those beautiful possessions, the duke had got for himself without the faintest effort of any kind. Most of them had been handed down to him, and all he'd ever had to do to get the others was write out a cheque—and he probably didn't even do that for himself but had a flunkey to do it. Never in his whole life had he known what it was like to be short of anything. Well, I had, and I don't think it was wrong to steal enough from him to subsidize me for a bit.

And those people, when they have something nicked, they've got it all insured anyway, so they don't suffer. Sometimes they advertise for its return—you know, 'Sentimental value' and all that. I'm sure I'd feel sentimental, too, about losing something worth a few hundred quid, only I'd be a bit more honest about it.

And the stuff I pinched from that particular house I appreciated, I did really. In fact, if it hadn't been too dangerous, I'd gladly have kept a lot of it to have around my own place, because it was so beautiful. But I never felt bad about taking it—why should I? I feel terrific. He'd got no cause for complaint, because it was taken, after all, by someone who could really appreciate its artistic merit, not one of those insensitive thugs who couldn't differentiate between Royal Worcester and a Woolworth's chamber-pot.

Oh yes, and one more thing. A couple of years later I read in the papers how this particular duke was involved in a real sordid court case. The details that came out about his private life then made me wonder if he ever did really appreciate those lovely possessions he had. From what they dragged out he sounded a right stinking bastard. But if I'd been caught that time I screwed his place he'd have been all up in arms about me—and the Law would have taken his side too. He was respectable and I wasn't, that's the way it would have been put.

But you don't confine yourself, like Robin Hood, entirely to stealing from the aristocracy, Bob, so let's consider another point as well. How do you justify wage-snatches for instance?

Could we get one thing clear first? I'm not trying to 'justify' anything. There's always two points of view on any subject, a wrong one and an even more wrong one. There's so much injustice in the world that we could start swopping one for another all the way along, like me turning round on you and saying: 'You justify some of your respectable society to me—like a managing director of a company taking five thousand a year for himself, from the efforts of people working for him whom he pays five hundred a year'—and so on.

So I'm not justifying anything; I'm just telling you what my point of view on a thing is when you ask me, and my point of view's probably as illogical and wrong as anyone else's is likely to be. I'm not saying: 'This is a hundred per cent right and everything else is wrong.' I'll put my point of view, but you're entitled to disagree with it and so is anyone else—in fact I wouldn't expect you to do anything other than disagree, because you belong in so-called 'straight' society.

Yes, O.K., Bob, but let's just stick to the point, shall we, and save the fireworks. What about wages-snatches?

Sure—but you can't blame me if you leave yourself wide open, can you? All right, wages-snatches. I'll try and take it from the beginning.

If I can see a chance of earning myself—or making myself, if you prefer it—a few thousand quid all at one go, naturally I'll do it. It's only what people, millions of them, are trying to do on the football pools every week. You could say: 'Yes, but they're trying to do it honestly'—to which I'd reply: 'It depends on your definition of honest, because while they're trying to get themselves several thousand of someone else's money for the outlay of a few shillings and no work, I'm trying to get it by some careful thinking and plotting, some bloody hard effort, and the risk of my own liberty into the bargain.'

So who's doing more to earn the money—me or the pools 'investors', as they're called? (By the promoters, of course. It's the old con-man's trick of persuading a mug you're going to give him something for nothing, playing on people's natural avarice and greed.) The 'investors' trust to luck to bring them a lot of money —well, I bank on my own efforts.

But there's a difference. Pools winnings come out of what the 'investors' hand over voluntarily, so those who lose have no complaint. Workers don't hand over their wages voluntarily for you to steal.

I'll say they don't. But look, don't try to break my heart. Who loses on a wages-snatch—the workers? Of course not. It's the company—and they can usually stand it. It's the same with banks —if I have a few thousand from a bank, theoretically it's their customers' money I've taken. But you never hear of a bank apportioning the losses round their customers, do you? 'We're so sorry, Major Bloodworthy, somebody blew our safe last night and took ten thousand quid—and it was your ten thousand that was in there!' Mind you, I'm not saying they shouldn't; to me it's quite an attractive idea.

No, let's face it, most of these people are insured against robberies, so it's only the insurance companies who pay up.

But this doesn't in any way defend the use of violence to get it, does it, by coshing the man carrying the wages-bag for instance?

There you go again, using words like 'defend' and 'justify'. I'm trying to tell you I'm not defending it, because fundamentally I don't believe you can defend the use of violence at all, in any circumstances. It's wrong whoever uses it and whatever they use if for. It's wrong when I use it, it's wrong when American maniacs drop an atom-bomb on Hiroshima or Nagasaki, when the South African police shoot down Africans at Sharpeville, when a man commits murder, when 'respectable' society takes him and hangs him as punishment, when Eden orders the British Air Force to bomb Port Said. This is all wrong, every time.

You get this in Parliament a lot, these politicians, usually the Tories, who start steaming off about the increase in crimes of violence, and how 'these thugs have got to be stopped'—these same fellers who were waving their order-papers and dancing up and down with delight when they thought we'd bombed the 'Egyptian wogs' into submission. Who are they to tell me that I'm beyond the pale for using violence?

Bob . . .

Yes, all right. So violence is wrong, on a fundamental level, I admit that. But on a day-to-day level it just happens that it's a tool of my trade and I use it—like an engineer uses a slide-rule, or a bus-driver the handbrake, or a dentist the drill. Only when necessary, and only when it can't be avoided. If I've got to whack a bloke with an iron bar to make him let go of a wages-bag he's carrying, O.K., so I'll whack him. If he lets go without any trouble, I don't. That's all.

I don't indulge in it, you know, for the sheer pleasure of the thing. I'm no sadist. This has always been my theory, that I'll take whatever job comes along. If there's a vanload of stuff to be pulled, I'll pull it; a screwing job, I'll screw it; a safe-blowing, I'll blow it—and so on. And if it's a coshing job, well then, I'll use a cosh.

There's another thing too that I think we ought to get straight. Violence is in a way like bad language—something that a person like me's been brought up with, something I got used to very early on as part of the daily scene of childhood, you might say. I don't at all recoil from the idea, I don't have a sort of inborn dislike of the thing, like you do. As long as I can remember I've seen violence in use all around me—my mother hitting the children; my brothers and sister all whacking one another, or other children; the man downstairs bashing his wife, and so on. You get used to it, it doesn't mean anything in these circumstances.

I've even seen, more than once, two men striping each other

with razors—and then, a few nights later, those same two men, with their faces covered with sticking-plaster, drinking together in a pub. I told you about Billy O'Lynn's father, and taking the gun for him, and how he said to us afterwards: 'Just you remember, that's the way to deal with people.' So you see, to me there's nothing all that terrible, or special in any way, about violence. It's just like any other form of activity: eating, sleeping, drinking, screwing, whatever you like.

Perhaps this might sound a bit odd, but it's true—as I've grown older, violence has got divided into two categories for me: the sort that's used for what you might call 'personal' reasons, and the sort to be used on a job.

The first sort, the 'personal' kind, I'm always struggling to get away from. Perhaps it's because I'm getting older or more mature: but I'm reaching the point now sometimes when I'm having an argument with somebody, and feel myself starting to lose my temper, I try and take a grip on myself, say to myself: 'No, I'm not going to whack him, it's wrong, it's sheer bullying, that's all. I've got to use my brains and argue myself out of this.' If I feel I'm not going to be able to do it, I try and make myself walk away from him altogether.

I never carry a knife or anything, no razor, nothing like that now. I used to, and I've used one in my time, striping people I'd got a big personal grievance against: but never light-heartedly, only after thinking about it a lot, and not more than six or eight times at the most. But God forbid, I've given up carrying a chiv now; it's not quite nice, one can so easily become a hooligan.

A few years ago it was different, I'd have whacked anyone soon as look at them, but it's childish, uncivilized, undignified, to be like that. Now, as I say, if I get in an argument, I try to get out of it by walking away. Yet if the self same bloke I'm arguing with was walking along the street one day, carrying a wages-bag that I was going to have, of course I'd whack him then. It wouldn't be personal bad temper, you see, only part of the job.

I've almost gone through a complete change-round. When I was a kid I was always looking for a fight. If someone offended me, whoever he was and however big he was, I'd be up to him waving my fists and offering to fight. But it worried me to have to hit someone on a job.

I can remember the first time quite clearly, I was only a kid, sixteen or seventeen, and thought myself a real tearaway of course. There was an old woman, a pawnbroker I think she was, lived in a little house just off Cable Street somewhere. Me and a couple of my mates heard that on Saturday nights she always had a bomb in there. Money was short and we decided to have it.

We went along about nine o'clock one Saturday night with shooters, banging on the door and shouting out: 'Mrs Rosenbloom, Mrs Rosenbloom!' or whatever her name was. 'Let us in, it's urgent, we've got to talk to you.' She opened the door, and seeing we were only kids she let us in. When we were inside we shoved her back into her kitchen and knocked her into a chair, telling her to keep quiet while we turned the place inside out looking for the money.

So of course she starts screaming and raving like a mad woman. Before we went in it'd been decided it was going to be my job to keep her quiet. I rammed my shooter up against her ear and said: 'Belt up, you old faggot, or I'll pull the trigger.'

It made not a blind bit of difference, she just yelled all the louder for help. The other two were tearing everything to bits trying to find where she'd hidden her money, and this racket she was making was really getting on their nerves, so one of them said: 'Oh, for Christ's sake hit the old bag, can't you? If you don't lay her out she'll have the whole neighbourhood on us.'

And I just couldn't do it. All I could do was stand there bleating: 'Shut up, will you! I'm warning you, I'll pull the trigger.' Naturally it didn't stop her. Finally one of the other two walked over, took the gun out of my hand, and belted her unconscious. He put the gun back in my hand, really angry, and he said: 'It's her or us, you silly bastard, can't you see that?'

It taught me the lesson, and after that I was all right. But I've never been keen on the idea of hitting old women, or old men for that matter. Just a personal weakness, but I don't like it, I don't think it's right. Nowadays I don't go in for it at all: if there's a job involving old people, I back out.

Gradually, you see, as you go on, most of the squeamishness about things gets knocked out of you. Not long after the old woman, I was on a job when we had to push around a wages clerk from a supermarket.

He used to be sent every week on his own to the bank to get
the money for wages, and then walk back carrying several hundred pounds in a bag. We followed him around for a few trips
first, and worked out the best place to stop him—at a corner
junction, where he usually had to wait to cross the road. We
came up by the side of him in a car, and hauled him in the back.
It's better than starting a fight in the street, because sometimes if
you do that passers-by try and join in and the thing develops into
a rough-house.

I was in the back of the car, holding his face down on the
floor so he wouldn't get a good look at us, and knocking him
about a bit to make sure he handed over the bag. He did that
without much trouble, and I told the bloke who was driving to
pull up so I could sling him out.

But the driver wouldn't. He said it was too dangerous to
stop, and I should push him out while we were going. It was the
attitude of 'him or us' again. So eventually I shoved him out
when we were going fairly slowly to get round a corner. Still a bit
squeamish, you see, even then.

But not long after that there was another job, in a ware-
house in Islington: and this one got rid of the last of my scruples
about violence. While we were in the place the night watchman
heard us moving about and he came up the stairs to the floor we
were on, to see what was going on. On the landing were a couple
of five-gallon oil drums. When I saw him coming up towards us, I
lifted one of them right over my head and let him have it. It
knocked him back all the way downstairs, but he lay at the
bottom yelling blue murder, so I took a fire extinguisher off the
wall and went down and laid him out with it. I didn't try to
batter him to death or anything, just put him out and stop his
noise. I didn't feel angry, savage, anything like that—I don't
think I felt anything, just dispassionate about it, knowing it'd
got to be done, because he was threatening us and our safety with
his noise.

You felt no compunction at all about hitting him like that?

No, none. I feel if someone takes a job as night watchman
he's got to be prepared to be hit if he tries to make a hero of
himself. I wouldn't have touched him if he'd left us alone, but
since he tried to stop us he got what he earned. Personally I

think he was stupid, he should have kept quiet and kept his nose out of it. What was he trying to do, win himself a medal? And what was he hoping to get from it, anyway—a pat on the shoulder from the guv'nor, 'Good feller, Jim,' a gold watch when he retired? Anyone who takes a job like that wants his brains testing, to me he does. Perhaps I'm missing something, but I can't see anything admirable in it at all, these heroes trying to win themselves medals for about nine-pounds-ten a week. You read it in the papers sometimes—'Last night Mr. Jim Smith tried to tackle some bandits and he's now in hospital recovering from concussion.' It always gives me a laugh, if it was a job I was on that it's referring to. O.K., so the bloke's a hero and got his name in the paper. So what's he got for it? Concussion. And what have I got? What I went for, which is what I would have got anyway, and he needn't have got his concussion trying to stop me.

But it's fortunate not everybody uses your methods, isn't it, or else we'd all be living in the jungle?

But we *are* living in a jungle. You've put your finger on it with that word, though, because that's all it is, a question of method. Lots of people take money off others, but they use other ways of doing it. Some of them are considered respectable. Personally I don't think they are—but it's a matter of opinion, that's all.

A landlord gets money out of people when he puts their rents up, by extortion, by playing on the fact they've got nowhere else to live. And the Law upholds him in doing it. Yet really all he's doing is stealing money from people. But if I go along and steal that money from him he screams to the Law, and they come after me to try and get his money back for him. If his tenant screams to the police that his landlord's robbing him, they do nothing of course. No: he perpetrates his crime upheld by all the respectability of society, without any risk on his part of going to prison. Well, personally, I think my method's a lot more straightforward and honest than his is. And I don't pretend to be doing anything other than what I am—stealing. But the landlord does. And, what's more, I don't go in for robbing poor people, either, like he does. Thieving off your own kind, that's terrible.

Or take the case of a jeweller. He's a business man, and he's in the game to make money. O.K., so I'm a business man too, and

I'm also out to make money. We just use different methods. The jeweller makes a profit—and often a very big profit—out of what he sells. On top of that he fiddles the income tax and the purchase tax, and even the customs duty as well if he can get away with it. That's considered all right by him and others like him, and if he makes enough to buy himself a big house and a posh car everyone looks up to him as a clever feller, a shrewd business man. But how's he got his money? By rooking people, taking advantage of soft young couples getting engaged to sell them a more expensive ring than they can afford, and fiddling the authorities whenever he can. But at least he didn't steal it. Well, what's in a name? Tell me exactly where the line is between thieving and 'shrewd business' and I might believe it. What's more, the jeweller can insure himself against people like me going and pinching his stock. But I can't insure against the police nicking me, can I? The Law's on one side only, the side of the pretenders, that's all.

It's funny, there's a few criminals, you do meet them from time to time, who won't do any violence. A firm I was with once, there was three of them besides me, we were discussing some job we had in view—a wages-snatch I think it was—where it was obvious we'd have to whack someone to get what we wanted. One of the three was one of these humanitarian types, you know, had what you might call a conscientious objection to using violence altogether. He went on about it so long the other two started to dither as well. We had a long argument about it, and my line was the one I've already explained: if violence needs doing, then you've got to do it. Some people won't hand over to you what you want just like that, so you've got to whack them. Well, this whole job fell through because they didn't look at it my way at all, they were scared about the thing. Once you start drawing lines here, there, and everywhere about what you will do, and what you won't, you might as well give up villainy altogether. It's amateurism—and the amateur's the curse of thieving like he is of any other game. The only approach I can go along with is to be a professional, and get on with whatever comes.

Bob, to get back to you yourself now . . . was there ever a point in your life when you made a conscious decision to be a criminal?

No, I can't think of one. I remember when I was doing my first lot of bird, I was quite determined I wasn't even going to try and go straight when I got out. I made up my mind that as soon as I was out I was going to get on with the business of having more money for myself, whatever way I had to use to get it. And going out to work for ten or twelve pounds a week wasn't one of the methods I even thought about. But there wasn't any one particular day when I got up in the morning and said: 'Im going to be a criminal,' like the kid who says: 'I know what I'll do, I'll be a fireman'—nothing like that. I more or less got accustomed to the idea gradually as I grew up, as I've tried to explain in the life-story part.

What really made you a criminal? Do you know?

This is the point, isn't it, where I should lay back in my chair, put my feet up on the mantelpiece, and say: 'I never had a chance!' But it just wouldn't be true. I don't say I've never had a chance, because I have, I've had plenty of chances if I'd wanted to take them. But I never did.

What made me a criminal? . . . I could reel off a whole lot of reasons, but they'd all only be part of the real answer. I'm always afraid of saying circumstances made me what I am, because I don't think they did entirely at all. Seeing my father, a straight man, getting only poverty all through his life for being straight . . . living in an environment where nearly everyone I knew was dishonest, where stealing was a necessity at some times, an adventure at others, but was always acceptable whatever the reason . . . wanting to impress other kids, getting a reputation for being a tearaway . . . seeing the terrifying dreariness of the lives of other people who were 'straight' . . . not being able to face working for a living because I hated the idea of work. . . .

Those were the circumstances, but they were only part of the answer. I still think I'd have been a criminal, whatever they'd been. For one thing, there's this tremendous hatred of authority which I've got, this compulsion, almost, to defy it. I was born with that, I'm sure. Or I could say it was because I'd always had a desire for adventure, for living dangerously. That was true when I was young, but it isn't true now, and I still go on. Now crime's just business, that's all.

There's so many facets, you see, aren't there, to what makes anyone what they are? I don't think there's one reason for me being a criminal, there's many, many of them. Some I know about, some I don't—but they all contribute to a greater or lesser degree. I might say: 'If only I'd had this, that, or the other,' or: 'If this had happened, or that hadn't . . .' My mother dying, for instance, when I was young: that's one example. . . . If I'd been thrashed less, or thrashed more. . . . I just don't know. I've never found one answer that convinced me, myself, in my own mind— you know, nothing I could think of and suddenly say: 'Yes, that's why I became a criminal.' I've thought about it a lot for many years and if I did know the answer, the answer you want, and could present it to you like that on a plate—well, I'd be a re- markable man. It seems to me that I've always been a criminal and always will be.

But, you know, you're asking me a question that far better people than me can't even answer. Some of them get paid for sitting in Chairs at universities and trying to work out the an- swer to this one, don't they? People like Grunhut and Mannheim and Radzinowitz. 'What makes criminals?'—they're working on it all the time, getting paid thousands a year to try and come up with the answer.

I've read a lot of books by those people, articles in the *Jour- nal of Criminology* and so on—after all, crime's the most inter- esting subject in the world to me, naturally—and none of them know, do they, however hard they try? And they're good people, those people, terrific brains—some of the work they do is first rate. I'm not knocking them, I wish there were more like them, working things out, trying to get other people to think deeply about these things instead of screaming all the time for more beatings, more imprisonment, more punishment. I think that fundamentally they're good and on the right lines. Dr. T. P. Morris, he's another one—I've read things of his, heard him on the radio, he knows his stuff, he talks sense.

And, well, sometimes some of them get near some of the answers. But they don't know *the* answer, any more than Lom- broso or Alexander Paterson did. They can tell you about condi- tions, environment, heredity, reactions to treatment of one kind or another—but they still can't tell you why under one set of circumstances some people go bent and others go straight.

Don't get me wrong, I'm all for them hammering away at it. But take any one of them, take—well, let's take Radzinowitz, for instance, he's about the top man now, I suppose, isn't he? I can't help feeling this, that all the time he's working in the dark, he's guessing. Because he's not a criminal himself, and so he can't know.

Hugh Klarc, he's another one. That Howard League of his, I think it's an organization working on the right lines: the pursuit of knowledge, that's always a good thing, a fine thing, there are some marvellous people in the Howard League. Even old man Butler, setting up his what-does-he-call-them, his research units on every little aspect of the problem—he's trying too. But there's one thing I think they're all missing, all of them—how do they ever think they're really going to find out what makes criminals tick if they go on looking on criminals just as specimens to experiment on?

You know, you can learn a lot about butterflies by catching one, sticking it on a board with a pin, and looking at it through a microscope. You can study its wing-structure, its anatomy, how it breeds, how it flies, its whole mechanism—but you're still nowhere near knowing what it's like to *be* a butterfly, are you?

Why don't these people sometimes set aside altogether the rights and wrongs of the matter, and get a few criminals to work in with them on the thing of what it's actually like to be one? Those who've given up crime now and reformed, they're no good, they're dead butterflies, their mental processes have atrophied—they've got too far away from it, mentally I mean. But an ordinary criminal, a working criminal, it's my guess if they could only dig down deep enough to find it in him—he'd know just by instinct some of the answers the butterfly inspectors are missing.

To return to yourself now, this feeling you have about being a criminal fundamentally—would it be right to say that in your case not only do you feel this, but, on an even deeper level perhaps, you feel you don't belong in 'respectable' society at all?

Yes, I think that's true. I do feel that now, very strongly. I don't want to mix at all with people who have what might be called 'suburban pretensions' or respectability. They don't inter-

est me: in fact, more than that, I don't like them, I actively
dislike them. To me it's much more interesting to be with a
group of criminals than a group of suburbanites, because there's
nothing about those people at all. I know what they're like, once
you've met one you've met them all, you can foretell everything
about them right down to the smallest detail. How their homes
are furnished—all in the same way: the telly in the corner, lace
curtains, a plaster dog in the window, a wooden clock on the
mantelpiece, photographs in chromium frames on the sideboard,
two armchairs in uncut moquette, four dining-chairs, one of
those hideous, glossy cocktail cabinets if they really want to impress . . . they're so stereotyped they're dead. And their talk . . .
the man, if you can get down to it, he always 'fancies' the woman
next door but of course he never gets round to actually doing
her. It's frightening, it's chronic. At least criminals have something interesting to talk about, their talk is deeper and more
real, the life they lead goes at a much faster tempo and has got
some excitement in it.

I think, if I'm going to try and be strictly honest about this
whole thing, that I ought to say, too, that now and again, on
some points, I don't feel I belong all that completely in my own
strata of society either. I'm not trying to flatter myself and say
I'm a cut above them or anything like that—but I do find sometimes, over certain things, that I don't belong.

I can remember before now on more than one occasion, for
instance, going into a public library near where I was living, and
looking over my shoulder a couple of times before I actually went
in, just to make sure no one who knew me was standing about
and seeing me do it. You get this in all walks of life, of course,
but I must admit a lot of the people I know aren't exactly what
you might call 'with it' on some things. I mean, I know blokes
who if you mentioned Leonardo da Vinci to them, their first
question would be: 'Whose mob's he with?' and if you were to
tell them he was a painter, they'd say: 'Well, how much docs he
make?'

But I think perhaps this isn't all that important anyway,
because certain types don't go much on this art business, and I
don't look down my nose at them for that. If I had to choose
between an art-addict and a sound, reliable screwsman for com-

pany, of course I'd choose the screwsman every time. It's the same with a woman—so long as she's reliable, and preferably a good screw into the bargain, that's far more important than she should be clever or things like that.

24 Albert Henry DeSalvo, the man accused of the numerous "Boston Strangler" murders, describes the interaction between a murderer and his victim.

"There is something about women . . ."

george william rae

This day I went to Salem and I rode around for a while and I ended up in Lynn. Just driving anywhere, not knowing where I was going, coming through back ways, in and out and around, and in my mind building this image up . . .

I don't know yet that I'm needing help . . . it's been getting worse very gradual . . . sometimes I'm driving to work and building the image up and then I get release right in my underwear but five minutes later I'm ready again and the image comes back and the pressure mounts up into my head, you understand me?

I find myself in Lynn, in front of 72 Newhall Street. I go around and start up the back stairs but someone is coming, so I go right to the front door and climb the stairs to the second floor and knock on a door.

I never been in this building before, I don't know nobody here, this woman, I don't know her, I don't know who lives in the apartment, whether or not it is a woman, but I knock and I know what I'll say when she opens the door, I don't think about it, I just know, see?

When she opened the door, she was wearing cotton pajamas, bottoms and tops, reddish white . . . stripes or some little design like this, here, I'll draw it, like this . . . you understand me?

"I come to do the work on the ceiling," I said, or something like that about work on the apartment.

"This is the first I've heard of it," she says.

"Well, lady, I'm telling you about it now," I say, smiling and looking down like I don't want to look at her standing there in her pajamas with the door cracked open five or six inches. "I don't want to bother you," I say, taking a step away, that's always a good one and it usually works—you are saying, what I mean, you know, I don't give a damn whether you let me in or not . . . and the funny thing is sometimes I hoped, almost prayed, that they wouldn't let me in . . . because I guess I knew what was going to happen, but I never really was sure if something would make me kill them—when that happened, there usually was a reason, like they turned the back of their heads to me and the pressure . . . but anyway, I say: "I really don't want to bother you and if I ain't done the work that ain't my fault but yours, so you can't complain to the super, okay, lady?"

"Well," she says, opening the door a little more, and I look away and move my feet, "it just seems funny that I never heard of it is all."

"I'm supposed to check the windows for leaks, too," I say and that one got her . . . a lot of these apartments around here got leaks at the windows where rain and snow blows in around the sash, see, so that's usually a good one, too.

"Well, it's about time," she said, "But I still don't know you."

The door opened a little more . . . so help me, this thing going in my head, this pressure, I want to say, don't open the door, but still I want it to open, it's funny, you know?

"I just do work for the boss of the apartment," I say, "you must've seen me around here sometimes . . . but, look, I ain't anxious to do this work, I got other things to do . . . I'll have the boss . . ."

Now the door was open pretty wide and she's standing in it in her cotton pajamas and, so help me, now I'm hoping she'll not let me in to do it to her and at the same time going on making her let me as if I couldn't stop the con I'm giving her and that is a very helpless feeling for a man to have, you understand me? The thing is, she never done nothing to me and I am going to do something to her, I don't know why, and she don't know me and I don't know her . . .

I had some more conversation with her. There is something about women, they like to talk, and they think that they get to know what a man is thinking by talking, like they get to know a man that way and that's a laugh, ain't it . . . when actually a man don't even know hisself what he's going to do when he gets the urge and ain't got nobody to work it out with and is thinking of hisself as what he's been told he is by somebody he loves very much, that he is dirty and that what he wants is dirty . . . how can a woman know just by talking to a guy at her door—or wherever, so long as it's just talking, talk is easy and you shouldn't have respect for a guy just because he talks, but only by what he does when he has the chance to do it and don't, you see?

So anyway she let me in and then it had to happen . . .

She went with me through the rooms and I worked my way through the rooms to the bedroom and when she turned her back, I put my arms around her neck and she went into a dead faint.

A little blood was coming from her nose. She was a heavy-set, big-breasted woman, very well built.

I picked her up and took her pajamas off. I took everything off and got on top of her. She was alive, but unconscious.

I remember biting her bust and other parts of her body, too . . . her stomach . . .

Then I took her bra . . . white . . . it was on the dresser, or on the chair, either one. There was panties there. They was large. I put the bra around her neck . . . a nylon stocking, too . . .

I think she was dead then and I could see the blood, just a little, coming from her nose, and the red marks of the bites on her big breasts and down her belly almost to the—what is the polite word for her privates?—yes, that's it—almost to the hair of that . . . I remember she had a big bush and for an old lady she was very well built . . . all the way down was these red bite marks, you see, and I remember looking at them and saying, gee, did I do that? . . . and it made me mad, somehow, to see her like that, dead, and with come on her hair and them bites and I gave

the stuff around her neck a good turn and then I went through
her place but I didn't take nothing . . . I don't know what I'm
looking for and am very angry and I don't know what about . . .
after a while I went into the bathroom and wiped the sweat off
my face . . . I left her about ten-twenty A.M. . . .

25 Final communications from persons who took their own lives.

Suicide notes

edwin s. shneidman

norman l. farberow

This is the last note I shall ever wright. No one should feel bad about my going as I am not worth it. I don't want to go but there is nothing else to do.

My Love kept after me until I lost control and struck at the only one I ever loved. The only thing that meant anything to me. Then I got tight. When I struck at her something snapped inside my head. I could feel it. I didn't want to hurt her ever. She is Mary Jones of 100 Main St. Los Angeles. Her aunt's phone is BA 00000. She lives close by. Please get in tutch with them at once. She keped after me until this is all I can do. I must.

My last request is not to be put 6 ft. under but burned and my ashes scattered over the mountains.

Please don't let my brother know how or why I died. To her it must be an acident. Mary is the most wonderful person on earth. I just wasn't the right one for her. It is not her fault I fell so madly in Love with her.

I have never been much good. I have only hurt everyone.

Well at least I have loved. I loved her and her two girls more than words could ever tell. They were like my own girls to me.

Well, that's it.

John W. Smith

Get in touch with Mary Jones at once. Call BA 00000. Tell Mrs. Brown. She will see Mary. Thank you.

John William Smith

Dear Mary, The reason for my despondency is that you'd prefer the company of almost anyone to mine. 2. You told me you had nothing to look forward to on week ends. You told me you preferred living alone. This led to more sedatives. I have lost the love of my two children. You blamed me for your vaginal bleeding. Your first husband was denied normal sexual inter-course because you said it hurt. I received the same accuse. You said it hurt even out of wedlock. This you cant help. But affec-tion would have been harmless. I had little of that. But gaiety you saved for strangers, but even so I loved you. My salary wasn't enough for a large family, with the car upkeep. I was happy regardless. So were you between moods also. You are free now to frequent the places where they drink and indulge in loose talk. Please refrain from giving Betty sips of beer, after all she is only 12. Make her love you some other way. Soon she'll dominate you and one thing leads to another. You don't want another child where your boy is. Your love for me would have endured if it had been the real thing.

Dr. Jones did all he could for my internal trouble. When we quarrel over other and younger men it was silly but you would have been hurt too. It's O.K. to be friendly but not hilarious. Nembutal has a tendency to make you tolerant rather than jeal-ous. It headed off many a quarrel because its quieting to the nerves. As you know I took them for sleep and spastic colon at nite; also migraine headache.

Well, I've loved you through 3 years of quarreling, adjusting the sex angle the way you said it pleased you. Your word for it was "ecstacy." Farewell and good fortune. I hope you find some-one who doesn't "hurt" you as you said 3 of us did. All the love I have,

Bill

Notify my kin by mail. Call Georgia St. Hosp. Ambulance.

Dear Mother and Mary, I am sorry to tell you this but Jo told you that I was drinking again. I won't lie about it. Because I quit for 5 week and never taken a drink. But Jo had come up home two nite a week after she got off from work and she would stay with me. But ever nite she came up she was drunk, and I would put her to bed. And on the nite of 12 of March she came drunk and when I went to work I left her in my bed and when she got up that was Wed. She went home she told me. But she didn't go home she went and got drunk, and I had been give her money to pay her room, and I give her money before I went that morning. But she go to the tavern and she got drunk and she got in a fight. I don't no who with, but it was on the street and she eather fell or got nook down and she got a black and blue place on her hip big as a teacup. I asked her how she got that but she said she done it on the ice box and she said it was like that and I no difference. The one that told me didn't no Jo was my wife. He seen it and told her she could do better then that. He said she was to drunk. I saw this and this made me mad and I did start drinking because she told me that she love me and I was so nice to give her money. I do love her and she love me. But I can't stand for her to drink like she does and do the way she do. Jo was up at my house Sun March 31, and she went home about 4 o'clock to go to work and I tryed to get to strating up. But she won't. If you can do anything with her I wish you would. Because I love her so much and she is killing herself. I wouldn't wrote you this if she hadn't told you I had started to drink again. I told her Sun. I would help her and I will if she will be half way write with me.

To my wife Mary: As you know, like we've talked over before our situation, I'll always love you with all my heart and soul. It could have been so simple if you had have given me the help that you alone knew I needed.

This is not an easy thing I'm about to do, but when a person makes a few mistakes and later tried to say in his own small way with a small vocabulary that he is sorry for what has happened and promises to remember what has happened and will try to make the old Bill come home again, and do his best to start all

over again, and make things at home much better for all concerned, you still refuse to have me when you as well as I know
that I can't do it by myself, then there's only one thing to do.

I'm sorry honey, but please believe me this is the only way
out for me as long as you feel as you do—This will put you in
good shape. Please always take care of Betty and tell her that her
Daddy wasn't too bad a guy after all. With all the love that's in
me. *Bill*

Yes, Mommie, now you have your car and a lot more too,
even more than you had hoped for. At least you are better off
financially than you were 6 years ago. The only pitiful thing
about the whole situation is the baby and the nice car that I
bought with blood money. I only hope I do a good job of it.
Then your troubles will be over with. I know this is what you
have been hoping for for a long time. I'm not crazy, I just love
you too much! ! !

I love you—*Daddy*—Goodbye forever.

Mary: The only thing you never called me was crazy. Now
you can do that. I loved you so.

Bill

Good by Kid. You couldn't help it. Tell that brother of
yours, When he gets where I'm going. I hope I'm a foreman
down there. I might be able to do something for him.

Bill

Madamhood as a vocation

sally stanford

I didn't set out to be a madam any more than Arthur Michael Ramsey, when he was a kid, set out to be Archbishop of Canterbury. Things just happened to both of us, I guess. At a time when most young girls decide to become schoolteachers, actresses, or lady lawyers, one doesn't after carefully considering all the vocations open to a female, say, "That's for me; I'm going to be a madam." Madaming is the sort of thing that happens to you—like getting a battlefield commission or becoming the Dean of Women at Stanford University. But I have never been the least bit touchy or sensitive about it—never. Many are called, I always say, but few are chosen; and for me it has been a steppingstone to bigger and more profitable things. (I started to say "bigger and better things," but is there really anything better, in the words of the poet, than "living in a house by the side of the road and being a friend to man?")

No, no one sets out to be a madam; but madams answer the call of a well-recognized and very basic human need. Their responsibilities are thrust upon them by the fundamental nitwittedness and economic shortsightedness of most hustling broads. And they become tempered and sharpened and polished to the highest degree of professional awareness by constant intercourse with men devoutly dedicated to the policy of getting something for nothing.

It doesn't take much to produce a good merchant of cash-

Reprinted by permission of G. P. Putnam's Sons from *The Lady of the House*, by Sally Stanford. © 1966 by G. P. Putnam's Sons.

and-carry love: just courage, an infinite capacity for perpetual suspicion, stamina on a 24-hour-a-day basis, the deathless conviction that the customer is always wrong, a fair knowledge of first and second aid, do-it-yourself gynecology, judo—and a tremendous sense of humor. Aside from these basic talents, a good madam must possess an understanding of female psychology (in the broadest sense), a knowledge of quick therapies for restoring drunks to a state of locomotion (so as to depart the premises), and a grasp of techniques for the eradication of pimps, who are the crabgrass of prostitution. Pimps are always moving in where the green stuff is thickest. With these qualities, and a few others, you may develop into a self-respecting madam. (A good Secretary of State could use some of the same.)

Morality?

As far as I'm concerned, morality is just a word that describes the current fashion of conduct. The Navajo Indians regarded it immoral for old people to live after they could no longer take care of themselves. When aging Navajos could no longer chew their pemmican, they were sent to their Happy Hunting Grounds. We civilized folks keep our elder citizens alive with drugs, intravenous feedings, and surgery, knowing full well we have prolonged only agony and pain.

The immoral Mohammedans can have as many wives as they can properly care for, a caper that our morality doesn't buy. Good old moral Christians like us can have all kinds of husbands or wives, as long as we keep them one at a time, and a good fib in court separates one from the other. Moral America finds itself practicing such noble customs as capital punishment (civil murder) and anti-birth control laws that spawn poverty.

Why is the bliss of ignorance considered so moral? My blood pressure goes up and my voltage charges when I realize that more attention is put drilling our young people on dental than on sexual hygiene. Syphilis and gonorrhea could go the way of smallpox and scarlet fever. They could be eradicated in a matter of months, but we stick our moral heads in the sand, sing hymns and say prayers, and cover the stinking problem as a cat buries its dirt.

People ask me what I hate. It's very simple. Phonies, ignorance, and poverty; and not necessarily in that order. I used to think that the primeval curse was the lack of money. Now I've licked that problem. But in my own life I find myself entangled in a jungle of spiritual poverty, intellectual poverty, and the rankest growth of all: the poverty of human kindness and concern about the pain and suffering of other people.

So why should I worry about being immoral in someone's daffy code book merely because . . . once upon a time . . . I permitted a generation of Adams to tarry in my Eden?

When I spoke of madamhood having served as a stepping-stone to bigger things, I was referring to my graduation into rehabilitation and respectability (rehabilitation being used here in the sense of my retirement from the professional life I once knew, and not as a form of repentant apology for something I've always considered a community service). Today, I own and operate one of the best restaurants the West has even seen—in Sausalito, that beautiful San Francisco suburb. I am one of the Directors of the Sausalito Chamber of Commerce and an officer on its "Ways and Means" committee. Here last year, and for the second time, I ran for a seat on the City Council and damn near made it both times, being defeated only because of a group of local matrons who'd rather have seen Judas Iscariot get the job, provided he was a Republican and would shave. I really consider it a wonderful honor to have received so many votes during those elections, and I will run again and again until I make it . . . if only to hear myself addressed as "Madam Councilman."

Respectability has come to me now, but I have a wonderful storehouse of memories of a full and gratifying life, as well as a damn good income—legitimately. True, I have not been asked as yet to address a girl's graduation class on the subject of the sporting life. But as for *my* life, I wouldn't change a day of it. In truth, I've always regarded my promotion of man's favorite indoor sport as thoroughly legitimate business and even, as I implied earlier, even a social service. Nobody sent for the customers. They arrived eager to barter and participate in the market place of love, and the doors of all my homes as well as my "houses" opened two ways.

As to my claim to performing a useful social service, every lusty, tourist-jammed seaport town like San Francisco needs safety valves and outlets for its males. Shut down a town and the rape rate soars higher than an astronaut while the economy of many a deserving "lady of the evening" drops and no one's really happy except the blue noses.

Mind you, I'm not trying to kid anyone that my journey along the primrose path has made easier for me my roles in life as a restaurateur, lady politician, real estate investor and steadily rising pillar of society. However, it is a fact that I have learned more of human values and of life than I ever would have anywhere else or in any other field; and that includes the ones I worked in as a child.

27 *The editor of a hippie publication discusses some misconceptions "normal folk" may have about the Haight Ashbury district of San Francisco.*

Notes to tourists

guy strait

Please remember as you approach Haight Street that you are about to see one of the most wondrous sights yet to come to the attention of mankind. It is far from perfect, but the mere fact that hundreds of thousands of tourists have spent many hours in traffic jams to see if there is any truth in the Love Generation testifies to the fact that all of us would like to find a better way of life. You may well be one of those wondering if it is truly possible to love your fellow man. Take it from Maverick, it is not only possible, but it is being done every day.

First let us apologize for the long hour that you have spent in the traffic jam. The San Francisco traffic engineers are mostly refugees from various looney bins. They are also handicapped by the San Francisco Police Department who have made no attempt to control traffic in The Haight. It is understandable—they are far too busy chasing pot-users (that is slang for marihuana), keeping the kids from sitting on the sidewalks, and passing out parking tickets. On that last note let us give you a warning: Be sure you know all the laws regarding parking . . . Tickets are passed out here like you have never seen before. As many as three parking-meter-minders are at work in this twelve block area at any one time. If you have not yet entered the Haight area be sure and check to see if all your stop lights are working, your windshield wipers are working, your brakes working, etc. This is because if you are stopped for anything you will be checked out

From *The Haight Ashbury Maverick*, 1. Reprinted by permission of Guy Strait.

minutely. It will help if you are cleanly shaven, have your Rotary Sticker on the bumper and most of all have a St. Christopher statuette on the dashboard. The latter is recommended throughout San Francisco.

Roll down your windows

Many tourists upon seeing the unshaven, unconventional clothed Love Generation roll up their car windows and lock the doors. This is not necessary and can be mightily inconvenient. Some of the hippies do bite but all of them have taken their rabies shots so their bite is not too bad. Honestly tho, you must consider that the unconventional attire would make it easy to describe your assailant to the police. By the way if it appears to you that there are no police in the area, have no fears—probably one out of every twenty males that you see between the ages of 25–35 are officers of some kind or the other.

Brands of hippies

Just like your normal folk, there are many brands of hippies . . . Some of you are vitally interested in politics . . . so are some of the hippies . . . We call that particular brand "activists." Probably you won't notice an activist on Haight since most of them stick pretty close to the home base—Berkeley. The activists run the gamut from a middle of the road (very rare) to the anarchist (not so rare).

Then there are the Flower Children . . . These are the most lovable of all the hippies. Early in the summer it was quite common to have them going down the streets passing out flowers and wearing garlands of flowers. But flowers are rather expensive to come by and even a small bunch of flowers are getting beyond the reach of those of moderate (or less) means.

Then there are the bikeriders. When you see them on the street they just plain look rough. And they damn well can be. But since they want the right to live their own life—as they choose—they respect the right of the others to do likewise. And might well be the ones who defend in acts the rights of those unprepared to defend those who are unprepared to do so. The riders primarily keep to a certain area but mix well in all the other areas of Haight Street.

And there are many many other tribes of hippies.

THE DRUG SCENE

We failed to warn you when we were talking about getting parking tickets that there are other areas of personal conduct that you must be careful about in the Haight-Ashbury area. If you have any unlabeled medicines or if you are a diabetic and must carry a hypodermic with you—we strongly suggest that you pass thru the Haight with as much speed as possible.

(However if you are a ballet star you need not worry because if you get arrested the police will apologize most resoundingly.)

But the ordinary person must be careful because the police cannot tell a hippie by just looking and those who have any drugs of any kind must be careful.

If you have come to the Haight looking for grass, then we suggest that you give up that long drive for these six blocks. There just isn't any around. Acid is also very scarce. Most tourists assume that they can pick up some for their private uses back in Oshkosh and Dallas. Sorry, it is just not so. Besides every nark (narcotics agent) in California is here and if there is any grass about it will be in their hands shortly. We strongly urge however that you might be able to get some in your home town and we further strongly urge that you smoke a joint before retiring and throw away those patent medicine Nytal, Sleepeze and so forth. Grass is so much better for relaxing. Try it instead of that martini before dinner; be sure, be safe and use pot instead of gin.

THE DRESS FOR THE HAIGHT

We would warn the tourists that our police department is highly uptight about dress here. Again they cannot tell a hippie from a straightie and those miniskirts are strictly out for the Haight. One girl was arrested for wearing a traditional Indian costume that came well below the midpoint of the upper leg. Some of the tourists who have ambled down Haight Street recently have caused consternation among the hippies (who you will admit are accustomed to wild dress), but those two-ax-handle-broad broads in phosphorescent orange slacks are a little much. Now if, on the other hand, if you have a burning desire to take that Indian blanket on the back seat and drape it over your shoulders and walk down the street, then you must do so. If you have a burning desire to take off your shirt (men only, there is a double standard here) and walk down the street bare breasted (chested) then do so, for that is called 'doing your thing.' But if you see a cop scowling at you, then retire back to your Mustang and drive off. That is unless you are prepared to defend your American right to do so. However you will find that American rights are largely disregarded by the municipal courts here. The one who dares to defy the mores (not the laws) here is bound to have a big legal bill to pay. All this is done in the name of "order."

FREE LOVE

If you have come to the Haight looking for 'free' love then we suggest that you turn around and leave—for you are wasting your time. This is of course assuming that our readers are males. If you are a female then sex is highly likely—for free even.

The mass media has played up big the idea that there is a lot of free nookey here. The ratio of male to female is about 5 to 1. As in other areas the females are tied up with permanent partners to a large degree. Some cats up for kicks from the oil fields of Texas and the Movie Moguls from Hollywood with 16 credit cards and a Hertz rented automobile have tried to impress the local chicks. It was a waste of time and money but we do thank them for feeding the chicks. In this case money won't buy anything at all.

28   *The first official statement of an organization identified with the New Left.*

Excerpts from the Port Huron Statement

students for a democratic society

AGENDA FOR A GENERATION

We are people of this generation, bred in at least modest comfort, housed in universities, looking uncomfortably to the world we inherit.

Our work is guided by the sense that we may be the last generation in the experiment with living. But we are a minority—the vast majority of our people regard the temporary equilibriums of our society and the world as eternally-functional parts. In this is perhaps the outstanding paradox: We ourselves are imbued with urgency, yet the message of our society is that there is no viable alternative to the present. Beneath the reassuring tones of the politicians, beneath the common opinion that America will "muddle through," beneath the stagnation of those who have closed their minds to the future, is the pervading feeling that there simply are no alternatives, that our times have witnessed the exhaustion not only of Utopias, but of any new departures as well. Feeling the press of complexity upon the emptiness of life, people are fearful of the thought that at any moment things might thrust out of control. They fear change itself, since change might smash whatever invisible framework seems to hold back chaos for them now. For most Americans, all crusades are suspect, threatening. The fact that each individual sees apathy in his fellows perpetuates the common reluctance to organize for changes. The dominant institutions are complex enough to blunt the minds of their potential critics, and entrenched enough to swiftly dissipate or entirely repel the energies of protest and reform, thus limiting human expectancies. Then, too, we are a materially improved society, and by our own improvements we seem to have weakened the case for change.

Some would have us believe that Americans feel contentment amidst prosperity—but might it not better be called a glaze above deeply-felt anxieties about their role in the new world? And if these anxieties produce a developed indifference to human affairs, do they not as well produce a yearning to believe there *is* an alternative to the present, that something *can* be done to change circumstances in the school, the workplaces, the bureaucracies, the government? It is to this latter yearning, at once the spark and engine of change, that we direct our present appeal. The search for truly democratic alternatives to the present, and a commitment to social experimentation with them, is a worthy and fulfilling human enterprise, one which moves us and, we hope, others today. . . .

VALUES

Making values explicit—an initial task in establishing alternatives—is an activity that has been devalued and corrupted. The conventional moral terms of the age, the politician moralities ("free world," "peoples democracies") reflect realities poorly, if at all, and seem to function more as ruling myths than as descriptive principles. But neither has our experience in the universities brought us moral enlightenment. Our professors and administrators sacrifice controversy to public relations; their curriculums change more slowly than the living events of the world; their skills and silence are purchased by investors in the arms race; passion is called unscholastic. The questions we might want raised—what is really important? can we live in a different and better way? if we wanted to change society, how would we do it?—are not thought to be questions of a "fruitful, empirical nature," and thus are brushed aside.

Unlike youth in other countries we are used to moral leadership being exercised and moral dimensions being clarified by our elders. But today, for us, not even the liberal and socialist preachments of the past seem adequate to the forms of the present. Consider the old slogans: Capitalism Cannot Reform Itself, United Front Against Fascism, General Strike, All Out on May Day. Or, more recently, No Cooperation with Commies and Fellow Travelers, Ideologies Are Exhausted, Bipartisanship, No Utopias. These are incomplete, and there are few new prophets. It has been said that our liberal and socialist predecessors were plagued by vision without program, while our own generation is plagued by program without vision. All around us there is astute grasp of method, technique—the committee, the *ad hoc* group, the lobbyist, the hard and soft sell, the make, the projected image —but, if pressed critically, such expertise is incompetent to explain its implicit ideals. It is highly fashionable to identify oneself by old categories, or by naming a respected political figure, or by explaining "how we would vote" on various issues.

Theoretic chaos has replaced the idealistic thinking of old— and, unable to reconstitute theoretic order, men have condemned idealism itself. Doubt has replaced hopefulness, and men act out a defeatism that is labelled realistic. The decline of utopia and hope is in fact one of the defining features of social life today. The reasons are various: The dreams of the older left were perverted by Stalinism and never recreated; the congressional stalemate makes men narrow their view of the possible; the specialization of human activity leaves little room for sweeping thought; the horrors of the twentieth century, symbolized in the gas ovens and concentration camps and atom bombs, have blasted hopefulness. To be idealistic is to be considered apocalyptic, deluded. To have no serious aspirations, on the contrary, is to be "tough-minded."

In suggesting social goals and values, therefore, we are aware of entering a sphere of some disrepute. Perhaps matured by the past, we have no sure formulas, no closed theories—but that does not mean values are beyond discussion and tentative determination. A first task of any social movement is to convince people that the search for orienting theories and the creation of human values is complex but worthwhile. We are aware that to avoid platitudes we must analyze the concrete conditions of social order. But to direct such an analysis we must use the guideposts of basic principles. Our own social values involve conceptions of human beings, human relationships, and social systems.

We regard *men* as infinitely precious and possessed of unfulfilled capacities for reason, freedom, and love. In affirming these principles we are aware of countering perhaps the dominant conceptions of man in the twentieth century: that he is a thing to be manipulated, and that he is inherently incapable of directing his own affairs. We oppose the depersonalization that reduces human beings to the status of things. If anything, the brutalities of the twentieth century teach that means and ends are intimately related, that vague appeals to "posterity" cannot justify the mutilations of the present. We oppose, too, the doctrine of human incompetence because it rests essentially on the modern fact that men have been "competently" manipulated into incompetence. We see little reason why men cannot meet with increasing skill the complexities and responsibilities of their situation, if society is organized not for minority participation but for majority participation in decision-making.

Men have unrealized potential for self-cultivation, self-direction, self-understanding, and creativity. It is this potential that we regard as crucial and to which we appeal—not to the human potentiality for violence, unreason, and submission to authority. The goal of man and society should be human independence: a concern not with image or popularity but with finding a meaning in life that is personally authentic; a quality of mind not compulsively driven by a sense of powerlessness, nor one which unthinkingly adopts status values, nor one which represses all threats to its habits, but one which has full, spontaneous access to present and past experiences, one which easily unites the fragmented parts of personal history, one which openly faces problems which are troubling and unresolved—one with an intuitive awareness of possibilities, an active sense of curiosity, an ability and willingness to learn.

This kind of independence does not mean egoistic individualism; the object is not to have one's way so much as it is to have a way that is one's own. Nor do we deify man—we merely have faith in his potential.

Human relationships should involve fraternity and honesty. Human interdependence is contemporary fact; human brotherhood must be willed, however, as a condition of future survival and as the most appropriate form of social relations. Personal links between man and man are needed, especially to go beyond the partial and fragmentary bonds of function that bind men only as worker to worker, employer to employee, teacher to student, American to Russian.

Loneliness, estrangement, isolation describe the vast distance between man and man today. These dominant tendencies cannot be overcome by better personnel management, nor by improved gadgets, but only when a love of man overcomes the idolatrous worship of things by man.

As the individualism we affirm is not egoism, the selflessness we affirm is not self-elimination. On the contrary, we believe in generosity of a kind that imprints one's unique individual qualities in the relation to other men, and to all human activity. Further, to dislike isolation is not to favor the abolition of privacy; the latter differs from isolation in that it occurs or is abolished according to individual will.

In the last few years, thousands of American students demonstrated that they at least felt the urgency of the times. They moved actively and directly against racial injustices, the threat of war, violations of individual rights of conscience and, less frequently, against economic manipulation. They succeeded in restoring a small measure of controversy to the campuses after the stillness of the McCarthy period. They succeeded, too, in gaining some concessions from the people and institutions they opposed, especially in the fight against racial bigotry.

The significance of these scattered movements lies not in their success or failure in gaining objectives—at least not yet. Nor does the significance lie in the intellectual "competence" or "maturity" of the students involved—as some pedantic elders allege. The significance is in the fact that the students are breaking the crust of apathy and overcoming the inner alienation— facts that remain the defining characteristics of American college life.

If student movements for change are rarities still on the campus scene, what is commonplace there? The real campus, the familiar campus, is a place of private people, engaged in their notorious "inner emigration." It is a place of commitment to business-as-usual, getting ahead, playing it cool. It is a place of mass affirmation of the Twist, but mass reluctance toward the controversial public stance. Rules are accepted as "inevitable," bureaucracy as "just circumstances," irrelevance as "scholarship," selflessness as "martyrdom," politics as "just another way to make people, and an unprofitable one, too."

Almost no students value activity as a citizen. Passive in public, they are hardly more idealistic in arranging their private lives; Gallup concludes they will settle for "low success, and won't risk high failure." There is not much willingness to take risks (not even in business), no setting of dangerous goals, no real conception of personal identity except one manufactured in the image of others, no real urge for personal fulfillment except to be almost as successful as the very successful people. Attention is being paid to social status (the quality of shirt collars, meeting people, getting wives or husbands, making solid contacts for later on); much, too, is paid to academic status (grades, honors, the med school rat-race). But neglected generally is real intellectual status, the personal cultivation of the mind.

Look beyond the campus, to America itself. That student life is more intellectual, and perhaps more comfortable, does not obscure the fact that the fundamental qualities of life on the campus reflect the habits of society at large. The fraternity president is seen at the junior manager levels; the sorority queen has gone to Grosse Pointe; the serious poet burns for a place, any place, to work; the once-serious and never-serious poets work at the advertising agencies. The desperation of people threatened by forces about which they know little and of which they can say less, the cheerful emptiness of people giving up all hope of changing things, the faceless ones polled by Gallup who listed "international affairs" fourteenth on their list of problems but who also expected thermonuclear war in the next few years—in these and other forms, Americans are in withdrawal from public life, from any collective effort at directing their own affairs.

Some regard these national doldrums as a sign of healthy approval of the established order, but is it approval by consent or by manipulated acquiescence? Others declare that the people are withdrawn because compelling issues are fast disappearing; perhaps there are fewer breadlines in America, but is Jim Crow gone, is there enough work and is work more fulfilling, is world war a diminishing threat, and what of the revolutionary new peoples? Still others think the national quietude is a necessary consequence of the need for elites to resolve complex and specialized problems of modern industrial society. But, then, why should business elites help decide foreign policy, and who controls the elites anyway, and are they solving mankind's problems? Others finally shrug knowingly and announce that full democracy never worked anywhere in the past—but why lump qualitatively different civilizations together, and how can a social order work well if its best thinkers are skeptics, and is man really doomed forever to the domination of today?

There are no convincing apologies for the contemporary malaise. . . . The apathy is, first, subjective—the felt powerlessness of ordinary people, the resignation before the enormity of events. But subjective apathy is encouraged by the objective American situation—the actual separation of people from power, from relevant knowledge, from pinnacles of decision-making. Just as the university influences the student way of life, so do major social institutions create the circumstances in which the isolated citizen will try hopelessly to understand his world and himself.

The very isolation of the individual—from power and community and ability to aspire—means the rise of a democracy without publics. With the great mass of people structurally remote and psychologically hesitant with respect to democratic institutions, those institutions themselves attenuate and become, in a fashion of the vicious circle, progressively less accessible to those few who aspire to serious participation in social affairs. The vital democratic connection between community and leadership, between the mass and the several elites, has been so wrenched and perverted that disastrous policies go unchallenged time and again. . . .

The first effort, then, should be to state a vision: What is the perimeter of human possibility in this epoch? . . . The second effort, if we are to be politically responsible, is to evaluate the prospects for obtaining at least a substantial part of that vision in our epoch: What are the social forces that exist, or that must exist, if we are to be successful? And what role have we ourselves to play as a social force?

THE CAMPUS REVOLT

Students for a Democratic Society has been continually interested in university reform, and may be credited with sparking anti-administration sentiment on many campuses since the appearance of the Port Huron Statement *in 1962. The following excerpt from the* Statement *is something of a manifesto against the social and political conservatism of academia.*

"Students don't even give a damn about apathy," one has said. Apathy toward apathy begets a privately constructed universe, a place of systematic study schedules, two nights each week for beer, a girl or two, and early marriage—a framework infused with personality, warmth, and under control, no matter how unsatisfying otherwise.

Under these conditions university life loses all relevance to some. Four hundred thousand of our classmates leave college each year.

But apathy is not simply an attitude; it is a product of social institutions, and of the structure and organization of higher education itself. The extracurricular life is ordered according to *in loco parentis* theory, which ratifies the administration as the moral guardian of the young. The accompanying "let's pretend" theory of student extracurricular affairs validates student government as a training center for those who want to spend their lives in political pretense, and discourages initiative from more articulate, honest, and sensitive students. The bounds and style of controversy are delimited before controversy begins. The university "prepares" the student for "citizenship" through perpetual rehearsals and, usually, through emasculation of what creative spirit there is in the individual.

The academic life contains reinforcing counterparts to the way in which extracurricular life is organized. The academic world is founded in a teacher-student relation analogous to the parent-child relation which characterizes *in loco parentis*. Further, academia includes a radical separation of student from the material of study. That which is studied, the social reality, is "objectified" to sterility, dividing the student from life—just as he is restrained in active involvement by the deans controlling student government. The specialization of function and knowledge, admittedly necessary to our complex technological and social structure, has produced an exaggerated compartmentalization of study and understanding. This has contributed to: an overly parochial view, by faculty, of the role of its research and scholarship; a discontinuous and truncated understanding, by students, of the surrounding social order; a loss of personal attachment, by nearly all, to the worth of study as a humanistic enterprise.

There is, finally, the cumbersome academic bureaucracy extending throughout the academic as well as extracurricular structures, contributing to the sense of outer complexity and inner powerlessness that transforms so many students from honest searching to ratification of convention and, worse, to a numbness to present and future catastrophes. The size and financing systems of the university enhance the permanent trusteeship of the administrative bureaucracy, their power leading to a shift to the value standards of business and administrative mentality within the university. Huge foundations and other private financial interests shape the under-financed colleges and universities, making them not only more commercial but less disposed to diagnose society critically, less open to dissent. Many social and physical scientists, neglecting the liberating heritage of higher learning, develop "human relations" or "morale-producing" techniques for the corporate economy, while others exercise their intellectual skills to accelerate the arms race.

The university is located in a permanent position of social influence. Its educational function makes it indispensable and automatically makes it a crucial institution in the formation of social attitudes. In an unbelievably complicated world, it is the central institution for organizing, evaluating, and transmitting knowledge. . . . Social relevance, the accessibility to knowledge, and internal openness—these together make the university a potential base and agency in the movement of social change.

1. Any new left in America must be, in large measure, a left

with real intellectual skills, committed to deliberativeness, honesty, and reflection as working tools. The university permits the political life to be an adjunct to the academic one, and action to be informed by reason.

2. A new left must be distributed in significant social roles throughout the country. The universities are distributed in such a manner.

3. A new left must consist of younger people who matured in the post-war world, and must be directed to the recruitment of younger people. The university is an obvious beginning point.

4. A new left must include liberals and socialists, the former for their relevance, the latter for their sense of thoroughgoing reforms in the system. The university is a more sensible place than a political party for these two traditions to begin to discuss their differences and look for political synthesis.

5. A new left must start controversy across the land, if national policies and national apathy are to be reversed. The ideal university is a community of controversy, within itself and in its effects on communities beyond.

6. A new left must transform modern complexity into issues that can be understood and felt close-up by every human being. It must give form to the feelings of helplessness and indifference, so that people may see the political, social, and economic sources of their private troubles and organize to change society. In a time of supposed prosperity, moral complacency, and political manipulation, a new left cannot rely on only aching stomachs to be the engine force of social reform. The case for change, for alternatives that will involve uncomfortable personal efforts, must be argued as never before. The university is a relevant place for all of these activities.

But we need not indulge in illusions: The university system cannot complete a movement of ordinary people making demands for a better life. From its schools and colleges across the nation, a militant left might awaken its allies, and by beginning the process towards peace, civil rights, and labor struggles, reinsert theory and idealism where too often reign confusion and political barter. The power of students and faculty united is not only potential; it has shown its actuality in the South, and in the reform movements of the North.

To turn these possibilities into realities will involve national efforts at university reform by an alliance of students and faculty. They must wrest control of the educational process from the administrative bureaucracy. They must make fraternal and functional contact with allies in labor, civil rights, and other liberal forces outside the campus. They must import major public issues into the curriculum. . . . They must make debate and controversy, not dull pedantic cant, the common style for educational life. They must consciously build a base for their assault upon the loci of power.

As students for a democratic society, we are committed to stimulating this kind of social movement, this kind of vision and program in campus and community across the country. If we appear to seek the unattainable as it has been said, then let it be known that we do so to avoid the unimaginable.

Epilogue

By definition, an epilogue functions to complete the plan of work. It ordinarily provides closure by suggesting a set of conclusions, key implications, or themes that should have become apparent as the work developed. But in keeping with our stated objectives, this book of readings was designed with the express purpose of opening rather than closing the reader's eyes to aspects of behavior often neglected or even totally ignored by experts. We have attempted to correct that bias, intentional or not, by providing a forum to achieve a broader understanding of the complex behavior represented in the selections. As social scientists, however, we would be remiss if we permitted our balancing effort to inadvertently tip the scales too far in the intended direction. After all, scientific study involves far more than the personal views of the persons being studied. It involves, for example, the processes by which behavior becomes identified as deviant, the specification of the conditions which precipitate such actions, and the differential attributes of different forms and types of behavior. In short, the social scientific investigation of deviance is far greater in scope and substance than the special concern of this book would indicate.

In an effort, therefore, to provide the ingredients for a broader perspective, we conclude this book by presenting a selective, annotated bibliography of relevant empirical and theoretical studies by social scientists. In keeping with the focus of the book, the intention of the bibliography is to acquaint readers with attempts to describe and analyze deviant behavior and its relationship to how the subjects perceive themselves and their world.

Bibliography

ABORTION

Ball, Donald W., "An Abortion Clinic Ethnography," *Social Problems*, 14 (Winter, 1967), 293–301.

A description of the manner in which an institution dealing in mass abortions minimizes the stigma of deviance for its clients.

Gebhard, Paul H., Wardell B. Pomeroy, Clyde E. Martin, and Cornelia V. Christenson, *Pregnancy, Birth and Abortion*, New York, Hoeber-Harper, 1958, Ch. 4.

A survey providing some indication of the prevalence of illegally induced abortions in the United States.

Schur, Edwin M., *Crimes Without Victims: Deviant Behavior and Public Policy*, Englewood Cliffs, N.J., Prentice-Hall, 1965, pp. 11–66.

A discussion of how the prohibitions against abortion have little effect on curbing the number of abortions but have adverse effects on the physical and psychological well-being of women who do obtain them.

ALCOHOLISM

Connor, Ralph G., "The Self-Concepts of Alcoholics," in *Society, Culture, and Drinking Patterns*, eds. David J. Pittman and Charles R. Snyder, New York, Wilcy, 1962, pp. 455–467.

A study comparing the self descriptions of male alcoholics and college students.

Jellinek, E. M., "Phases of Alcohol Addiction," *Quarterly Jour-*

nal of Studies on Alcohol, **13** (1952), 673–684.

An analysis of the developmental stages of alcoholism.

*Jessor, Richard, "Toward a Social Psychology of Excessive Alcohol Use," *Proceedings Research Sociologists' Conference on Alcohol Problems*, eds. Charles R. Snyder and David R. Schweitzer, Southern Illinois University, April 30–May 1, 1964.

Alcoholism viewed as an adaptation to strain at both the social and personality levels.

Drug Use

Becker, Howard S., "Becoming a Marihuana User," *American Journal of Sociology*, **59** (November, 1953), 235–243.

A description of the learning process which is involved in using and enjoying drugs.

Lindesmith, Alfred R., *Opiate Addiction*, Bloomington, Indiana University Press, 1947.

A social psychological study of the process of becoming addicted.

Sutter, Alan G., "The World of the Righteous Dope Fiend," *Issues in Criminology*, **2** (Fall, 1966), 177–222.

Although this article concentrates on a specific type of drug user, it includes a comprehensive discussion of many aspects of the illicit drug world.

Homosexuality

*Gagnon, John H. and William Simon, "Homosexuality: The Formulation of a Sociological Perspective," *Journal of Health and Social Behavior*, **8** (September, 1967), 177–185.

Approaches homosexuality as a developmental process which includes not only sexual behavior but a wide range of nonsexual roles and commitments.

Leznoff, Maurice and William A. Westley, "The Homosexual Community," *Social Problems*, **3** (April, 1956), 257–263.

*Starred articles may be found in Mark Lefton, James K. Skipper, Jr., and Charles H. McCaghy, eds., *Approaches to Deviance: Theories, Concepts, and Research Findings*, New York, Appleton-Century-Crofts, 1968.

A discussion, based on research, of the functions of homosexual groups for coping with a hostile society.

Schofield, Michael, *Sociological Aspects of Homosexuality: A Comparative Study of Three Types of Homosexuals*, Boston, Little, Brown, 1965.

An empirical study which includes, among other things, a description of the process by which homosexuals are pressured by society into a homosexual subculture.

Juvenile Delinquency

*Ball, Richard Allen, "An Empirical Exploration of Neutralization Theory," *Criminologica*, 4 (August, 1966), 22–32.

A study of whether delinquents perceive more justifications for law-breaking behavior than do nondelinquents.

Dinitz, Simon, Frank R. Scarpitti, and Walter C. Reckless, "Delinquency Vulnerability: A Cross Group and Longitudinal Analysis," *American Sociological Review*, 27 (August, 1962), 515–517.

The terminal report on a longitudinal study concerning the relationship between self-concept and future delinquency.

*Hall, Peter M., "Identification with the Delinquent Subculture and Level of Self-Evaluation," *Sociometry*, 29 (June, 1966), 146–158.

A study of a transitional process of becoming committed to delinquency and its relationship to self-concept.

Short, James F. and Fred L. Strodtbeck, *Group Process and Gang Delinquency*, Chicago, University of Chicago Press, 1965, chs. 6–7.

A study of self-concepts of gang members in the context of their groups and how these concepts are related to behavior and other variables.

Mental Disorder

Kleiner, Robert J. and Seymour Parker, "Goal-Striving, Social Status, and Mental Disorder," *American Sociological Review*, 28 (April, 1963), 189–203.

An excellent review of the literature on the relationship

between psychopathology, on the one hand, and such social and psychological factors as social status, social mobility, and mobility orientation, on the other.

*Lefton, M., S. Angrist, S. Dinitz, and B. Pasamanick, "Social Class, Expectations and Performance of Mental Patients," *American Journal of Sociology*, **68** (July, 1962), 79–87.

A key idea contained in this paper is that disease manifestations are perhaps more significant than social class and role expectations as criteria of posthospital adjustment.

Scheff, Thomas J., "The Role of the Mentally Ill and the Dynamics of Mental Disorder: A Research Framework," *Sociometry*, **26** (December, 1963), 136–453.

This paper proposes a model in which the dynamics of mental disorder occur within the system constituted by the deviant and those reacting to his behavior. Of special concern to the reader is the distinction made between a sociological and a psychological explanation of the dynamics of mental disorder.

NUDISM

llfred, Fred, Jr. and Roger Lauer, *Social Nudism in America*, New Haven, College and University Press, 1964.

A comprehensive discussion of several aspects of nudism.

Weinberg, Martin S., "Becoming A Nudist," *Psychiatry*, **29** (February, 1966), 15–24.

An empirical study of the process by which persons contemplate nudism, visit a camp, and become nudists.

*Weinberg, Martin S., "Sexual Modesty, Social Meanings, and the Nudist Camp," *Social Problems*, **12** (Winter, 1965), 311–318.

Utilizing a "typography of immodest behavior," an investigation is made of the existence of the various types within a nudist camp.

POLITICAL EXTREMISM

Almond, Gabriel A., et al., *The Appeals of Communism*, Princeton, N.J., 1954.

A study of 221 ex-Communists: their characteristics, why they joined the Party, and why they left.

Lincoln, C. Eric, *The Black Muslims in America*, Boston, Beacon Press, 1961.

An account of the Black Nationalist organization: its problems and the philosophies of its members.

*Rush, Gary B., "Status Consistency and Right-Wing Extremism," *American Sociological Review*, **32** (February, 1967), 86–92.

An empirical study which discovers a relationship between status inconsistency and attitudes compatible with those of right-wing political groups.

Sibley, Mulford Q. and Philip E. Jacob, *Conscription of Conscience: The American State and the Conscientious Objector, 1940–1947*, Ithaca, N.Y., Cornell, 1952.

A detailed study of the treatment of conscientious objectors during the second world war.

PROPERTY CRIME

Cameron, Mary Owen, *The Booster and the Snitch*, New York; Free Press, 1964.

A study of professional and amateur shoplifters with an emphasis on their self-concepts and rationalizations.

*Lemert, Edwin M., "An Isolation and Closure Theory of Naive Check Forgery," *Journal of Criminal Law, Criminology and Police Science*, **44** (September–October, 1953), 296–307.

One type of check forgery is described in terms of the offender's social isolation, the situation, and the private meanings which check writing has for this individual.

Maurer, David W., *Whiz Mob: A Correlation of the Technical Argot of Pickpockets with Their Behavior Pattern*, New Haven, Conn., College and University Press, 1964.

Although primarily a study of the "social structure of language," this work contains a comprehensive view of the professional criminal.

PROSTITUTION

*Bryan, James H., "Apprenticeships in Prostitution," *Social Problems*, **12** (Winter, 1965), 287–297.

The process by which novice call girls become acquainted with the skills and values of the trade.

Davis, Kingsley, "Sexual Behavior," *Contemporary Social Problems*, 2nd ed., ed. Robert K. Merton and Robert A. Nisbet, New York, Harcourt, Brace & World, 1966, pp. 322–372.
Contains a sociological discussion of the relationship between society's institutional control of sex and the existence of prostitution.

Jackman, Norman R., Richard O'Toole, and Gilbert Geis, "The Self-Image of the Prostitute," *Sociological Quarterly*, 4 (April, 1963), 150–161.
An investigation of the values and rationalizations of prostitutes.

SUICIDE

*Gibbs, Jack P. and Walter T. Martin, "A Theory of Status Integration and Its Relationship to Suicide," *American Sociological Review*, 23 (April, 1958), 140–147.
An attempt to explain variations in suicide rates by variations in patterns of status occupancy.

Jacobs, Jerry, "A Phenomenological Study of Suicide Notes," *Social Problems*, 15 (Summer, 1967), 60–72.
A classification of suicide notes based on the perspective of the writers.

Wilkins, James, "Suicidal Behavior," *American Sociological Review*, 32 (April, 1967), 286–298.
A comprehensive critical review of empirical studies on suicide with suggestions for the direction of future research.

VIOLENT PERSONAL CRIME

Amir, Menachem, "Patterns of Forcible Rape," in *Criminal Behavior Systems: A Typology*, ed. Marshall B. Clinard and Richard Quinney, New York, Holt, Rinehart and Winston, 1967, 60–75.
Characteristics of rapists, their victims, and the offense situations plus a subcultural interpretation of the recurring patterns of such offenses.

Gebhard, Paul H., John H. Gagnon, Wardell B. Pomeroy, and
    Cornelia V. Christenson, *Sex Offenders: An Analysis of
    Types,* New York, Hoeber-Harper, 1965.
    A comprehensive, descriptive study of all types of sex of-
    fenders with Chapters 7 through 9 dealing specifically with
    "aggressive" offenders.
Wolfgang, Marvin E., "Victim Precipitated Criminal Homicide,"
    Journal of Criminal Law, Criminology and Police Science,
    48 (May–June, 1957), 1–11.
    A survey and discussion concerning murder victims whose
    own behavior contributes to their death.